Collected Plays
Volume Two

For several decades, Girish Karnad has been recognized nationally and internationally as one of the pre-eminent playwrights of contemporary India. Born in 1938, he belonged to the generation of writers who came to maturity shortly after independence and collectively reshaped Indian theatre as a national institution in the later twentieth century. Karnad's *Collected Plays* brings together the playwright's own English versions of all his important plays and makes them available to audiences around the world. Together, these volumes span the varied and celebrated career of Girish Karnad, from his very first play to his recent works.

Collected Plays
Volume Two

Talé-Daṇḍa
The Fire and the Rain
The Dreams of Tipu Sultan
Two Monologues:
Flowers
Broken Images

GIRISH KARNAD

With an Introduction by
Aparna Bhargava Dharwadker

OXFORD
UNIVERSITY PRESS

OXFORD
UNIVERSITY PRESS

Oxford University Press is a department of the University of Oxford.
It furthers the University's objective of excellence in research, scholarship,
and education by publishing worldwide. Oxford is a registered trademark of
Oxford University Press in the UK and in certain other countries.

Published in India by
Oxford University Press
22 Workspace, 2nd Floor, 1/22 Asaf Ali Road, New Delhi 110002, India

First Edition published in 2005
4th impression 2024

ISBN-13: 978-0-19-012768-8
ISBN-10: 0-19-012768-6

Typeset in Minion in 10.5/14
by Excellent Laser Typesetters, Pitampura, Delhi 110034
Printed in India by Manipal Technologies Limited, Manipal

CONTENTS

for
SHARAD PATIL
the Phule-Ambedkar-Marxwadi philosopher

INTRODUCTION

I

In terms of the chronology of composition, the plays of Girish Karnad written between 1961 and 2004 constitute two natural and distinct sequences, the first beginning with *Yayati* in 1961 and concluding with *Hittina Hunja* in 1980, and the second beginning with *Nāga-Mandala* in 1988 and continuing with the two monologues, *Broken Images* and *Flowers* (2004). In terms of form and content the plays reveal equally distinct and recurrent patterns of thematic engagement with ancient myth (*Yayati, Hittina Hunja, Agni Mattu Malé*), premodern and modern history (*Tughlaq, Talé-Daṇḍa, The Dreams of Tipu Sultan*), the timeless but recognizably traditional world of folktales (*Hayavadana, Nāga-Mandala, Flowers*), and carefully chosen aspects of contemporary life (*Anjumallige, Broken Images*). In terms of effect and significance, however, Karnad's oeuvre has been less orderly: the attention he had attracted with *Yayati* was followed by the spectacular successes of *Tughlaq* and *Hayavadana* in print and performance (circa 1964–74), but *Anjumallige* (1977) and *Hittina Hunja* (1980) had little impact in either medium, and did not appear in English translations (in Karnad's authorial practice, a certain sign of his dissatisfaction with the plays). In hindsight, therefore, *Nāga-Mandala* emerges as his first successful play after a seventeen-year interval, and its composition signals the end of an unusually unproductive period in Karnad's life as a playwright.

I have discussed the plays of the 1961–88 period in the Introduction to volume one of this collection. An apt point of departure for a discussion of the later plays, collected in the present volume, is the event that brought forth *Nāga-Mandala* and launched the second significant phase in Karnad's theatrical career: his tenure as a Fulbright Fellow at the University of Chicago in 1987–8. Oddly reminiscent of the Rhodes Scholarship period during which Karnad had written his first two plays, the year-long Fulbright grant offered him the intellectually stimulating environment of a major international university, the relative freedom of a research appointment, and perhaps most important, daily contact for several months with his friend and acknowledged mentor, A. K. Ramanujan. Two folktales that Ramanujan had shared with Karnad some years earlier resurfaced to form the core of *Nāga-Mandala* when C. M. Naim, Chair of the Department of South Asian Languages and Civilizations, encouraged Karnad to write and direct a new play at the University Theatre. The student production of *Nāga-Mandala* in Spring 1988 represented an unusual collaboration between a major contemporary Indian playwright and the diasporic scholarly community, as well as the atypical beginning of what has subsequently been a distinguished performance history for the play. In many respects, *Nāga-Mandala* is a companion piece and 'sequel' to *Hayavadana* rather than a work of striking originality: it continues the turn from the public to the private and the personal that the earlier play had begun, and takes a more elemental approach to the complication and subversion of conjugality. Its unique significance in Karnad's career, however, is that it re-energized and refocused his playwriting, and led later to collaborations that resulted in other major work.

Karnad returned from Chicago in the summer of 1988 to a high-profile five-year appointment as Chairman of the Sangeet Natak Akademi, and a political sphere far removed from the delicate play of fancy and fantasy in *Nāga-Mandala*. Four years after Operation Bluestar and the assassination of Indira Gandhi, the secessionist Khalistan movement among the Sikhs in Punjab had become quiescent, but the country was poised on the verge of that radical renegotiation of majority–minority relations, secularism, and protective discrimination that was to shape the crisis-ridden politics of the next decade and more. In 1989, the National Front Coalition government of V.P. Singh decided to implement the recommendations of the Mandal Commission that 27% of the positions in the central administration and public sector corporations should be reserved for members of the Other Backward Castes (OBCs). Supporters of the policy promoted it as a necessary corrective measure; opponents described it as a political ploy for creating a large 'vote bank' that would favour candidates eager to woo socially disadvantaged groups. The perceived divisiveness of the Commission's recommendations, and the opportunity they offered for cynical political manipulation, sparked off nationwide protests and horrific acts of self-destruction on the part of young upper-caste students who claimed that their future had been irredeemably compromised. The Bharatiya Janata Party withdrew its conditional support from Singh's government, and in September of the same year L.K. Advani began a 'Rath Yatra' (in a Toyota-Chariot) from Somnath to Ayodhya, where he promised the demolition of the controversial sixteenth-century mosque, the Babri Masjid, and the construction of a temple to Lord Rama on the same site.

The mutually contradictory nature of these events was self-evident to any reflective observer. The Mandal Commission's recommendations underscored the ritual divisions and economic inequalities within mainstream Hindu society; in direct negation of this fragmentation, Advani's rhetoric sought to claim a monolithic, benevolent identity for Hinduism, reimagine India as a unified Hindu nation, and inflame collective sentiment against the largest group of religious others, the Muslims. In actuality, in both inter-religious and intra-religious perspectives (Hindus vs Muslims on the one hand, the upper castes vs the 'untouchables' on the other), the deep divisions within the Indian polity had emerged fully, and were generating conflicts more destructive than the 'disenchantment and cynicism that marked the end of the Nehru era'. A quarter century earlier Karnad had intuited the crisis of India's secular nationhood in *Tughlaq*; written in 1989, *Talé-Danda* is a play about the nation that acknowledges and contends with the reconfiguration of Indian politics in the post-Indira Gandhi years.

II

The essential method of *Talé-Danda* is the same as that of *Tughlaq*: to understand the present one must return to the past, because the premodern history of India prefigures and encompasses the drama of modernity. But where *Tughlaq* confronts the problem of majority and minority religions (Hinduism and Islam) turning against each other, *Talé-Danda* goes further back in time to uncover the history of the majority religion turning against itself. This is a necessary move because the play responds to a later moment in the political evolution of India-as-nation— the decisive shift in the late-1980s from secular to religious (and more specifically Hindu) nationalism, which suppressed individual styles of charismatic leadership in favour of mass politics fuelled by communal feeling. In pursuing their program Hindu nationalists follow what T. N. Madan describes as the 'basic premise of communalism...that the political interests of a religious community are unaffected by ethnic, linguistic, class, or any other divisions within the community. Rather, these interests are defined antagonistically in relation to other similarly conceived religious communities' ('Religion' 61). The second claim, put forward not so much by Hindu ideologues as by political theorists attempting to explain the rise of religious extremism in modern societies, is that the simultaneous appearance of secularization and fundamentalism is only 'apparently contradictory, for in truth it is the marginalization of faith, which is what secularism is, that permits the perversion of religion. There are no fundamentalists or revivalists in traditional society' (Madan, 'Secularism' 749).

Karnad's play is a rejoinder to the claims that Hinduism is a monolithic cultural unity which can unproblematically oppose rival systems of belief like Islam, and that religious intolerance is a problem created by a secularized modernity. The play's historical narrative centers on the twelfth-century *Virasaiva* movement of religious reform and protest, led by the poet-saint Basavanna, which flourished for a time in the city of Kalyan (in present-day Karnataka) under the patronage of King Bijjala, but ended in violence when the new community translated its opposition to caste into practice by arranging a marriage between a brahmin girl and an untouchable boy. To focus on the hierarchical disunity of Hinduism, Karnad foregrounds the problem of caste and relegates the devotional, mystical, and poetic features of the movement to the background. And to highlight the pervasiveness of violence in a 'traditional' society, he incorporates the conflicts not only across caste boundaries within brahminical Hinduism, but also between Hinduism and reformist religions like Buddhism and Jainism. Two further arguments emerge from this representation: for Hinduism to claim an exclusive right in the constitution of an Indian nation is to flout a long-term history of racial and religious diversity, and for Hinduism to claim a pristine pre-Islamic past is to deny its own history of reform, protest, sectarianism, and violence.

Caste appears in *Talé-Daṇḍa* as the basis of Hindu socioreligious organization across class divisions, and the play presents the philosophical dialectic of caste as well as the practical consequences of the opposing positions. The *Virasaiva* communitarians (who call themselves *sharanas*) have exchanged the boundaries of caste for the bonds of friendship, fellowship, equality, humanity, and social change. The radicalism of such a fellowship inspires King

Bijjala, especially because as a caste barber whose ancestors reinvented themselves as kshatriyas, he has found full acceptance only among the *sharanas*. The contrary position is set forth by the priest Damodara Bhatt, who defends caste's 'logic of inequality' by arguing that 'a hierarchy which accommodates difference is more humane than an equality which enforces conformity'. For him the beauty of Hindu *dharma* is that it allows all individuals to be always and only themselves: 'One's caste is like one's home— meant for oneself and one's family. It is shaped to one's needs, one's comforts, one's traditions. And that is why the Vedic tradition can accommodate all differences from Kashmir to Kanya Kumari' (56). The conceptual difference here is between fellowship and family, affiliation and filiation, corresponding to the opposing conceptions of caste as extrinsic or intrinsic. For the orthodox it is like a skin that cannot be cast off; for the *sharanas*, it is a cast of mind that can be separated from the corporeal body and neutralized through reason. Karnad's pessimistic conclusion, which applies to the twelfth-century history of the *sharanas* as well as to present-day cultural politics in India, is that caste *is* ultimately untranscendable, even for those who repudiate it. The movement of the *sharanas* remains an oasis of reform and protest in a desert of orthodoxy, and their own opposition to caste is too self-conscious and obsessive, devolving merely into a desire to challenge brahminism at every opportunity. The brahmin-untouchable marriage is thus a classic example of the right deed done for the wrong reason, and the ensuing blood-bath destroys the very movement the union was meant to celebrate.

In the short Preface to the English translation of *Talé-Daṇḍa* (1993), Karnad commented that he wrote the play in 1989 'when the "Mandir" and "Mandal" movements were beginning to show again how relevant the questions posed by these thinkers [the *Virasaivas*] were for our age. The horror of subsequent events and the religious fanaticism that has gripped our national life today have only proved how dangerous it is to ignore the solutions they offered'. The events within the play offer a covert commentary on both facets of the present crisis because Karnad seeks to enforce the identity between communal and caste violence, and to show that the effects of intra-religious conflict are very similar to those of inter-religious conflict. Throughout *Talé-Daṇḍa* we could substitute the category of religion for the category of caste, and the terms 'Hindu' and 'Muslim' for the terms 'brahmin' and 'untouchable', without modifying the play's thematics or its interlocked movements of transgression and punishment. This possibility of substitution nullifies the argument that one kind of violence or fanaticism is godly while another is godless, a point emphasized in Basavanna's most transportable insight: 'violence is wrong, whatever the provocation. To resort to it because someone else started it first is even worse. And to do so in the name of a structure of brick and mortar is a monument to stupidity' (29). With caste and communalism persisting as the dominant sources of present-day political violence in India, the relevance of *Talé-Daṇḍa*, like that of *Tughlaq*, appears overdetermined and inexhaustible, and both plays have taken on cautionary and prophetic qualities of a similar kind.

This thematic density, however, is at variance with the stage history of *Talé-Daṇḍa*, which appears especially truncated in comparison with the rich theatrical life of *Tughlaq* and *Hayavadana*. Since the play deals with a central event in the history of Karnataka that continues to resonate (in some ways, ironically) in the present-day practices of *Virasaivism*, its most notable productions have fittingly been in Kannada. Of these, Jayateertha Joshi's version for the Karnataka Nataka Rangayan (Mysore), and C. R. Jambe's production for Ninasam (Heggodu) in 1992 attracted special attention. Ramgopal Bajaj translated the play into Hindi under the title *Rakt-Kalyan*, and Ebrahim Alkazi directed that version for the National School of Drama Repertory Company in 1992, returning to a history play by Karnad exactly a decade after his London revival of *Tughlaq*. But there has been no major

English production of *Talé-Daṇḍa*, and several prominent directors who have distinguished records in relation to Karnad—B. V. Karanth, Satyadev Dubey, Shyamanand Jalan, and Rajinder Nath, to name a few—have not taken up this play. When *Talé-Daṇḍa* was published in Kannada in 1990, many reviewers, especially those in Karnataka, saw it as Karnad's return to serious playwriting and placed it beside *Tughlaq*. Thirty years later it continues to be regarded as a significant commentary on the relation of religion to politics, but there is evidently less interest in maintaining a consistent presence for it on the stage.

At an intertextual level quite removed from the public life of the play, *Talé-Daṇḍa* is also an extended tribute to A. K. Ramanujan, and the culmination of a long-standing intellectual relationship between two leading post-independence authors from Karnataka. Karnad was drawn to his older contemporary from early adulthood because Ramanujan's brilliance as a poet, translator, and scholar of Tamil and Kannada literature seemed to offer an exemplary model as well as an antithesis to his own interests as a playwright, actor, and filmmaker (he sometimes jocularly described his entire creative career as an attempt to give artistic form to Ramanujan's intellectual insights!). The Fulbright fellowship year in Chicago channelled the earlier exchanges into new and concrete directions. Karnad dedicated the 1989 English translation of *Nāga-Mandala* to Ramanujan in acknowledgment not only of the folktales he had passed along, but the rich conversations between them that had circled endlessly around oral culture, folklore, and the *Virasaiva* tradition. *Talé-Daṇḍa* was substantially indebted to these discussions as well as to *Speaking of Siva* (1973), the brilliant collection of Kannada *vacanas* in which through translation and commentary Ramanujan had accomplished the first major recuperation of this premodern socioreligious and literary movement for a contemporary readership in English. In *Talé-Daṇḍa* Karnad breathed a different kind of life into the poetic texts and historical events by developing a dramatic structure that would 'explain' the relation of poetry and religious mysticism to political economy and social radicalism, and in the English version of the play he incorporated a generous selection of old and new translations of the *vacanas* by Ramanujan. Following his mentor's example (though not his method), he also avoided the sentimental simplifications of hagiography and sought to invent an action around the figure of Basavanna that was psychologically complex, historically plausible, and theatrically sustainable. The Author's Note to *Talé-Daṇḍa* speaks of Ramanujan's pervasive presence in the play, made more poignant by the circumstance that he died in July 1993 a few months before the English text appeared in print.

III

In the summer of 1993 Garland Wright, Artistic Director of the Guthrie Theatre in Minneapolis, directed *Nāga-Mandala* as part of the theatre's thirtieth anniversary season, and then commissioned Karnad to write a new play for possible production during the 1994–5 season. Karnad found his subject in the rather obscure myth of Yavakri(ta) that he had encountered decades earlier in C. Rajagopalachari's prose retelling of the Mahabharata. The play, titled *Agni Mattu Malé* (The Fire and the Rain) was written originally in Kannada but rendered immediately into English for a workshop with professional actors at the Guthrie, and the entire process of change and revision took place in English. The production at the Guthrie did not materialize due to Garland Wright's departure from the theatre, but in Kannada, Hindi, and English, *Agni Mattu Malé* has chalked up perhaps the most extraordinary performance record and range of reader responses among Karnad's plays.

A surprising feature of this reception is a persistent violation of authorial intent that goes beyond the 'artistic licence' theatre directors usually exercise and playwrights usually accept (Karnad, in particular, has always allowed directors the freedom to interpret his plays according to their artistic understanding). In C. Basavalingaiah's well-received Kannada production, the play concluded with the entrance of a pregnant Vishakha, carrying the child of the lover (Yavakri) whose death she herself had brought about. In 1998, for the first and only time in his career Karnad took public exception to a director's handling of his work when he described Prasanna's Hindi production of the play for the National School of Drama Repertory Company (titled *Agni aur Barkha)* as a 'travesty'. On the questionable grounds that the performance was well over three hours long, Prasanna had cut the last fifteen minutes of the play and eliminated the role of the Brahma Rakshasa entirely, thus creating unexplained gaps and inconsistencies in the action. By common consensus, the most spectacular and successful production of the play was by Arjun Sajnani in English (Bangalore, 1999), but when Sajnani reworked the play as a commercial Hindi film titled *Agnivarsha* (casting Amitabh Bachchan as Indra), he failed to mention Karnad as the author of the original! In contrast, readers ranging from the philosopher Ramachandra Gandhi to the historian Ramachandra Guha and the theatre critic Shanta Gokhale have lavished praise on the play, and the composer Bhaskar Chandavarkar has described it as not only Karnad's best work but one that he will be unable to surpass.

The attributes of *Agni Mattu Malé* as a text and performance vehicle more than explain the intensity of these responses, both negative and positive. It is a dense, intellectually ambitious, autumnal play structured around ideas (witness the long and unusual 'notes' at the end of the English translation) and a plethora of tangled relationships which unfold with a rare economy and intensity of words and emotions. Karnad noted that the year spent in the company of South Asia scholars at the University of Chicago had stimulated his interest in orthodox Hinduism and the complex organization of Hindu society. In *Talé-Daṇḍa* this interest was directed at the sociopolitics and psychology of caste at a specific moment in premodern history; in *Agni Mattu Malé* Karnad reimagines the world of Hindu antiquity and constructs a story of passion, loss, and sacrifice in the contexts of Vedic ritual, spiritual discipline (*tapasya*), social and ethical differences between human agents, and interrelated forms of performance still close to their moments of origin.

Once again Karnad amplifies and alters an obscure myth for a multilayered reflection on cultural codes, modes of representation, and forms of attachment. The story of Yavakri in Chapters 135–8 of the Vana Parva in the Mahabharata is a cautionary tale about the misapplication of powers that human beings receive from the gods after great penance. Yavakri, the son of sage Bharadwaja, acquires knowledge of the Vedas from Indra after years of *tapasya*, but uses it to molest the daughter-in-law of sage Raibhya, whom he resents. Raibhya in turn creates a demon (*rakshasa*) and a spirit in the form of his daughter-in-law, both of whom pursue Yavakri and kill him. Bharadwaja places a curse on Raibhya—that he will die at the hands of his own son—and then kills himself in remorse. Sometime later Paravasu indeed mistakes the deerskin his father Raibhya is wearing for a wild animal, and accidentally kills him. Involved with his younger brother Aravasu in a fire sacrifice, Paravasu initiates another cycle of evil when he falsely accuses the latter of patricide (and hence of brahminicide). Aravasu then begins his own penance to the Sun God, and when granted a boon, asks for Yavakri, Bharadwaja, and Raibhya to be restored to life. Lives that were destroyed due to human lapses are restored through divine intervention.

In his elaboration of the myth, Karnad forges closer connections between the principal characters, gives them rounded personalities, and inserts an unambiguous intentionality into their actions. Yavakri and Vishakha are not strangers in *Agni Mattu Malé* but lovers whose relationship both precedes and follows Vishakha's marriage to Paravasu, making her more than merely a passive object of Yavakri's lust. Her marriage itself appears to be an arid contract: after a frenzy of sensual gratification Paravasu has abandoned Vishakha to Raibhya's care, and the relationships between the three are startling in their lovelessness and malevolence.

The real Vishakha (not a spirit) also brings about Yavakri's death because of her very desire to keep him alive: what is a magical act of vengeance in the Mahabharata turns into tragic irony in *Agni Mattu Malé*. Similarly, Paravasu kills his father out of deliberate hatred, not accidentally or in ignorance, and although he does not instigate the destruction of the fire sacrifice at the end, he does choose death within the *yajna* enclosure as an act of expiation. The same quality of active volition extends to the play's supernatural characters. In the Mahabharata version the Rakshasa is a device for bringing about Yavakri's death; in Karnad's play, his return to the spirit world becomes entangled with painful ethical choices in the human world.

In a more radical move, Karnad invents the parallel story of Aravasu's relationship with the tribal girl Nittilai, and develops Arvasu (his variant spelling of the name) as the antithesis to Raibhya, Paravasu, and Yavakri. As an actor and as Nittilai's lover, Arvasu counterpoints the brahminism and asceticism of the other male characters, and enables Karnad to systematically contrast the life of discipline and sacrifice with the life of instinct and emotion. This split between nature and culture, body and mind appears in such earlier plays as *Hayavadana* and *Bali*, but in *Agni Mattu Malé* the duality is expressed for the first time as the explicit opposition between brahmin and shudra, with Arvasu functioning as the connective link between the two worlds. As ascetic males Yavakri, Raibhya, and Paravasu have a will to power that empties their spirituality of moral value, and Paravasu's patricide and his false denunciation of Arvasu are of course acts of deliberate evil. Arvasu, in contrast, has committed himself to love and community, and is prepared to renounce his twice-born status for the sake of Nittilai. The play thus associates brahminism with mind-games, egocentrism, sterility, and ruthlessness, and shudra culture with love, compassion, freshness, and hope, although the contrast is not simplistic or absolute. As Karnad himself points out, among the brahmins the transgressive woman (Vishakha) is chastized but not punished, whereas among the hunters Nittilai pays with her life for choosing Arvasu over her husband. Ironically, Arvasu loses Nittilai because of his inability to abandon orthodoxy at a crucial moment—even as he lags behind to perform the last rites for Yavakri, Nittilai is given away to another man.

Arvasu's identity as actor further complicates the treatment of brahminism, because in terms of both origin and practice theatrical performance complements Vedic ritual and has a place within it, although the *profession* of acting is particular to the shudra caste. In the Notes to the play Karnad argues pointedly that theatre as theorized and practiced in antiquity is not the 'secular' counterpoint to a *yajna* but a parallel performance that can even offer a welcome diversion from the rigours of ritual. The distinction here is not between the sacred and the secular, but between two complementary forms of the sacred, performed by agents on different rungs of the caste hierarchy; the actor's shudra identity is an accepted part of the hierarchy of roles, not a violation of it. The metatheatrical commentary on the actors' craft in the play thus becomes an occasion for revisiting, and celebrating, the myth of the divine origins of theatre. But the most intricate relationship Karnad explores is that between representation and reality—the 'reality' of the fictional characters, that is. When Paravasu contaminates the fire sacrifice by his acts of murder and betrayal, the distinction between fiction and fact is erased in the performance as well. The demonic role Arvasu has assumed in the play-within-the-play temporarily becomes his real self, leading to the desecration of the *yajna* site and the death of Paravasu. A little later, Nittilai loses her life because she cannot resist her human impulse to rush to Arvasu's aid when the enclosure erupts in flames, even though she is in hiding from her tribe. Finally, the redemptive act that ends the crisis within the community is not performance of either kind (the *yajna* or the inner play), but Arvasu's 'real-life' decision to sacrifice his own happiness with Nittilai for the sake of the Brahma Rakshasa's release. All these interlinked elements make *Agni Mattu Malé* Karnad's most ambitiously metatheatrical play, one in which performance is not just a framing device but a thematic preoccupation and an intrinsic part of the main action.

In the broadest sense, *Agni Mattu Malé* is a drama of sacrifice and expiation. The fire sacrifice is a propitiatory ritual intended to end the community's suffering, but it is corrupted in multiple ways by Paravasu; his death is a form of personal atonement, but the communal crisis is resolved through other painful resignations. Paravasu also offers up Vishakha's life, first to his sensual appetite and then to his lust for fame, while Vishakha unwittingly sacrifices Yavakri to her very love for him. Nittilai dies for the sake of Arvasu, and Arvasu surrenders Nittilai for the common good. The play's unusual capacity to move readers and audiences is certainly bound up with this succession of victims and a pervasive sense of loss.

IV

After *Agni Mattu Malé*, the primacy of Kannada as the language of original composition in Karnad's drama comes to an end. For three decades he had argued that he could be a playwright only in Kannada—what happened to his plays after composition and initial publication was a matter not of his intentions but of the multilingual conditions of print and theatrical performance in India. In an interview that appeared in the *Sunday Herald* on 21 February 1999, Karnad reiterated that 'a language is something you need to develop over a whole lifetime. After having written in Kannada for about 25–30 years, I feel I know how to write in Kannada now...I don't have time to go into a new adventure, looking at and mastering an entire new subject because to be able to speak is not enough. You have to go into the language, you have to go into its possibilities'. In rendering his plays into English, he also often expressed regret that some particular social or dialectal aspect of the original Kannada could not be captured in translation, making English a less precise medium for his work. Kannada thus retained its primary position in his playwriting, despite the reciprocal relationship between the two languages.

However, all of Karnad's new plays between 1994 and 2004—*The Dreams of Tipu Sultan* (1997), *Broken Images* (2004), and *Flowers* (2004)—were written originally in English and then translated by him into Kannada. Two older plays, *Anjumallige* and *Hittina Hunja* were written and published originally in Kannada in 1977 and 1980, respectively, but in Karnad's own words they were 'rewritten so completely in English that you could consider them virtually new creations in English'. This shift in language accommodated new circumstances and contexts in Karnad's career as a playwright. *The Dreams of Tipu Sultan* was commissioned by the BBC and broadcast as a radio play in London on 15 August 1997, the fiftieth anniversary of India's independence. It was directed by Jatinder Verma of Tara Arts, and cast Saeed Jaffrey in the title role. Karnad chose to write it originally in English because that was the language of first performance, as also of the historical source material he had consulted. The play was performed in Kannada (as *Tipu Sultan Kanda Kanasu*) by the Karnataka Nataka Rangayan under C. Basavalingaiah's direction in 1999, and in English again by the Madras Players (under N. S. Yamuna's direction) in 2000, the same year that the Kannada text was published. Karnad rewrote *Anjumallige* in English as *Driven Snow* for a workshop with British actors organized by Jatinder Verma in 2000, and *Hittina Hunja* as *Bali* for a production at the Haymarket Theatre, Leicester, in 2002. English is a peculiarly appropriate medium for *Broken Images* (2004) because the play deals with a Kannada woman writer who unexpectedly produces an international bestseller in English. The play was, however, promptly translated into Kannada under the title *Odakalu Bimba*, and received simultaneous Kannada and English productions in Bangalore in 2005, both directed by Karnad in association with K. M. Chaitanya, with Arundhati Nag and Arundhati Raja, respectively, in the role of Manjula Nayak.

Nag won in the best actress category at the 2008 Mahindra Excellence in Theatre Awards (where the play was performed in Hindi), and an English production featuring the well-known film actress Shabana Azmi toured internationally in 2010. The second monologue in English, *Flowers* (2004) premiered at the Ranga Shankara Theatre in Bangalore in 2006, with Rajit Kapur as the solo performer and Royston Abel as director. This acclaimed production was featured at the Bharat Ranga Mahostava, the National School of Drama's annual international theatre festival, and the play has had several other performances within and outside India.

With the post-1994 plays, therefore, Karnad ceased to be 'a playwright only in Kannada' and emerged as the only truly bilingual practitioner in contemporary Indian theatre. His renegotiations of language are obviously determined by multiple factors, both private and public. Karnad's 'real' mother-tongue, Konkani, was not the first language of his childhood because he grew up in Karnataka. Kannada, in turn, was not the first language of communication within his family because his wife as well as his children were brought up speaking only English. Beyond this, the growing imperialism of English in both the private and public spheres in urban India means that balancing its claims against those of even a major literary language such as Kannada was a much more difficult task at the turn of the century than it was in the 1960s or 1970s. Broadly speaking, published translations and productions in English have widened Karnad's audience at home, while the various commissions by theatre companies abroad have given him increasingly greater international visibility. More than other contemporary Indian-language playwrights, he appears to have benefitted from the global reach of English without relinquishing his firm hold on the language-world of Kannada. As the plays after *Agni Mattu Malé* demonstrate, this versatility opened up a whole new range of subjects for Karnad, and diversified his drama both formally and thematically.

V

The Dreams of Tipu Sultan (1997) can be described as the long-awaited history play in which, after dealing with precolonial Indian history in two earlier works, Karnad confronts British colonialism in its crucial early stages of military expansion—paradoxically, at the invitation of the British, and for a celebration of Indian independence. The playwright notes that his 'obsession' with Tipu was something else he inherited from A. K. Ramanujan, who had begun but left unfinished a novel in English on the subject, and mentioned to him the secret diary in which Tipu had recorded his dreams. In 1987 Karnad located a copy of this diary at the University of Chicago's Regenstein Library. In 1990, he was among the public figures who voiced strong support for Sanjay Khan's teleserial, *The Sword of Tipu Sultan*, on the grounds that Tipu needed to be given his due as a major figure in Karnataka history, a visionary, and a patriot. When the BBC approached Karnad in 1996 about a play relating to the independence theme, he 'didn't have to think twice' about the subject, and produced a work in which the impulse towards a complex poetic rehabilitatation of Tipu is clearly evident. The historical symbolism of the play was realized brilliantly in 1999 when C. Basavalingaiah staged it in the precincts of Tipu's summer palace, Daria Daulat in Srirangapattna, to commemorate the two hundredth anniversary of the sultan's death.

In many important respects *Tipu Sultan* follows the model of the history play established in *Tughlaq* and *Talé-Daṇḍa*. It draws upon a range of historical sources to present convincing portraits of the principal characters, but creates an imaginative plot and resonant dialogue to contain their experience. It deals with a controversial protagonist who can be characterized in radically opposite ways, depending on the observer's viewpoint— as a heroic figure of anticolonial resistance (comparable to the Rani of Jhansi) in one perspective, and a treacherous but fallible (and even foolish) adversary in another. The image in the play of a polity in crisis, both because of internal dissensions and the presence of a powerful alien adversary, carries the same potential for application to contemporary problems that had made the history of *Tughlaq* and *Talé-Daṇḍa* politically relevant in present-day India. As in *Tughlaq*, the presence of a court historian, Hussain Ali Kirmani, among the play's characters enables Karnad to reflect on the process of history-writing and the many conduits of history—oral and written, unofficial and official, objective and subjective, dominant and subaltern. The play also juxtaposes larger-than-life figures such as Tipu, Haidar Ali, Nana Phadnavis, Lord Cornwallis, and Arthur and Richard Wellesley against a large cast of less prominent historical individuals (Kirmani, Tipu's principal queen and sons, numerous courtiers, and military officials), as well as ordinary citizens and soldiers. The result, as in the earlier plays, is a historical reconstruction that succeeds as a dramatic fiction through its polyphony of voices.

In other respects, *Tipu Sultan* stands apart in Karnad's oeuvre because as a play about colonialism it has to grapple with the inescapabale psychodrama of East vs West, Europe vs the non-European other, white vs non-white, and colonizer vs colonized. Avoiding any partisan parade of heroes and villains, Karnad creates ambitious and determined players in both camps who are sucked into the vortex of a major transitional moment in Indian history, politics, and culture. There are several important strategies in the portrayal of Tipu Sultan that unfold simultaneously. Karnad interlineates 'textualized' history with legend, lore, and memory because all these modes of transmission are germane to the story of Tipu. The ruler's fabled persona as the Tiger of Mysore thus figures prominently in the action, both as oral legend and as a military reality that the English must contend with. Karnad also casts his protagonist in multiple and contradictory roles—as a beloved ruler, legendary warrior, loving father, and visionary dreamer, but also as the Machiavellian schemer who plots with the French against the English, the defeated soldier who enters into humiliating treaties with the enemy, and the gullible commander who is eventually betrayed by his own side. The perceptions of Tipu that have the greatest energy, however, are those with Brechtian-materialist overtones: they underscore Tipu's excitement over the 'new ideas' of Europe, his understanding of political economy, his interest in the link between commerce and empire, and his desire for an up-to-date army. In this analysis, the tragedy of Tipu's fall is not only that it made way for a full-scale colonial takeover, but that it destroyed a visionary who shared the modernizing impulses of the European Enlightenment, and could meet the English on their own terms (much to their chagrin).

Karnad's portrayal of the English characters, while near-Manichean in some scenes, is more in line with the conventional view of colonial conquest and the attendant cultural relations. Ethically, the main English characters in the play are rational, calculating, pragmatic, and ruthless, although their resentment of Tipu's apparent invincibility is also an aspect of what Homi Bhabha terms colonial ambivalence, while their racist contempt for all natives anticipates the unqualified colonialist denigration that Edward Said calls orientalism. Karnad's principal thematic argument is a familiar one: the English succeeded in India not only (or even principally) because of their superior weapons and warfare, but because of their ability to play off members of the native ruling elite against each other. This accounts for the crucial quadrangulation between the Wellesleys, Tipu Sultan, the (absent) Nizam of Hyderabad, and Nana Phadnavis, and the dynamic is interesting from the teleological perspective of the postcolonial present because it depicts the decentered nature of power relations in the absence of a 'national' idea. Karnad's Tipu is a proto-nationalist who resists as long as he can the Englishman's schemes to rob his land, even as he understands that the English 'believe in the destiny of their race' and are willing to die in faraway places for their dream of England. At home, however, his appeals to a common faith fail to rally the Muslim Nizam to his side, and the instinctive hostility between Hindu and Muslim princes alienates him from the Marathas, although he issues a prophetic (and purely political) warning to the Nana about England's territorial ambitions. The pained scenes of Tipu's peace treaties with the English emphasize that a complex, civilized, and prosperous culture was betrayed into subjection because of the pursuit of petty self-interest by key functionaries. In hindsight, the 'traitorous' collaboration between English and native armies across racial and cultural lines thus becomes the perfect prelude and antithesis to the invention of India-as-nation by nineteenth- and twentieth-century nationalists.

The three-layered structure that contains this drama of colonial encounter is perhaps the most striking feature of *The Dreams of Tipu Sultan*. The basic division—between the scenes from the present which show Hussain Ali Kirmani's attempts to write an 'objective' account of the dead Tipu for the English, and the intermittent scenes from the past which portray the sultan—gives the play a powerfully elegiac quality, because Tipu's life is framed throughout by his death. For Kirmani, a participant-observer in Tipu's tragedy, the matter of history consists not of facts (which concern the English) but with the memories of a fabled ruler that are fading all too quickly. The play begins and ends with memory: Kirmani and Colin Mackenzie serve as the chorus for a highly selective and reflexive history that unfolds cyclically, beginning with the day of Tipu's last battle and returning to it via crucial stages in his slide towards defeat and death. In a subtle, deconstructive move, Karnad also reveals that the interests of the appointed historian are at variance in some respects with 'actual' history. Kirmani disclaims that Tipu ever sent an embassy to Malarctic, the French governor-general of Mauritius, whereas the very first scene with Tipu shows him talking about Malarctic's role in arranging a royal delegation from Mysore to France. The third layer of the action contains Tipu's dreams—partly narrated and partly enacted—along with his interpretations of three of them. Each of the four dreams is a political allegory of his reign; some contain imaginary characters while others conjure up key historical figures like Lord Cornwallis and Haidar Ali. The last dream is the most poignant because it is a fantasy of victory in the midst of defeat and death. The insertion of this dream text into history introduces a level of experience even more evanescent than memory, and maks *The Dreams of Tipu Sultan* Karnad's most poetic play.

VI

The two short monologues in English that conclude this collection— *Broken Images* and *Flowers* (2004)—form a radical provisional coda to Karnad's career as a playwright until that date because they initiate new subjects and forms. *Broken Images* takes up a debate that has grown steadily edgier since independence—the politics of language in Indian literary culture, specifically in relation to the respective claims of the modern Indian languages and English, which must also be recognized now as an Indian, though not an indigenous, language. As a successful author of short and long fiction in Kannada and a teacher of English in a Bangalore College, Manjula Nayak, the play's only character, has led a rather typical literary life. When she unexpectedly publishes a stunning first novel in English that transforms her into the Literary Phenomenon of the Decade, the breakthrough arouses admiration, but also dismay and resentment that she has 'betrayed' Kannada for the sake of fame, fortune, and a vastly expanded audience. (So far, these are the standard terms of the debate over language, and except for the missing Booker Prize, Manjula's story is a transparent send-up of Arundhati Roy's runaway success with the *The God of Small Things*.) Manjula's conversation with her own television image (her doppelgänger) soon reveals, however, that she is an impostor who has passed off her dead sister Malini's novel as her own. The switch to English, hailed as an inspired act of self-fashioning on the author's part, turns out in reality to be an act of dishonesty, desperation, and cowardice, the implication being that the material lure of English as a medium can only lead the Indian-language author to prostitute herself. Significantly, the value of the novel itself is not in dispute—titled *The River Has No Memories*, it is a superbly accomplished autobiographical fiction about a lifelong invalid who 'breathed, laughed, dreamt in English'. What the play impugns is the opportunism of the Kannada author who tries to cash in on a dead sibling's talent.

This almost-Aristotelian structure of revelation and reversal encapsulates the basic arguments in the language debate as they have unfolded in the post-independence period, and points to the striking tenacity of certain oppositions. During the 1950s and 1960s, the difference between the indigenous tongues and English was routinely cast as a choice between integrity and corruption, wholeness and fragmentation, rootedness and rootlessness, decolonization and recolonization. Conversely, Indian-English writers (especially vocal spokesmen such as Nissim Ezekiel, P. Lal, Keki Daruwalla, and Arvind Krishna Mehrotra) claimed that English was not a deliberately chosen or elitist medium, but simply a 'natural' expression of their private and social experience. In *Broken Images* Manjula Nayak presents the same arguments in defence of her sudden transition—her novel, she insists, spontaneously 'burst out in English', and she was somehow able to intuit and emphasize with the experience of a crippled woman well enough to craft a masterpiece about it. But all these 'literary' justifications are discredited when Manjula is exposed as a plagiarist. What remains is her self-interested argument that looking for larger audiences and making money are not illegitimate pursuits for a writer, leading to a rather bald conclusion about the contaminating effects of English.

By all accounts, this dialectic faithfully represents the impassioned charges that major authors across the spectrum of Indian languages (U. R. Anantha Murthy, B. Jayamohan, Rajendra Yadav, and Gurdial

Singh, to name some) have continued to level against English in public forums of all kinds. What is remarkable is that, framed in these terms, the debate sidelines three developments that have transformed the language issue in India since the 1980s, for better or for worse. First, in the aftermath of the 'Rushdie revolution' the quality and quantity of writing in English by Indians bears little relation to the traditions of 'Indo-Anglian writing' as they had emerged before and after independence, so that a new theoretical and critical vocabulary is necessary to deal with the body of English works that counterpoints writing in the Indian languages. The generation of R. K. Narayan, Raja Rao, and Mulk Raj Anand has to be distinguished from the generation of midnight's children or midnight's orphans, however one may wish to name the new literary progeny. Second, the rapid growth of the global Indian diaspora has also repositioned many of the major Indian-English writers and absorbed them into the international literary establishment, so that India is no longer the primary context for their writing. Novelists such as Githa Hariharan and Shashi Deshpande, who live and publish in India, inhabit a qualitatively different literary landscape from novelists such as Amitav Ghosh, Rohinton Mistry, Bharati Mukherjee, and Vikram Seth. Admittedly, regardless of location Indian writers in English reach much larger audiences than those who write in the 'regional' Indian languages or even in the majority language, Hindi, and one may use this commonality of medium as a reason to reject them equally. But the differences between them still have to be recognized in a circumspect assessment of literary contexts: globalism has rapidly eroded the status of *all* stay-at-home writers, whatever their medium, although its effect on Indian-language authors has been especially dire. Third (and somewhat paradoxically), through the phenomenon of translation into English and other languages, Indian-language authors do inhabit a larger and more dynamic literary world than their predecessors—a change that Karnad knows well at first hand.

Indeed, it is intriguing to consider the figure of Manjula Nayak as a displaced version or anti-self of Karnad himself, in terms of both gender and experience. Karnad occupied a special place in the language debate by virtue of writing originally in Kannada as well as in English, and in translating from one language into another. Due to the quality and versatility of his talent he did not lead a life of struggle or obscurity as an author, and did not spend his life in a humdrum profession. Instead of remaining a 'regional' author, he commanded national visibility from the beginning of his career—not in the genre of fiction but drama. He is also one of the best-known contemporary Indian playwrights abroad. Karnad's own authorial career, in short, seems to counteract the premise in *Broken Images* that English is the necessary bridge to literary and material success for Indian authors, or that English and the Indian languages are mutually exclusive media. The discussion in the play is a complex and accurate recapitulation of the classic grounds of the language debate, but a partial gloss on conditions at the beginning of the twenty-first century.

In another perspective Karnad's portrayal is especially insightful, because the issue of a class system in contemporary Indian literature involves not only language but genre. Karnad could have chosen to portray a fellow playwright in *Broken Images*, but he is well aware that a *play* in English, however successful its author, cannot compete with a *novel* in English, because of the qualitative differences between novels and plays as literary artifacts. Fiction in English by Indian and Indian diaspora authors now commands a global readership and appears in academic curricula around the world; Indian plays in English occupy a distinctly subservient position, not only in relation to print genres such as fiction, non-fiction, and criticism in English, but also in relation to plays in Indian languages such as Bengali, Marathi, Kannada, Hindi, Malayalam, and Manipuri. The same is true of theatre professionals in the Indian diaspora who write and direct plays in English, such as Jatinder Verma in London or Rahul Varma in Montréal. Their works remain outside the cultural mainstream and command an audience infinitely smaller than the audience for the fiction of Rushdie, Mistry, Ghosh, and others. Accordingly, when Karnad takes on literary politics in *Broken Images* he immediately relates language to genre. The central issue in the play does not involve drama at all but the radically unequal status of fiction written in two contemporary languages, Kannada and English. The exclusion of Karnad's own lifelong form from the discussion is both an acknowledgment of the power of fiction in English and an imaginative leap into the world of other writers. The formal device of a character being interrogated by her own mechanically reproduced self, the crisp dialogue, and Karnad's fine ear for an up-to-date conversational idiom also make this a technically accomplished play.

Flowers, in contrast, returns to the world of folklore, and is the first work in this genre to focus on male rather than female desire, thus registering a small but important shift in Karnad's dramaturgy. The legend of Veeranna on which the play is based belongs to the Chitradurga region, and became widely known when the Kannada writer T. R. Subbanna (known as TaRaSu) included it in his 1952 novel, *Hamsageethe* (Swan Song). The protagonist of the novel is a singer called Venkatasubbayya, and early in the narrative Subbanna briefly inserts him into the tale of Veeranna, *archaka* of the Hidambeshwara temple. The married priest has been passionately in love with a mistress to whom he takes the offerings from the temple after the evening prayers. One day the *palegar* (chieftain) discovers a hair in the *prasada* and demands an explanation from Veeranna, who claims that the hair belongs to god. Challenged by the chieftain to prove the truth of his claim, the priest in turn challenges god to display hair or accept his head in punishment, and enters a meditative trance to the accompaniment of Venkatasubbayya's song. When the chieftain arrives the next day to expose Veeranna's lie, the *shivalinga* has indeed sprouted long silken hair, and when (urged by the singer) he pulls out a tuft to test its authenticity, blood begins to ooze from the crown of the *lingam*. Overwhelmed by a sense of sin at having injured his deity, Veeranna beheads himself in the sanctum.

In Subbanna's version of the legend the priest's wife and mistress are mentioned only in passing at the beginning. The heart of the narrative is the triangulated contest between the priest, the temple singer, and the chieftain, and the contrast between the brahmins' moral certainty and the insecurity of the shudra king. Karnad preserves the core event of the *shivalinga* sprouting hair, but recasts the legend as a conflict between religious devotion and erotic love, undergirded by the priest's guilt at his daily betrayal of his wife. The monologue is a swan song of another kind, a recounting of the nameless priest's experience as he prepares to drown himself in the temple tank. As in Karnad's earlier folk-based plays, the relationships in *Flowers* form a pattern of triangulated desire, this time between a man and two women. The drama highlights the spiritual and aesthetic intensity with which the priest has devoted himself to the task of worshipping and beautifying the *lingam*—an intensity that is transferred to the body of the courtesan-mistress. This mingling of the spiritual and the carnal is short-lived, however. The miracle of the *shivalinga* confirms the power of the priest's worship and marks him as one of the chosen, but it also ends his life.

The introspective, confessional male voice of the priest in *Flowers* has no precursor in Karnad's drama. Instead, it evokes the figure of Praneshacharya, the priest whose role Karnad had created in the celebrated 1970 film version of U. R. Anantha Murthy's *Samskara*. As the 'crest jewel of Vedantic learning' Praneshacharya is the spiritual leader of a community rather than a caretaker in a local temple, but both men sublimate their sexuality into religious fervour, and find sudden release after a lifetime of repression in an illicit union. In both works, renunciation gives way to sensuality, resistance to temptation, purity to pollution. Praneshacharya's liaison with the untouchable prostitute Chandri precipitates a sexual and spiritual crisis that is still unresolved at the end of the novel, though it ends his circumscribed existence in the *agrahara*. Similarly, in *Flowers* the priest's sexual awakening in the home of the courtesan Ranganayaki turns his world of ossified routine upside down, and begins the cycle of falsehood and concealment that culminates in the lie about the *lingam* sprouting hair. He therefore enacts Praneshacharya's extended crisis in a highly accelerated form, and by the end of the monologue is poised on the verge of self-destruction. Furthermore, both works offer an ironic variation on what the West calls the whore-madonna syndrome: sensuality is the province of the always ripe and ready courtesan, the world of dull duty and routine belongs to the shrivelled wife. This is arguably a chauvinistic position, though in Karnad's portrayal the priest's voice has an endearing innocence and honesty rather than an alienating—qualities successfully embodied in the performances by Rajit Kapur, the most notable actor to create the role in English.

VII

The body of journalistic, performance-related, critical, and scholarly commentary on Girish Karnad is already one of the most extensive in post-independence theatre, so that a general introduction to his drama does not need to go beyond a sequential overview of the qualities and contexts of his major plays. There are three aspects of his career, however, that deserve brief consideration because they have a direct as well as indirect bearing on the plays: his place in a multilingual theatre culture; the relation of playwriting to his work in the media of film and television; and his presence as an engaged intellectual in the always volatile Indian public sphere.

It is important to recognize that Karnad's translations of his own plays from and into Kannada and English are only a small part of the process by which his work has circulated within and outside India, and acquired an enduring afterlife. As the last five decades have demonstrated, in Indian theatre the prompt recognition of new plays as contemporary classics does not depend so much on publication or performance in the original language of composition as on the rapidity with which the plays are performed and (secondarily) published in other languages. Works such as *Tughlaq* and *Hayavadana* are showpieces of this process of dissemination-through-translation, including between them every major Indian language, as well as European languages such as Hungarian, Spanish, Polish, and German. The multidirectional movement is of central importance in a polyphonous culture because a classic in one language enriches theatre in numerous other languages: it makes a playwright's work available to major interpreters in multiple locations, and generates notable performances and texts for reading. Alyque Padamsee's English production of *Tughlaq* in 1970, Arvind Deshpande's Marathi production of 1971, Ebrahim Alkazi's Urdu productions of 1972, 1974, and 1982, and Satyadev Dubey's Marathi production of 1989 were landmark events in their respective languages as well as a confirmation of the play's 'national' standing. Similarly, Vijaya Mehta's Marathi productions of *Hayavadana* and *Nāga-Mandala* (1983 and 1991) extended her range as a director, while her German productions (1984 and 1992) transplanted the plays in a unique European venue, the Deutsches Nationaltheater in Weimar. Hence, while B. V. Karanth, C. Basavalingaiah, and C. R. Jambe are the most important interpreters of Karnad's plays in Kannada, the major directors of his plays in other languages (in addition to those mentioned above) include Om Shivpuri, Kumar Roy, Shyamanand Jalan, Rajinder Nath, Prasanna, Amal Allana, and Neelam Mansingh Chowdhry. It is no exaggeration to say that theatres in Hindi-Urdu, Bengali, Marathi, and Punjabi, among other languages, are infinitely richer for having absorbed Karnad's drama. This performance-centered activity has an important textual parallel when the translator is also a major playwright. The Marathi translation of *Tughlaq* is by Vijay Tendulkar, paralleling Karnad's translation of Badal Sircar's *Evam Indrajit* into English (1974), and of Mahesh Elkunchwar's *Wasansi Jeernani* and *Dharmaputra* into Kannada (2004). While an editor at Oxford University Press, Madras, in the 1960s, he persuaded the company's head office in London to publish A. K. Ramanujan (a fundamentally bilingual author and a leading translator) in the Oxford Poets series. Karnad has thus contributed at multiple levels to the all-important contemporary culture of translation—as the translator of his own and others' work, as a facilitator, and as a playwright whose work can be widely appropriated in other languages.

Karnad's extensive work in the media of film and television is remarkable for other reasons, and raises a different series of issues in relation to drama. As a literary playwright he maintains an authorial persona similar to that of contemporaries such as Dharamvir Bharati, Mohan Rakesh, G. P. Deshpande, and Mahesh Elkunchwar, all of whom approach drama primarily as a verbal art and a mode of sublimated self-expression. These authors engage with the processes of performance and production exclusively in connection with their own work, and at the invitation of other directors and theatre groups because they do not direct themselves (the English and Kannada productions of *Broken Images/Odakalu Bimba* in 2005 mark Karnad's debut as a stage director of his own work in both languages). Yet in another respect Karnad stands apart from all the playwrights mentioned above, because outside the theatre he was a prize-winning actor, director, and screenwriter for film and television in Kannada, Hindi, and English. His first significant screen role was as Praneshacharya in *Samskara*, under Pattabhi Rama Reddy's direction, in 1970. The following decade witnessed a vital partnership between Karnad as actor, Vijay Tendulkar as screenwriter, and Shyam Benegal as director. His leading roles in *Nishant* (1973), *Manthan* (1976), and *Umbartha* (1982) helped to launch and sustain the Middle Cinema movement in Hindi, while the commercial but 'serious' film *Swami* (1978) drew him into the competitive world of Bombay cinema. Over the same period Karnad also directed a number of significant feature films: *Vamsha Vriksha* (with B. V. Karanth, 1971), *Kaadu* (1973), and *Ondanandu Kaaladalli* (1978) in Kannada; and *Godhuli* (with B. V. Karanth, 1977), *Utsav* (1984), and *Cheluvi* (1993) in Hindi. *Samskara* won the national award for best film in 1971, *Vamsha Vriksha* the national award for best direction in 1972, and *Kanaka-Purandara* the award for best documentary in 1988.

What does this unique engagement with multiple media in multiple capacities imply for Karnad's life as a playwright? His simplest explanation is economic: he took on work in film and television so that he could earn a living and pursue his first love, drama. The trajectory of his career also shows that his leanest years as a playwright, from 1972 to 1987, were among his busiest in film and television, so that drama and the popular media would seem to stand in an inverse relation to each other—one waxing while the other wanes. When Karnad received the Jnanpith Award and the Kalidasa Samman in 1999, he commented that the two prizes would contribute greatly to his financial independence and enable him to 'retire' from films, giving him more time to write. In moments of candour, he has also repeatedly expressed great dislike for the actor's job. These may have been Karnad's private sentiments, but the distinctions he earned for his work in cinema and television also confirmed his talent for these media, and his ability to engage a serious audience. There was also an unmistakably 'literary' bent to his acting and filmmaking. *Samskara* brought a major novel to the screen; Benegal's films had screenplays by Tendulkar; *Utsav* was based on Shudraka's Sanskrit play, *Mrichchakatika*; *Ondanondu Kaaladalli* was a Kannada adaptation of Akira Kurosawa's *The Seven Samurai*; *Cheluvi* was based on 'The Flowering Tree', a folktale transcribed by A. K. Ramanujan; and so on.

A different kind of connection between playwriting, film, and television appears in Karnad's personalized conception of 'drama': human beings pretending to be someone else and acting out a story that is of interest to the viewers. Drama in this sense is common to all the media that represent human beings in action, although for Karnad plays occupy the centre, and the other activities—acting, directing, screenplay-writing, and television production—are ancillary occupations that feed off an essentially dramatic sensibility and feed back into it. In his 1993 interview with me Karnad expressed satisfaction at the fact that 'we see much more drama around us than ever before...[and] more people are involved in the "business" of drama than ever before' ('Performance' 363). In his International Message on World Theatre Day (27 March 2002) he returned to the account of the first-ever dramatic performance in the *Natyashastra* to re-emphasize the uniqueness of theatre in relation to the mechanical media:

Radio, films, television and video inundate us with drama. But while these forms can engage or even enrage the audience, in none of them can the viewer's response alter the artistic event itself. The Myth of the First Performance points out that in theatre, the playwright, the performers and the audience form a continuum, but one which will always be unstable and therefore potentially explosive. That is why theatre is signing its own death warrant when it tries to play too safe. On the other hand, that is also the reason why, although its future often seems bleak, theatre will continue to live and to provoke.

There is perhaps no better summation of Karnad's work as a playwright than his move to locate the strength of theatre in its potential for failure; notwithstanding a charmed career, he is eventually a poet of incompleteness, fallibility, and loss.

In yet another perspective, Karnad's success in multiple cultural modes also made him an unusually visible artist-intellectual for several decades. His activities in theatre, film, and television were reported regularly in the journalistic media, and his positions on various issues, both regional and national, carried considerable weight. During the 1960s and 1970s, Karnad's contributions to public discourse were mainly in the spheres of cultural practice and cultural policy, as evidenced in his Bhabha Fellowship from 1970–2, his participation in the Sangeet Natak Akademi's National

Roundtable on the Contemporary Relevance of Traditional Theatre in 1971, and his Directorship of the Film and Television Institute in Pune from 1974–5. As Director of the Sangeet Natak Akademi (1988–93) and the Nehru Centre in London (2000–3), and as a frequent commentator on Indian theatre and the arts in numerous national and international forums, he continued these forms of cultural engagement. He is also not a 'political' playwright of the same kind as Utpal Dutt, G. P. Deshpande, or even Vijay Tendulkar. But like many other Indian intellectuals, after the late 1980s Karnad had to negotiate a difficult new phase in the politics of the nation, and his stand against religious nationalism led inevitably to confrontation and controversy.

The experience of writing *Talé-Daṇḍa* appears to have been the turning point in this respect. Karnad was the first Kannada writer to denounce Advani's Rath Yatra (on Bangalore Doorsdarshan) the very day that it began, and prepared the way for similar criticism by other writers. In 1994, when the BJP accused the Muslim community in Hubli of impeding a flag-raising ceremony at Iddgah Maidan (although the rights to the Maidan were then under litigation), Karnad held a press conference in New Delhi to focus attention on the harrassment of the Muslims. In 1997 he delivered the keynote address (entirely in Marathi) at the 70th annual Marathi Sahitya Sammelan before an audience of 70,000 in Nagar, pointing to the irony that a country in which the military has been famously neutral in political matters, political parties with an adversarial agenda have adopted a militaristic mode of organization in the name of 'discipline'. Interpreted (and hailed) widely as a much-needed castigation of groups like the Shiv Sena and the RSS, the speech was published in the *Economic and Political Weekly* under the title 'Citizen as Soldier', and remains remarkable for the clarity with which it analyses the fundamentalist urge to stifle debate. In 2003, Karnad was among a group of Kannada writers who insisted that the government of Karnataka curb BJP and Bajrang Dal activism over Baba Budan

Giri, a Sufi hill in the Chikmagalur district that had long been known for its multi-religious following, but was being claimed as another Hindu shrine 'forcibly taken over by Muslims'. In 2015 he was involved in a controversy over the naming of the new international airport in Bengaluru, and not long before his death in June 2019 he memorialized the murdered journalist Gauri Lankesh by ironically proclaiming himself an 'urban Naxal'. Each one of these events after 1989 made Karnad the target of demagogic denunciations and threats of retaliation; each one reconfirmed his cosmopolitan commitment to an open society based on respect for the rights of others. As the representation of large-scale political *processes* in plays such as *Tughlaq* and *Talé-Daṇḍa* shows, the principles of secularism and human fellowship are difficult values that founder in the face of self-interested opposition. But in the quotidian world Karnad affirms what the plays imply: unexamined certitudes are synonymous with death; doubt and uncertainty are the signs of life.

APARNA BHARGAVA DHARWADKER
ASSOCIATE PROFESSOR OF ENGLISH AND INTERDISCIPLINARY
THEATRE STUDIES
UNIVERSITY OF WISCONSIN-MADISON

Works Cited

Karnad, Girish. 'Citizen as Soldier.' *Economic and Political Weekly*, vol. 32, no. 11 (15 March 1997): 523–5.

———. 'Performance, Meaning, and the Materials of Modern Indian Theatre.' Interview with Aparna Dharwadker. *New Theatre Quarterly* 44 (1995): 355–70.

Madan, T. N. 'Religion, Ethnicity, and Nationalism in India,' in *Religion, Ethnicity and Self-Identity: Nations in Turmoil*, Martin E. Marty and R. Scott Appleby (eds). Hanover: University Press of New England, 1997. 53–71.

———. 'Secularism in its Place.' *Journal of Asian Studies 46. 4 (1987):* 747–59.

TALÉ-DAṆḌA

NOTE

During the two decades ending in AD 1168, in the city of Kalyan, a man called Basavanna assembled a congregation of poets, mystics, social revolutionaries and philosophers. Together they created an age unmatched in the history of Karnataka for its creativity, courageous questioning and social commitment. Spurning Sanskrit, they talked of God and man in the mother-tongue of the common people. They condemned idolatry and temple worship. Indeed, they rejected anything 'static' in favour of the principle of movement and progress in human enterprise. They believed in the equality of sexes and celebrated hard, dedicated work. They opposed the caste system, not just in theory but in practice. This last act brought down upon them the wrath of the orthodox. The movement ended in terror and bloodshed.

Talé-Daṇḍa literally means death by beheading (*Talé*: Head. *Daṇḍa* Punishment).

Offering one's head, either on completion of a vow or in penitence, was a common practice in medieval Karnataka.

Basavanna often uses the word to express his outrage at a particularly unpleasant situation or accusation, to mean something like 'May my head roll' or 'I offer my head—'.

The translations of the free verse lyrics by Basavanna used in the play are all by A. K. Ramanujan, who brought this extraordinary body of work to the attention of the world outside. Three of them have already appeared in his anthology, *Speaking of Siva* (Penguin Books, 1973). The rest he translated specially for this English version. Tragically, Ramanujan died a few months before it was published.

In Karnataka, as elsewhere in India, a man has only to open his mouth and his speech will give away his caste, his geographical origins, even his economic status. In the original Kannada version of *Talé-Daṇḍa*, the language of the play engages with the implications of this fact for a situation in which a group of people are trying to fight caste and social inequality. For obvious reasons, this aspect of the problem is not explored in the English translation.

GIRISH KARNAD

SAMBASHIVA SHASTRI	Brahmin, Jagadeva's father
AMBA	Jagadeva's mother
BHAGIRATHI	Brahmin woman
SAVITRI	Jagadeva's wife
JAGADEVA	*Sharana*, Brahmin by birth
MALLIBOMMA	*Sharana*, Tanner by birth
SOVIDEVA	Bijjala's son
RAMBHAVATI	Bijjala's queen
DAMODARA BHATTA	Queen's priest
KALLAPPA	Bijjala's bodyguard
BIJJALA	King of Kalyan
BASAVANNA	The great *Sharana* saint poet
MANCHANNA KRAMITA	Brahmin, adviser to the king
GUNDANNA	*Sharana*
KALAYYA	*Sharana*
KAKKAYYA	*Sharana*, Skinner by birth
GANGAMBIKA	Basavanna's wife
HARALAYYA	*Sharana*, Cobbler by birth
KALYANI	Haralayya's wife
SHEELAVANTA	Haralayya's son
MADHUVARASA	*Sharana*, Brahmin by birth
LALITAMBA	Madhuvarasa's wife

KALAVATI	Madhuvarasa's daughter
INDRANI	Courtesan
MARAYPPA	Boy attendent
BANKANNA	Boy attendent
EERAVVA	Queen's maid
RACHAPPA	Palace guard

Brahmins, palace servants, crowds, tribals, *sharanas*, Indrani's woman, soldiers and messengers.

Scene One
AD 1168

The Brahmin quarter of the city of Kalyan. Sambashiva Shastri's house. The Shastri is lying in bed in a room. He is ill. Next to him sit his wife, Amba, and her friend, Bhagirathi. Savitri, the Shastri's daughter-in-law, aged about fourteen, mixes medicine in the kitchen. Suddenly the Shastri begins to call out.

SHASTRI: Jagganna—Jagadeva—Come here, son. Where are you? Come soon.

AMBA: Please stop that. You have ripped your throat to shreds calling for him.

SHASTRI: Get him here, immediately. Tell him I want him here. I feel scared when he's not near me. Jagganna—

BHAGIRATHI: Poor soul! How he torments himself! Can't you send for Jagganna again, Ambakka?

AMBA: I would have. But is there any point? They say there is a crowd of about twenty thousand people around the Treasury. Govind says he was almost trampled to death reaching Jagganna. And after all that, Jagganna had no time for him. He was only concerned about the Treasury. If he cared, don't you think he would have looked in here some time during these four days? He knows his father is ill—

SHASTRI: Is Jagganna here? Why hasn't he come? Jagadeva... Jagganna...

AMBA (*wiping her tears*): Jagganna's inflicting every torture in hell on us for having borne him.

BHAGIRATHI: Besides, is it wise to antagonize the Yuvaraj and the royal family like this? Robber barons, after all. I wouldn't put anything past them.

SHASTRI: I'm afraid. Jagganna...

AMBA: He has seen with his own eyes what happened to his father when he stood up to the King. The whole world collapsed around us.

SHASTRI (*enraged*): I'm screaming my head off here and all you do is stand there. Go, bring him. Instantly. Go. Jagadeva—
(*He tries to get up but, racked by a vicious coughing fit, falls back panting.*)

AMBA: Savitri—Savitri—

BHAGIRATHI: Is the medicine ready, Savitri? Hurry up.
(*Savitri rushes from the kitchen with the medicine. She hands it over to Amba, who pours it into the Shastri's mouth. He quietens down.*)

BHAGIRATHI: Why can't that Basavanna see some sense? In every household in Kalyan, it's the same story. Father against son—brother against brother.

AMBA: And our son sent Savitri back to her parents just to show us how annoyed he is. But why blame Basavanna, Bhagirathi? We must suffer what's written in our foreheads.
(*Jagadeva and Mallibomma enter the street in front of the house. They are both around nineteen. They are in high spirits.*)

JAGADEVA: Come in.

MALLIBOMMA: Don't be silly. I shouldn't have even stepped into this Brahmin street. And you want me to come into your house? No, thank you.

JAGADEVA: Come on. Let's show them.

MALLIBOMMA: You go in now. I'd better return home, too.

JAGADEVA: That won't do. You must come in. Don't be afraid. I'm here. Come on!

(*He starts dragging Mallibomma by his arm. Mallibomma resists.*)

BHAGIRATHI (*getting up*): Jagganna's come. I'll be off.

(*She goes out. Savitri follows her to the door and watches her husband from a distance.*)

JAGADEVA: Don't make a fuss, Malli. Or else—

MALLIBOMMA: No, please, listen to me—

BHAGIRATHI (*at the door*): Why, Jagganna, your poor father is killing himself there crying out for you. And you hold court here?

JAGADEVA: How does that concern you? You'd better look after your husband. You know where he is—

BHAGIRATHI (*to Mallibomma*): Who are you, boy?

JAGADEVA: He's my friend, Mallibomma.

BHAGIRATHI (*ignoring Jagadeva*): This is a Brahmin household. Do you mind standing a little aside so the women of the house can move about freely? What are we to do if you plant yourself on the doorstep like a feudal chieftain?

(*Mallibomma, mortified, tries to move aside but Jagadeva doesn't let him.*)

JAGADEVA: This is my house, Bhagakka, and he is a friend of mine. My friends will come here when they like and stand where they choose. If that's not to your liking, you are free to stay as far from here as you wish.

BHAGIRATHI: I'd do just that, son, except that your mother, poor thing, is alone and without help. And I gather that before taking off with your *sharana* cronies, you sent your wife home to her family—just to spite your parents?

AMBA (*comes out*): Come in, Jagga. Why are you standing on the steps like a stranger?

JAGADEVA: Mother, you tell Mallibomma yourself. I won't set foot in the house unless he comes in with me.

MALLIBOMMA: No, really, I must go.

AMBA: Come in, Malli.

MALLIBOMMA (*explaining*): You see, Ma'am... I'm the son of Tanner Kariya.

(*Pause.*)

AMBA: My son won't come into the house unless you do. So come in, please. I'll have the house purified later. Please, I beg of you—with folded hands—

MALLIBOMMA (*horrified*): Oh, Ma'am. Please don't say such things.

AMBA: Then come in.

(*The doors of neighbouring houses fill up with women, children and old men watching.*)

JAGADEVA: Look how they've collected! You'd think there were some kind of acrobatics going on here. (*Loudly*) Are you all listening? All attention? This is my friend Mallibomma. He is the son of a tanner. And I am taking him inside our house. Are you satisfied? Come on, Mallibomma—

(*The three step into the house. Mallibomma is half dead with embarrassment. Jagadeva is surprised to see Savitri behind the door.*)

JAGADEVA (*growls*): When did you come back? Didn't I say I would send for you?

AMBA: *I* sent for her. I was alone here. You went off with the *sharanas* and didn't even bother to check if we were dead or alive here. How much can one ask of the neighbours? So embarrassing to—

JAGADEVA: But I had no choice, Mother. I had to go. It would have been disastrous if I hadn't! Listen. That day, Accountant

Kishtachari's son casually mentioned to me that the Prince was planning to open the doors of the Treasury. And instantly I smelt mischief! The King is not in town. Basavanna is away. And the lock of the Treasury cannot be touched unless either the King or his Treasurer is physically present: that is the law. So why should Prince Sovideva pick this moment to inspect the accounts? Most intriguing...

AMBA (*spreading a mat*): Sit down, Malli. (*To Jagadeva*) I hope you don't need to be reminded that you have a father—and that he has cried himself hoarse calling out to you.

JAGADEVA (*looks into the bedroom*): He's asleep? Good! (*Comes out.*) I went from door to door, immediately, waking up the *sharanas*. I lost my voice telling everyone that something sinister was going on. But no one would move.

AMBA: Can't the King's Treasurer handle his own affairs?

JAGADEVA: I told you, Basavanna wasn't in town. He was away in Bannoor with Kakkayya, initiating the untouchables there into our fold. (*To Mallibomma*) Do you know—Basavanna himself told me—all the untouchables there have accepted our faith and become *sharanas*!

MALLIBOMMA (*excited*): Marvellous! (*To Amba*) The problem, Ma'am, is that once Basavanna involves himself in such matters, nothing will make him budge. Even if we had sent for him, he would have ignored us. One can't say what might have happened if Jagganna hadn't taken it upon himself to rally the *sharanas* that day. The Prince would have fixed the accounts and ruined Basavanna's reputation!

JAGADEVA (*laughing*): But once the *sharanas* were up, there was no stopping them. No less than five to six thousand—

MALLIBOMMA: Five to six? More, more. There were at least ten—

JAGADEVA: But that was later. Initially, no one would react. There were barely—

MALLIBOMMA: Ma'am, you should have seen how they treated Jagganna—like a real leader! For the past four days fifteen thousand *sharanas* have been following his commands implicitly—

AMBA: I see, and he gave up all that glory for the sake of his ailing father! Very noble of him, I'm sure.

JAGADEVA (*pleading*): Please, Mother, try to understand. I would have come home sooner. But there was no way I could leave till Basavanna himself returned and took charge. That Prince was in the Treasury—and no trick is too filthy for him. Basavanna returned from Bannoor just half an hour ago. Didn't even go home. Came to the Treasury direct and, do you know, the first thing he said was 'I am sorry to hear your father is unwell. You go home. I am here. I'll come and meet your father later.' Can you imagine? In the middle of all that confusion! (*To Mallibomma*) He is no ordinary man, I tell you. I'm sure he's the incarnation of the divine bull, Nandi.

(*The Shastri moans inside. Jagadeva gets up and goes in.*)

MALLIBOMMA: Jagganna, take your father's head on your lap. Rub his forehead. He'll feel better.

(*Jagadeva does as told, but awkwardly. Mallibomma speaks to Amba.*)

We didn't know his father was so ill, Ma'am. I would certainly have sent him home sooner—

SHASTRI: Put it down on the floor.

AMBA: He's up.

(*She goes in. Mallibomma watches from the outer room.*)

SHASTRI: Why are you sitting idle? Pick it up. Put it on the floor.

JAGADEVA: Father, I'm here. I shan't go away again. Don't be afraid.

SHASTRI: Take it off the bed. Be quick. Why are you ignoring it? Pick it up—

JAGADEVA: Pick what up, Father?

SHASTRI: Me.

JAGADEVA: What are you saying?

SHASTRI: It's lying there unattended. Put it on the floor, fold its legs, otherwise it won't fit on the bier. Jagganna—where is Jagganna? Send for the bamboos and rope.

JAGADEVA: I'm here.

SHASTRI: Not you—I want my son! There is so much to do. Your mother. Attend to her hair. Her head has to be shaved—

AMBA: I can't take this. God, what have I done in my past lives to have to put up with all this?

(*She runs in weeping. Mallibomma, seeing the seriousness of the situation and aware that his continued presence will only create more problems, quietly slips away. Savitri stands in the doorway, watching Jagadeva, and weeps.*)

SHASTRI: Jagga—

JAGADEVA: I'm here.

SHASTRI: Not you. My son! He has to be there for the cremation. Tell him the corpse is beginning to stink. It'll get worse. Call him. Jagganna—come. Remove the corpse—

Scene Two

Bijjala's palace.

The Chamber of Queen Rambhavati. She is unwell and mostly sits on a couch, reclining against the wall. Sovideva, her son, aged twenty, paces up and down. Adjacent to the Chamber is the god's room with a linga in it. In size, the linga is large enough to be worthy of the palace. The priest, Damodara Bhatta, aged thirty, is performing the pooja.

SOVIDEVA (*screaming*): I shall bury them alive! Hack them to pieces and feed them to my hounds!

RAMBHAVATI: Calm yourself! Don't get into a fight with those *sharanas*, son. If your father comes to know, there'll be—

SOVIDEVA: It's he who encourages those sons of slaves. It's because of him that the vermin can be so brazen, so impudent. I am the Yuvaraj of the Kalachurya dynasty—and those louts have the insolence to make a fool of me in front of the whole city? They know they can get away with anything—

(*Damodara Bhatta does* arati *before the* linga. *Mother and son stand and fold their hands. The priest steps out of the room, extends the* arati *towards the two. They spread their palms to receive the warmth of the flame and put a few coins in the plate.*)

RAMBHAVATI: Come, Sovi. Sit next to me.

SOVIDEVA: No, I won't.

RAMBHAVATI: Come on.

(*She forces him to sit by her side.*)

Why do you want to tangle with those *sharanas*? Leave the King's affairs alone—

SOVIDEVA: Stop telling me what to do! I'm sick and tired of being at the receiving end all the time. I won't put up with it any more—

RAMBHAVATI (*tired*): Do as you wish. Just don't upset your father, that's all. He takes out his bad temper on me and I've just had enough.

SOVIDEVA: Basavanna has been systematically defrauding the Treasury. Accountant Kishtachari has evidence to show he had bilked us of thirty thousand sovereigns. And yet he continues to be the King's Treasurer—our Minister of Finance! Father is totally in his thrall, I tell you. And so are you!

RAMBHAVATI: What am I to do? Do you think your father ever listens to me?

SOVIDEVA: Why not? If only you would put your mind to it! Each one of your stepsons was awarded his own independent domain by the time he was eighteen. That mongrel brood! They get their claims! You are a princess of the Hoysala dynasty. Bijjala's favourite Queen. And I am your only son. And what do I have? A jangling bell to keep me occupied.

RAMBHAVATI: Don't say that, son. Who do I have other than you?

(*Damodara Bhatta has finished his* pooja. *He comes out.*)

DAMODARA: Forgive me for interrupting, Your Majesty. It was a mob no less than fifteen thousand strong that encircled the Treasury. Yet you should have seen how disciplined they were, how restrained! For four days they sat there, surrounding the building, ungrudging, even cheerful, until Basavanna himself came on the scene and sent them home. It was a prodigious display of loyalty to Basavanna. Would the *sharanas* be as loyal to the King? One wonders.

RAMBHAVATI (*dubious*): I don't know. Basavanna can be obstinate. But I don't think he is treacherous.

SOVIDEVA (*explodes*): There you are! So I am the villain. I should now humbly crawl…

DAMODARA: 'Miraculous' is the only word for the speed with which the news spread. Barely an hour had elapsed after the Yuvaraj had the locks opened—and there they were, thousands of them, swarming from every corner of Kalyan. Certainly points to an efficient network of spies within the court, doesn't it?

RAMBHAVATI: But did you find any evidence against Basavanna?

DAMODARA: I had warned the Yuvaraj against this—this adventure, Your Majesty. Basavanna is not one to drown in shallow waters. And suppose we had managed to prove our charges. What of it? He would merely be proven a corrupt officer of the court, like any other. If one aims to catch a tusker, one must dig a pit capacious enough to take him in entire.

(*Kallappa enters.*)

KALLAPPA: I fall at your feet, Ma'am. The Master is here.

RAMBHAVATI (*getting up, flustered*): Already? Why couldn't he let us know a little in advance? (*Shouts.*) Eeravva! Eeravva! Go call Eeravva, for heaven's sake. Ask her to get the *arati* ready—

KALLAPPA: The master doesn't want any of it, Ma'am. He's already in the palace, on his way here.

RAMBHAVATI: Eeravva! (*Suddenly noticing Damodara Bhatta.*) You may go, sir. You know how he is—

(*Damodara Bhatta nods and leaves with a smile. Sovideva tries to go out with him.*)

KALLAPPA: The young Master is to remain here.

SOVIDEVA: Which snivelling spy informed him I was here? I must go. (*To Rambha*) You make some excuse for me—

(*Sovideva tries to go out. But Kallappa steps in his way, quietly but firmly.*)

SOVIDEVA (*to his mother*): So you see how I am treated in my own house—like a toothless hound?

BIJJALA (*roars from outside*): Where is that son of a whore?

RAMBHAVATI: Come here, son. And whatever he says, keep your mouth shut.

(*Bijjala enters.*)

BIJJALA: Is he hiding in here?

RAMBHAVATI: What nonsense is this? You shouldn't rush in like this—without *arati* or saffron-water to cast out the evil eye. Wait there now. Beyond the doorstep. Eeravva!

BIJJALA: May your Eeravvas and Paaravvas be cast to perdition. Is that accursed fruit of our family here?

(*He sees Sovideva.*)

Come out. Come out. Aren't you ashamed to hide under a woman's backside, your blood-sodden rag, you—

(*Sovideva steps out.*)

What were you up to in my absence? Who gave you the right to tamper with the Treasury locks?

(*He starts beating up Sovideva. Sovideva does not resist.*)

RAMBHAVATI: I beg you, don't. Don't beat him, please. I implore you in the name of our family God, I touch your feet. He's a grown-up man. Don't humiliate him like this.

(*To Sovideva*)

Go—go away from here!

BIJJALA: What! He's not leaving his mother's home empty-handed, is he? Eeravva, a sari and a blouse-piece for our son. And be quick—

RAMBHAVATI: Stop it. Please! At least for my sake. Or do away with me first. Once you're rid of me, do what you will with him. But I can't bear this. Please. I fall at your feet!

BIJJALA: Rambha! Rambha! All this is your doing. You, with your pampering and swaddling, you have turned him into a royal eunuch. And I am the greater fool for having let your tears stop me. If only I had birched the skin off his back as I had with his brothers. If only I had tied him up in a bundle and dowsed him in the river. But you had to get in the way and cry and wail. It's all your doing...

RAMBHAVATI: You treat him as one shouldn't even one's bitterest enemy. Why? What has my son done to deserve this from you?

BIJJALA: What hasn't he done? He fiddles with the Treasury locks when he shouldn't have. And then, on top of it, when Basavanna actually arrives on the scene, he attempts to run away, like a rabbit. Fifteen thousand people blocked his way and applauded and roared with laughter as Basavanna led him back by hand into the Treasury and had the doors sealed behind them. I reached the city gates this morning, exhausted, aching all over, and what news greets me, do you think? 'Basavanna and the Yuvaraj were closeted in the Treasury for eleven days, checking accounts. They have only just finished'! Checking accounts, my bloody foot. (*To Sovideva*) Did you find a broken cowrie missing from the coffers? A counterfeit coin unaccounted for in the books?

(*No reply.*)

When Basavanna puts something down on paper, it's there for good. As if planted by Brahma himself. And that's why he continues to be the King's Treasurer. Are you listening, nincompoop? Are you? Then speak out. You are quick enough to find the wrong limb to do the wrong things. But you can't find your bloody tongue—

RAMBHAVATI: Please, don't be abusive!

BIJJALA: Madam, this is not your parental home. Let's not have any of your Hoysala sanctimonious humbug here. I am a Kalachurya. Rough-hewn. Blunt. I have asked my son a question. And I am waiting for an answer. You keep out of it!

RAMBHAVATI: And what have you done to justify calling him your son? He has come of age and you haven't even thrown a scrap of land at him—

BIJJALA: Land? At this bumpkin? I give him a kingdom—And what do I do with the people in there? Push them into a bottomless pit? I fetched him a golden bride. He only had to conduct himself with a bit of sense and his father-in-law would have given him half his kingdom. He couldn't keep her. And now he aspires to be a king, does he? Let's see. Kallappa!

(*Kallappa enters.*)

Kallappa, this scion of the Kalachuryas craves to be a king, we are told. Now, in order to be a ruler, what is the primary qualification? Surely the ability to kick people around? That is why they say to be born a king in this life you need to have been a donkey in your last. You've heard that? Good. Now my son and heir will try to deliver a kick on your behind. But you must not let it land. If his foot touches you, I shall skin you alive, mind. Now honourable Yuvaraj, proceed. Go on. Kick him.

(*Sovideva tries to kick Kallappa. But Kallappa is too agile for him. Sovideva makes several attempts but to no avail. Bijjala is red with excitement and frustration as he watches.*)

Faster, son. Move. Why are you stuck there, leg out, like a dog pissing? Hit out. From the hip, you oaf.

(*Exasperated, he turns to Rambha.*)

This is the first lesson they teach in the gymnasium. And he can't manage it!

(*Impatient, he jumps in.*)

My turn now, Kallappa. If my toe so much as grazes you, you'll pay with your head.

(*Bijjala takes aim and kicks. The kick catches Kallappa squarely on his behind. He crashes to the floor. Bijjala roars triumphantly. Then turns to Sovideva.*)

You next. Ready?

(*He sends Sovideva reeling with a well-aimed kick.*)

Kallappa, two gold sovereigns for you. Tell the clerk. He'll pay you. It's not your fault you lost. Bijjala hasn't lost his touch yet.

(*Kallappa bows to him and exits, brushing his behind. Bijjala glares after him.*)

That sly bastard! I shall never know if he hasn't made an ass of me.

(*Rambhavati, who has not watched any of the above, opens her eyes and pushes Sovideva out. Then she sits back, crying. Bijjala sits next to her, tired, defeated.*)

BIJJALA: So many, so many women came and went. Not one of them could keep hold of me. Then you came. The world knows there hasn't been another. And then... (*Spits.*) this rat has to crawl out of your womb.

(*Noise outside.*)

What's that commotion, Kallappa?

Kallappa (*enters*): Basavanna is here for an audience, Master.

BIJJALA: I knew it! Seat him in the inner chamber. Not the audience hall, mind you. He is too unpredictable.

(*Kallappa exits.*)

RAMBHAVATI: I'm baffled by your infatuation for that man. He mocks your son in front of the world, and instead of tarring his face in public you invite him into the inner chamber?

BIJJALA (*glares at her*): You and your son! In all these fifteen years, you haven't understood a thing about Basavanna, have you? Or about me, for that matter! Who am I? I am Bijjala, the Emperor of Kalyan, the strong-shouldered Kalachurya conqueror! And yet—what is my caste? Tell me.

RAMBHAVATI: What has that to do with it?

BIJJALA: I have asked you a question. Answer it!

RAMBHAVATI: We are Kshatriyas.

BIJJALA: Your family—the Hoysalas, *you* may be Kshatriyas. But

I am a Kalachurya. Katta churra. A barber. His Majesty King Bijjala is a barber by caste. For ten generations my forefathers ravaged the land as robber barons. For another five they ruled as the trusted feudatories of the Emperor himself. They married into every royal family in sight. Bribed generations of Brahmins with millions of cows. All this so they could have the caste of Kshatriyas branded on their foreheads. And yet you ask the most innocent child in my Empire: what is Bijjala, son of Kalachurya Permadi, by caste? And the instant reply will be: a barber! One's caste is like the skin on one's body. You can peel it off top to toe, but when the new skin forms, there you are again: a barber—a shepherd—a scavenger!

(*Pause.*)

In all my sixty-two years, the only people who have looked me in the eye without a reference to my lowly birth lurking deep in their eyes are the *sharanas*: Basavanna and his men. They treat me as—as what?—(*Almost with a sense of wonder.*) as a human being. Basavanna wants to eradicate the caste structure, wipe it off the face of the earth. Annihilate the varna system. What a vision! And what prodigious courage! And he has the ability. Look at those he has gathered around him: poets, mystics, visionaries. And nothing airy-fairy about them, mind you. All hard-working people from the common stock. They sit together, eat together, argue about God together, indifferent to caste, birth or station. And all this is happening in the city of Kalyan—*my* Kalyan!

RAMBHAVATI: Then why don't you join them too? That may solve the problem—

BIJJALA: It'll solve nothing. They are insufferable moralists. You know that verse of Basavanna's?

Do not steal.
Do not kill.
Do not ever lie.
Do not rage...

and so on. It's not, as you can see, an ethics designed for rulers. Worse still is their *bhakti*, their relentless devotion, their incessant craving for the Lord's grace. I've built temples to keep my subjects happy. But the one truth I know is that I exist and God doesn't.

(*She giggles.*)

What are you giggling about?

RAMBHAVATI: Suddenly, you were as you used to be in those days— our early years together, when you'd talk and talk and insist on my listening. Remember?

BIJJALA: Is that all you have to say? Doesn't anything interest you women except marriage and husbands and children?

RAMBHAVATI: Have you left us anything else?

(*Commotion outside.*)

BIJJALA: What the devil's that noise, Kallappa?

KALLAPPA (*enters*): Crowds, thronging to take a look at Basavanna, Master.

BIJJALA: Why? Don't the numb-skulls know he lives in this city?

KALLAPPA: Well, Master, it's this thing they say that happened in the Treasury—

BIJJALA: What?

KALLAPPA: This morning, Master... They say Basavanna performed a miracle. That's why these crowds—

RAMBHAVATI: A miracle?

KALLAPPA: Yes, Ma'am. A miracle. There was a miracle. And the whole city was witness to it.

Scene Three

The inner chamber of the palace. Basavanna is talking to an old woman. Three or four domestics are grouped around them, listening.

BASAVANNA: But, Guddevva, your daughter-in-law is still young. So it's up to you to take a sensible view of things. May I suggest something?

GUDDEVVA: Will anyone say no to you?

BASAVANNA: They say you have a sweet voice and that you know many songs by the Tanner Chennayya—

GUDDEVVA (*blushing*): *Ayyo!* Who told you all that?

BASAVANNA: Why don't you hand over your house to your daughter-in-law for a few days? Let her look after it. You come over to our house...

GUDDEVVA: No, thank you. You collect all those low-caste people in your house, don't you—even the untouchables? I'd rather not rub shoulders with them—

BASAVANNA (*laughs*): They'll be there, certainly. But you can choose where you want to sit. Sing what you feel like singing. They'll sing too. Then you decide whether you would like to visit us again. What do you say?

(*The heralds proclaim the King's entry from outside.*)

HERALDS: *Mahārajādhirāja Kālanjarapurādhīshwara Suvarna-Vrishabhadhwaja Damaru-toorya-nirghoshana Kalachūrya-Vamsha-Kamala-Bhāskara Triambaka-pāda-padma-madhupa Nisshankamalla Bhujabala-Chakravarti Bijjala-Devaraj (Crescendo.) Bho parāk! Bho parāk!*

(Bijjala enters followed by his Brahmin adviser, Manchanna Kramita. Basavanna bows. The King looks at him expectantly. Basavanna says nothing. A long pause.)

BIJJALA: I presume you don't like our new titles.

BASAVANNA: The ears overflow, Your Majesty.

MANCHANNA: I am acutely aware they do not do full justice to His Majesty's achievements.

BASAVANNA: Perhaps His Majesty's glory would have been better served if there had been a little less Sanskrit and a little more of our mother tongue.

BIJJALA: There! Ask the honourable Manchanna Kramita: I predicted you would react like that. He composed the titles. I had to have a new stone inscription erected and he kindly obliged.

MANCHANNA: One cannot expect the common tongue to possess the grandeur and resonance of Sanskrit.

BASAVANNA (*ignoring him*): If Your Majesty's titles continue to proliferate at this pace, I fear that all the rocks in our kingdom stacked together will not be enough to contain them.

MANCHANNA: What greater spur to expand our Empire beyond its present confines? It's fortunate for us that the neighbouring kingdoms of the Chola and Pandya are better known for their boulders than for their arts.

BASAVANNA (*flares up*): A new rock inscription. And to justify it, a new campaign. A dozen battles. A hundred new hero stones, to be greeted by the wails of a few thousand fresh widows and orphans. And then to finance this senseless self-indulgence, another wave of taxes, demands and extortions.

MANCHANNA: This life is transient, Basavanna. We shall all be gone one day. But these inscriptions will outlast the ages and sing of our King's magnificence to distant generations.

BASAVANNA: Inscriptions need eyes to decipher them. Panegyrics need tongues to sing them. Meaning is generated by this moving body and it is this human body that should be our primary concern.

(*Manchanna is about to retort, when Bijjala decides to take matters in hand.*)

BIJJALA: Why don't you visit the court more often, Basavanna? Having you here is like adding a dose of strong spices to bland food.

BASAVANNA: Forgive me, sir. I got distracted.

(*He offers the King a bunch of keys.*)

These are the keys to the Treasury. Your Majesty was kind enough to entrust them to my care. But they feel heavy now. I must implore you to relieve me of this weight.

BIJJALA: And if I refuse?

BASAVANNA: I shall leave them by the Shiva-*linga* in the palace.

(*Pause.*)

BIJJALA: These last couple of years I've barely seen you at the court, except on an occasional festival day. The kingdom bristles with gossip about the deteriorating relations between the King and his Treasurer. I gather you have even written songs mocking my kingship and sung them to your congregation. Yet I have not uttered a word of rebuke nor asked you to surrender the keys—

BASAVANNA: I hope my stand has been clear, sir. I work in the Treasury not for the King's pleasure but because that wealth belongs to the people. As a guardian of the people, the King

has a right to it. But no other member of the royal family is
entitled to have access to it.

BIJJALA: Answer my question first. Would any other king have
been as lenient and accommodating as I?

BASAVANNA: No, sir. I accept. And I am most grateful for Your
Majesty's indulgence.

BIJJALA: Good then. Listen to me. Let the past be forgotten. It was
a childish prank. My son is an imbecile—

MANCHANNA: Your Majesty, that's a preposterous...

BIJJALA (*ignoring him*): Shall I have him brought here, bound and
gagged, and roll him at your feet?

BASAVANNA: It would be wrong to attribute my resignation to the
Prince alone. Our congregation grows day by day and has
started making greater demands on my time.

(*Pause.*)

BIJJALA: That's one of the things that irks me about you. 'The
Prince'! Why do you insist on calling him a Prince? It's a title
which even the King's bastards flaunt. It would make the
Queen happy if you called him the Yuvaraj. I would be
pleased. The court knows that—

BASAVANNA: A Yuvaraj is an heir to the throne, sir. I was not aware
Your Majesty had so anointed him.

BIJJALA: Of course, I haven't. Dear man, do you imagine for a
moment that my other sons will sit by meekly while I bestow
that privilege on this ass? They'll tear me to shreds. Nevertheless, when only one prince is present in the capital, it's
customary to address him as the Yuvaraj.

BASAVANNA: Perhaps a new custom, sir? I'm not aware of it. But
it matters little what he is called, except that the title of
Yuvaraj entails certain responsibilities.

BIJJALA: You aren't going to start on that again—

BASAVANNA: Yes, I am, sir. For it can bear repetition. Kingship is a calling. A source of living, yes, but also a duty and a service to humanity. It is not an inheritance, not a family gift but a right to be earned, to be justified by diligent application.

BIJJALA (*soothing*): Don't I know it? We discussed all this threadbare fifteen years ago—

(*To Manchanna Kramita, smiling.*)

—when I threw out the Chalukyas and grabbed their throne!

BASAVANNA: But the same words are unacceptable to you when applied to your son.

BIJJALA (*explodes*): Yes, because he's my son. My son! Do you have even the faintest idea of what a son means? My dear fellow, there are over a hundred and ninety-six thousand *sharanas* in this city of Kalyan who light the lamp every evening in your name for having given them a new life. And though they all know you have a son, a good half of them don't even know what that poor devil is called. What kind of a father are you? Have some sense, Basavanna. Or, at least, read the sacred texts to acquire some. A son is the final goal of human existence! It may be that he drinks your blood and chews your bones to mash. But he is the one who'll keep your soul fed till eternity.

BASAVANNA: For a *sharana*, physical parentage is of no consequence. A person is born truly only when the guru initiates him into a life of knowledge.

BIJJALA: That's what *you* believe. As a child, you tore up your sacred thread and ran away from home. Birth, caste and creed mean nothing to you. But don't you delude yourself about your companions, friend. If you really free them from the network of brothers, sisters, sons, daughters, uncles and second cousins, and let them loose in a casteless society, they will merely sputter about like a pile of fish on the sands and die! (*Suddenly*) You don't wish to look after the Treasury any more? So be it. Give me the keys.

BASAVANNA: It's not bare relationships that matter but the meanings one brings to them. I know why Prince Sovideva tried to
set a trap for me. Because he hungers for your attention. He
wants a few nods of affection from you. Seat him next to you,
talk to him—

BIJJALA: Perhaps that's how Brahmin boys are reared. But he is a
Kshatriya. His only problem is that he hasn't tasted the lash
enough. Let's not worry about my son any more. Shall we
turn to your bhaktas instead?

BASAVANNA (*puzzled*): Sir?

BIJJALA: Kallappa, let them in.
(*To Basavanna*)
We'll start with the servants of the palace, who've known you
over the years.
(*Kallappa lets a group of half a dozen people enter. They ignore the
King, rush in and fall at Basavanna's feet. Some cling to his legs.
Others weep.*)

BASAVANNA (*taken aback*): What's all this nonsense? What are you
doing?

OLD MAN: Forgive us. Forgive us, Basavanna. We didn't realize you
were such a great soul—

BASAVANNA: What's got into you?

WOMAN: I've been married four years. Four children, all dead at
birth. Save the next one for me, please.

KALLAPPA: Enough now. You'll get more time later. You know
there are others waiting outside. Move on.
(*He herds them out, and lets in a new lot who also rush to clasp
Basavanna's feet.*)

BASAVANNA: No! No! What foolishness is this? (*To a woman*)
Rangavva, will you at least tell me what this is all about?

RANGAVVA: Is there anything you don't know, Basavanna? You
performed the miracle—

BASAVANNA (*aghast*): I did what?

OLD MAN (*placating*): Not you, but Lord Shiva. On your behalf—
He performed it—

RANGAVVA: They say you had borrowed money from the Treasury.
For your good works. Fifty thousand sovereigns. And Shiva
replaced the whole amount. When the young Master tried to
catch you, there was nothing amiss.

BASAVANNA: No, never!

OLD MAN: Each empty coffer filled up right in front of their eyes.
They actually had to shake the sacks to fit the coins in. Money
kept pouring in.

BASAVANNA (*anguished*): Do you really believe I would steal money
from the Treasury?

OLD MAN: It's not like that. Not for yourself. It was all to feed the
sharanas—to give alms and—

RANGAVVA: Not for your own expenses, but for God's work.

BASAVANNA: So the Prince is right. I'm a thief!

RANGAVVA (*her eyes filling up*): Why do you say such dreadful
things? May our tongues rot if we malign a saint like you!
Don't tease us...

(*She goes out wiping her tears, followed by the others. Bijjala signals
Kallappa to stop further admissions.*)

BIJJALA: Hope you're enjoying this outburst of devotional ectasy.

BASAVANNA (*anguished*): What's all this, Your Majesty?

MANCHANNA: In the good old days, fire sacrifices had to be
performed and animals ritually slaughtered before the Vedic
gods consented to descend to the earth. But since the winds
of *bhakti* started sweeping across the continent, the gods
seem only too eager to act. The devotee weeps and God
performs a miracle. The devotee laughs and He performs
another. Our gods have been transformed into a mob of
perpetual conjurers.

BIJJALA (*to Basavanna*): Today your companions would rather you were a thief so they can turn you into a wonder-worker. Tomorrow the same enthusiasts may damn you as a murderer so they can prove you've experienced Lord Shiva himself! I am an ordinary king. I want no truck with the gods. I go by the laws of the land. Which is why this mass hunger for divine grace bothers me greatly. It should bother you too.

BASAVANNA: Let them damn me as a thief, condemn me as a miracle-monger. I don't care. But to be damned as a devotee in the presence of all the great devotees! *Talé-daṇḍa!*

> I don't have in me
> *bhakti* enough
> to equal a sixth
> of a mustard seed.
> I'm an ekke, a swallow-wort
> among mangoes.
> How can I shamelessly
> call myself a devotee
> in front of the *sharanas*
> of our Lord of the meeting of rivers?

Will Shiva perform miracles for the sake of a buffoon like me, a shameless buffoon? I beg Your Majesty to excuse me.

BIJJALA (*calls*): Kallappa! (*To Basavanna*) Are you going home?

BASAVANNA: No, sir. I've distressing news from Maddur. If I leave now, I may reach by sun-down.

BIJJALA: Oh, yes! Some of your young followers have got into a fight with the Jains there, haven't they? Good. You'll have a restraining influence on them. Situations rarely seem to improve when left to my officers.

BASAVANNA: I shall look to it, Your Majesty. Along the way I want to call on Jagadeva and his mother. I was in the Treasury when his father died—

BIJJALA (*ignoring the last remark*): Kallappa, have a pair of guards ready to accompany Basavanna—

BASAVANNA: I need no escort, sir.

BIJJALA: The throngs outside are bursting with the delirium of bhakti. I don't want any more miracles right now, thank you.

BASAVANNA (*bows*): *Sharan*, Your Majesty.

BIJJALA: Good-bye.

(*Basavanna leaves along with Kallappa. A long pause.*)

MANCHANNA: You can't blame the Yuvaraj, sir. Not if you've seen the goings-on in Basavanna's house. Food for all the devotees that flock there, day and night. Gifts. Clothes. How can he afford such lavish hospitality? His affluence is a source of dismay to the whole city.

BIJJALA: I'm happy to know my son is not alone in his benighted existence. With a hundred and ninety-six thousand *sharanas* resident in the city, do you think I would choose to remain ignorant of their finances? I can account for every penny spent in that house.

(*Manchanna Kramita tries to hide his astonishment.*)

I came to this city ten years ago and I brought Basavanna with me as my Treasurer. Along with him came the *sharanas*, each one convinced that work is worship, that his work is no mere profession but a calling.

Every *sharana* seeks only to earn the day's keep, makes no extra demands, treats profits with contempt. So who benefits? From every corner of the country, trade and commerce have come pouring into Kalyan, and now the city is bursting at its seams with money and activity. Even those who despise the *sharanas* for their beliefs need them for their economic enterprise—as indeed I do—and so they pour money into the *sharana* coffers. Basavanna does not need to defraud me! If only my idiot son had asked me first—(*Calls out*) Kallappa!

Has the mob thinned? It's time we proceeded to the audience hall.

KALLAPPA (*enters*): Thinned, Master? Vanished is more like it. They've all followed Basavanna out. There isn't a soul left behind to swat a fly!

Scene Four

The Brahmin quarter of Kalyan. Sambashiva Shastri's house. The post-funeral rituals are going on. The mantras can be heard. Basavanna and Kakkayya enter the street in front of the house, followed by a noisy crowd, mostly consisting of men and children. Basavanna stops, turns, folds his hands before the crowd.

BASAVANNA: I beg of you. Don't follow me around like this. There was no miracle in the Treasury. Don't shame me with this wanton talk of God's miracles!

MAN: There are those who saw with their own eyes—and you deny it? Not ten but fifty thousand witnesses swear to it—

MAN 2: How many miracles have you performed so far, Basavanna?

BASAVANNA: How many shall I say? Will eighty-eight do?
    Showing off my eighty-eight miracles
    my *bhakti* has become
    a carnival wardrobe.
It's in such tatters, I can't find a patch large enough to hide my shame.

CROWD (*shouts*): Basava is Shiva! Shiva is Basava! Victory to Saint Basavanna! Glory to the Treasurer of Faith!

(*Basavanna stands, non-plussed.*)

KAKKAYYA: You go on, Basavanna. I'll hold them here. (*To the crowds*) You stay here with me. Stand back!

BASAVANNA: Thank you, Kakkayya.

(*Basavanna enters the house. Some members of the family, who had collected at the door to watch the crowds, disperse hurriedly when they see Basavanna come in. No one greets him. He sits quietly in a corner. Amba comes in. Long pause.*)

BASAVANNA: I heard of his illness in Bannoor. I hoped to call on him as soon as I returned to Kalyan, but there was this business at the Treasury. Never got to see him again. God's will.

AMBA: You used to come here often, with my husband. But you haven't been here in a long while. You've become a big man.

BASAVANNA: What am I to say, Ambakka?

AMBA: People are under your spell. They say Lord Shiva performs miracles for you. That's good. God did nothing for us in this house—not that we are worthy of it!

(*She starts crying.*)

BASAVANNA: Why the tears, Ambakka? You have your son Jagadeva—

AMBA: Yes, he is there. But will he stay? Why have you come here, Basavanna? I have this cold fear in the pit of my stomach...why have you come? My son is home again. He has brought his wife back. There are signs that he may settle down again to a normal life. But to accomplish this his father had to give up his life. Have you come to take him away again? Let today's ceremony be over. Let the house be cleansed to set up life again. Then do as you wish.

BASAVANNA: Do you want me to go away?

(*A side door opens and the Head Priest enters.*)

PRIEST: The Brahmins have received their parting fee and are ready to leave. No one may remain here.

(*Amba hurries out. Basavanna doesn't move.*)

The rites are over. The Brahmin who has invoked the departed sprit on himself is about to leave. No outsider may see him. It's a bad omen.

BASAVANNA: Omens don't bother me.

PRIEST: As you wish.

(*He peeps into the room.*)

Please, come.

(*Three Brahmins step out, followed by Jagadeva, who is now clean-shaven and wears a sacred thread. He is startled to see Basavanna. The Head Priest signals one of the Brahmins to go out by the back door. He does so.*)

PRIEST: Jagadeva, go, sweep the floor after him and apply cowdung, so the ground he's stepped on is purified again.

(*Commotion outside. Shouts of 'Basavanna!' 'Victory to the Treasurer of Faith!' are heard. Basavanna turns to go out.*)

JAGADEVA: Sit, Basavanna. Don't go. Please. I'll be back—

(*Jagadeva goes out by the back door.*)

PRIEST (*to Basavanna*): Rituals for the departed are being performed in this house. Couldn't you find a different venue for your antics?

(*The Priest and the Brahmins depart. Jagadeva enters hurriedly. Long pause.*)

JAGADEVA: Are you angry with me—that I should have reverted to my caste? This sacred thread—these rites—

BASAVANNA: No.

JAGADEVA: Then perhaps you find it comic—this Brahmanical masquerade—

BASAVANNA: What I feel is beside the point.

JAGADEVA: I had to do it. For my mother's peace of mind.

(*Pause.*)

Father kept calling out for me in the last few days of his life. His throat gave out but I didn't come. Now, these last eleven days I have been seeking him, invoking him limb by limb on two absurd little pebbles. I am calling out to him, now that he's gone! Isn't that just like me?

(*Pause.*)

Just like my father too. For all his fire sacrifices, penance
and meditations, when it came to facing death, he couldn't
take it. He was afraid. He used to weep with fear. Do you
think my life too will be like that? A tale of fear, defeat,
futility?

BASAVANNA: It needs courage to accept that one is afraid. To be
able to say 'This fear of mine—This is my truth now'—that
may be the ultimate triumph.

(*Commotion outside. The crowds are getting more riotous. Basavanna
makes a move to go.*)

JAGADEVA: Where are you going?

BASAVANNA: They won't leave you in peace while I stay here.
Besides, I must reach Maddur before dark.

JAGADEVA: I have to talk to you, Basavanna. I have so much to
discuss. Must you go to Maddur today?

BASAVANNA: Yes, some of our people have occupied a Jain temple
there by force. They are threatening to smash the naked idols
in it and turn it into a Shiva temple. Things could go out of
hand—

JAGADEVA: And what will you do once you get there? I know.
Rebuke our own people. Hold them responsible. You don't
know how the Jains bait us, provoke us—

BASAVANNA: Violence is wrong, whatever the provocation. To
resort to it because someone else started it first is even worse.
And to do so in the name of a structure of brick and mortar
is a monument to stupidity.

> The rich
> will make temples for Shiva.
> What shall I,
> a poor man,
> do?
> My legs are pillars,
> the body the shrine,

the head a cupola
of gold.
Listen, O lord of the meeting rivers,
things standing shall fall,
but the moving shall ever stay.

JAGADEVA: Haven't you heard? In Ablur, Ramayya, the Solitary Saint, led the attack on a Jain temple. He threw the non-believers out and established his rights to their temple by performing a miracle. His head flew around like a pigeon—

BASAVANNA: Isn't this life abundant enough? Do we need more miracles?

JAGADEVA (*suddenly*): There was no miracle in the Treasury.

BASAVANNA: No, there wasn't. I know that.

JAGADEVA: So long as I was there, there was not a whisper of it.

BASAVANNA: It's sad, but even among the *sharanas* there's no shortage of credulity.

(*Pause.*)

JAGADEVA: Tell me. Who started this rumour about a miracle? Was it you?

(*Pause.*)

BASAVANNA: Since you ask, you must think so.

JAGADEVA (*excited*): I led the march to the Treasury. Here my father was breathing his last. My mother, alone and helpless, was banging her head against the wall. And I was at the Treasury! You know why? To make sure that Basavanna's honour remained untarnished. To establish his glory in perpetuity. That's why! Tomorrow I shall be the talk of the town, I told myself. I shall be the hero of the *sharanas*. I could see myself taken out in procession, hoisted on the shoulders of my friends and companions! And what happened? I came home. For eleven days I immersed myself in these death rituals. And this morning, as I emerged from them, I was told—Basavanna has performed a miracle. Basavanna! No mention of me. In front of my own house, only hosannas to Basavanna!

BASAVANNA: I too have been performing rituals of sorts these last eleven days. Locked up in the Treasury. (*Pause.*) All this glory!

> My men in their love for me,
> with praise and more praise,
> have impaled me on a stake of gold!

JAGADEVA: Everyone my father trusted let him down. The King, you, I, even God. Finally, there was nothing left for him but to shed tears. Do you know how a man crumbles when he loses power? In the service of the court, father was tall and imposing and walked with long, confident strides. Weighed each word before parting with it. But the moment Bijjala threw him out, he shrank, like a piece of soaked cloth. Even his voice went shrill. It was loathsome—

BASAVANNA (*gently*): You must not judge too easily.
(*Pause.*)
I have just left the King's service myself.
(*Jagadeva looks at him in astonishment. Then slowly.*)

JAGADEVA: Do you know what you are? You are a manipulator. A clever, conniving trickster.

BASAVANNA (*pained*): Why do you say that?

JAGADEVA: Father had seen through you. 'Don't trust Basavanna', he would say, 'He's an impostor—'

BASAVANNA: I'm sorry. But I don't believe your father would ever say that.

JAGADEVA: Do you mean...I'm lying?

BASAVANNA: Yes, you are. But why?

JAGADEVA: You and I must have been enemies through the last seven births. That's why, no matter what I say, you can still make me feel small. You turn me into a worm in the eyes of the people.

(*Commotion outside. The Chief Priest enters.*)

PRIEST: If you don't leave now, they'll break in. Please—

JAGADEVA: Look, I'm here to worry about that. Why don't you keep out of it?

PRIEST: Your mother asked me. So...

(*He goes out.*)

BASAVANNA (*gets up*): I'd better go.

JAGADEVA: Don't, Basavanna. Please. Who's there to talk to if you go? Who else will even have an inkling here of what I'm saying? Perhaps I'm stupid. Perhaps you have cast one of your spells on me. But there's no one left for me but you.

BASAVANNA: Come here. Shut your eyes.

(*Jagadeva does as told. Basavanna places his palm on his head.*) Repeat after me: *Om namah Shivāya.*

(*Jagadeva repeats the words. This is done three times. Then Basavanna withdraws his hand.*)

JAGADEVA: You torment me till my heart screams murder. Then to be soothed back to sleep, who do I need but you?

BASAVANNA: No one is on his own. The Lord has tied us to one another with bonds beyond our comprehension. I'll tell you something—something I have not breathed to anybody else. One night the mystic Allama and I were sitting talking late into the night. He is one of the few I know to have attained a state of grace. So I asked him: 'What is this I? How do I recognize it?' And Allama replied: 'I'll show you. Watch.' And right there, even as I was watching, his whole life poured out of his body.

(*Pause.*)

Like shadow puppets, row after endless row. His birth. Childhood. His youth in Banavasi. His lust for the dancer Kāmalatā. Her death. The *linga* he found on the palm of a buried skeleton. A procession of events. A pantomime in which I even saw myself and my associates. Everything. Not just the ordinary or the simple or the holy or the beautiful. Along with that, the grotesque and the evil. Filth beyond belief. As though a river full of spring blossoms also carried decaying flesh, rotten limbs, uprooted hair, a flood of pus—the stench interwoven with the fragrance. I couldn't bear it. 'No, this is not you, Great Saint', I cried out. He smiled and said: 'You are watching, aren't you?' Then there was, suddenly, a point when I was so overwhelmed by the beauty and the horror that I shut my eyes for a moment. When I opened them, he was there but fast asleep. We didn't talk about it the next day—or ever again. Even now, as I think of it, I can feel myself shiver.

JAGADEVA: Why are you telling me all this?

BASAVANNA: I don't know. Just felt like telling you. I don't know why Allama treated me to that vision either.

(*Stones crash on the roof. There is a roar from the crowd outside. Shouts of 'Basavanna, come out!' 'Darshan!' 'Darshan!' are heard. Amba enters.*)

AMBA: Spare us, Basavanna. Your devotees are throwing stones for you—

BASAVANNA (*gets up*): I did not mean to trouble you. But I seem to have succeeded in doing just that. (*Smiles.*) My life seems to have become one long apology.

(*He says 'Sharan' and goes out. The crowd surrounds him with enthusiasm, follows him out. Jagadeva, Amba, Savitri and the Head Priest watch.*)

PRIEST (*relieved*): Well, the rest is easily attended to. Nothing utilized in today's rituals may be put to use again. Not the wood, not the pots, not the left-overs. Burn what you can. Consign the rest to the river. Everything should be disposed of.

JAGADEVA: But I too was used in the rituals. So what do I do with myself?

Scene Five

Basavanna's house. He is with two sharana *youths—Kalayya and Gundanna. Kakkayya, the untouchable saint, who is in his seventies, is sitting near by.*

BASAVANNA (*angry*): Shall I come in person then and tell him?

GUNDANNA (*laughs*): That will be hurling a thunderbolt at a sparrow. He isn't a bad fellow, really, that officer! Someone has been setting him up—

BASAVANNA: There's such a thing as common humanity!

KALAYYA: Basavanna, these tribals have brought their god with them. You should see that idol. Rolling eyes. A tongue lolling out. It's very funny.

GUNDANNA (*laughs*): I think—the sooner you initiate them into our fold the better!

BASAVANNA: A roof over their head first, and a piece of land to spread their mats on. We can minister to their spiritual needs later.

GUNDANNA: All right. We'll keep you informed.

(*While the above conversation is going on, a group of visitors enters: Madhuvarasa, a Brahmin by birth, with his wife Lalitamba, and daughter Kalavati, aged about twelve; Haralayya, a cobbler by*

*birth, along with his wife Kalyani and son Sheelavanta, of about
fifteen years; their friends. They are led in by Gangambika, wife of
Basavanna.*

*They all greet each other with 'Sharan, Basavanna', 'Sharan,
Kakkayya', etc.)*

GANGAMBIKA: Gundanna, I have kept a few bags of paddy, lentils,
salt and spices for them in the room outside. Pick them up
on your way out.

GUNDANNA: Yes, Gangakka.

BASAVANNA (*restless*): I really ought to go with you now. But I'm
expecting Kukke Shetty, the trader. If I finish with him soon,
I'll follow. Otherwise I'll be there the first thing tomorrow
morning.

KALAYYA: That may not be necessary though. *Sharan.*

(*Gundanna and Kalayya exit.*)

HARALAYYA: Is that about the refugees from Andhra, Gangakka?
They say a band of tribal shepherds is camping on the river-
side.

BASAVANNA: There's famine raging in Andhra. These poor souls
have trecked for weeks in search of food and shelter. But our
people won't let them stray this side of the river because of
their low caste. I tell you, for sheer inhumanity our people
have no equal.

MADHUVARASA: Had you been the Treasurer to the King now, a
thing like that wouldn't have taken a moment! But our
sharanas mocked you then, for serving a worldly King.

(*Basavanna shrugs vaguely, goes to the door and looks out.*)

GANGAMBIKA: Are you expecting someone?

BASAVANNA: Some dispute in Kukke Shetty's family. They want me
to adjudicate.

GANGAMBIKA: They aren't here yet. So you might at least talk to
those who are!

BASAVANNA (*abashed, to the visitors*): Oh! Oh! So you're here to see me? (*Explaining*) You see what it is. I have a formula. If a visitor wears a smile on his face as he approaches this house, he's here to see my wife. If he's scowling, he's here to see me.

GANGAMBIKA (*blushing*): Enough now!

BASAVANNA: All of you seemed so happy, I naturally assumed— (*He notices that they are dressed up.*)
Well, now! What's on! Some festival? New sarees, new turbans. You look grand. Is it some special occasion? But Lalitakka, you don't look too happy—

MADHUVARASA (*laughs*): Heh! Heh! Isn't it to be expected that a mother will feel a little upset at the prospect of her daughter's wedding?

BASAVANNA (*excited*): Truly? So Kalavati is getting married, is she? Did you hear that, Ganga?

GANGAMBIKA: They just told me. I'm so happy—

MADHUVARASA: We have the engagement ceremony tomorrow evening. You must all come. Kakkayya, you too—

BASAVANNA: Of course, we'll be there. (*To Gangambika*) Just think—that little girl who was toddling around only the other day now at the threshold of life! I feel my bones creaking.
(*Laughter all round.*)

KALYANI: Go on, Sheela, touch their feet. Don't stand there like a wax doll—

HARALAYYA: He's grown into a proper buffalo. Still needs to be told everything.
(*Sheelavanta touches Basavanna's feet.*)
We expect you at the betrothal tomorrow, Basavanna.

BASAVANNA: God be praised! There must be some extraordinary conjunction of stars tomorrow. Two betrothals on the same day!
(*Laughter.*)

GANGAMBIKA: You're the limit! Where are you? There's only one betrothal.

KALYANI: It's been decided to bring Kalavati for our Sheela. Bless them, Basavanna—

BASAVANNA: What's that?

(*His eyes suddenly fill with tears. He cannot speak. Kakkayya looks stunned, uncomprehending. A long, strange silence. Then Madhuvarasa starts, with great deliberation.*)

MADHUVARASA: Naturally, we are gratified to notice that even you are taken by surprise. It's evident you did not anticipate that your efforts would bear fruit so soon—

GANGAMBIKA: Sheelavanta is waiting for your blessings.

BASAVANNA (*with a start*): Bless you! Bless you! Our good wishes are always with you. You must seek the blessings of elders—

(*Basavanna gestures towards Kakkayya. Sheelavanta touches Kakkayya's feet. Basavanna relapses into silence. A strange anxiety fills the room. Haralayya's face reddens; he turns to his wife, perplexed but also angry.*)

MADHUVARASA (*clears his throat*): We came here secure in our belief that you would welcome this alliance with joy. Instead, we see you both startled—even troubled.

HARALAYYA: Your hand wouldn't even bless the boy!

KAKKAYYA (*slowly, gently*): You know my profession is tanning. In terms of 'caste', that's low, even lower than you, Haralayya. When one grows up that far down, there's nothing one doesn't know about the horror of caste. So I ask you: have you given this alliance enough thought?

MADHUVARASA: How can you even ask? Kalavati is our only daughter, Sheelavanta their only son—

KALYANI (*looking at her husband for support*): We have given enough thought to the wedding arrangements, Kakkayya. A *sharana* boy marries a *sharana* girl. No need for much fuss there, is there?

(*Pause.*)

But if you're going to see it as a Brahmin girl marrying a cobbler's son—well, we don't know how to answer you.

GANGAMBIKA: Sister, you know my husband would never think like that! It's not like him—

KALYANI: Who knows what thoughts will strike whom at what time.

KAKKAYYA: We are all *sharanas*. We have surrendered ourselves to Lord Shiva. There is no caste among *sharanas*, neither Brahmin nor cobbler. This alliance is a cause for celebration. And yet—

MADHUVARASA: Yes?

KAKKAYYA: The worldly surround us. Will they take kindly to it? Will they accept?

HARALAYYA: What do they have to do with this wedding?

MADHUVARASA: Should we care if the ignorant scream their heads off? Should it affect us? Why should I sneer at others, Kakkayya? Till the other day, even I mocked the *sharanas*, ridiculed them at the slightest pretext. And then one day, enlightenment dawned. It'll happen to others too. You'll see.

KAKKAYYA: And will they sit patiently until then?

HARALAYYA: They'd better. We'll see to it that they do.

BASAVANNA: Until now it was only a matter of theoretical speculation. But this—this is real. The orthodox will see this mingling of castes as a blow at the very roots of the *varnashrama dharma*. Bigotry has not faced such a challenge in two thousand years. I need hardly describe what venom will gush out, what hatred will erupt once the news spreads.

MADHUVARASA: So be it. Like Lord Shiva himself, we shall drink that venom and hold it blocked in our throats!

BASAVANNA (*angry*): This is no time for pretty speeches! It's a question of life and death for these children. From tomorrow the wrath of the bigoted will pursue them like a swarm of snakes, to strike as they pause to put up a roof or light an oven. Who will protect them then? Elementary prudence demands that—

HARALAYYA: So you don't approve of this alliance! I knew it, Kalyani. So what if it's the saintly Basavanna or the revered elder Kakkayya? Let a cobbler rub shoulders with a Brahmin and the *sharanas* will be the first to object.

BASAVANNA: Some day this entire edifice of caste and creed, this poison-house of varnashrama, will come tumbling down. Every person will see himself only as a human being. As a *bhakta*. As a *sharana*. That is inevitable. But we have a long way to go. You know the most terrible crimes have been justified in the name of *sanatana* religion.

MADHUVARASA: Then let me say this: I shall not hesitate to sacrifice my daughter's life to forward the cause of our great movement.

KAKKAYYA (*horrified*): Madhuvarasa!

BASAVANNA: No one has a right to sacrifice anyone—not even himself.

HARALAYYA (*to Madhuvarasa*): The word 'sacrifice' strikes terror in me. Too long have my people sacrificed our women to the greed of the upper castes, our sons to their cosmic theories of rebirth. No more sacrifices, please.

(*Long silence.*)

KAKKAYYA: What does Sheela say?

HARALAYYA (*surprised*): What can he say? He'll do as told.

KALYANI: He's still wet behind the ears. What does he know?

KAKKAYYA: But *he* has to face the ordeal.

(*He turns to Sheelavanta.*)

So, Sheela, what do you say? Is this alliance acceptable to you?

(*Sheelavanta looks at his parents, perplexed.*)

Don't look at them. Look at me—

SHEELAVANTA: I—I—

GANGAMBIKA (*to Kalavati*): You and your friends should go out and play in the garden. We'll send for you.
(*Kalavati and friends run out.*)

BASAVANNA: Yes, Sheelavanta?

SHEELAVANTA: I don't want the marriage.

HARALAYYA: Are you in your sense, you—

KAKKAYYA (*silences everyone*): Why? Don't you like Kalavati?

SHEELAVANTA: *Ayyo*, Shiva-Shiva! It isn't at all like that. She is—like a flower, I swear. Poor thing.

KAKKAYYA: Then why?

SHEELAVANTA: I have told my parents...

KAKKAYYA: Tell us too. Why are you afraid?

SHEELAVANTA (*tearful*): I don't want to hurt her. Don't want to ruin her life. They'll tease her tomorrow, call her a 'cobbler's priestess'.

KAKKAYYA: Who will?

SHEELAVANTA: The children. In our own neighbourhood.

KAKKAYYA: *Sharana* children?

SHEELAVANTA: Yes, sir. Besides—I'm not willing to give up my father's calling. What's wrong with stitching footwear?

BASAVANNA: Is anyone asking you to give up your ancestral calling, Sheelavanta?

SHEELAVANTA (*scared*): No, sir, no one. But—Kalavati can't stand the smell of leather. I've seen her. Whenever she passes a cobbler's shop she holds her nose. Will she spend her whole life like that?

LALITA (*bursts out*): I have been silent all along. I can't be any longer. Sheela is a gem. You won't find another boy like him in all the Brahmin quarters! But what he says is true.

BASAVANNA: Yes?

LALITA: Till the other day our daughter ran around barefoot. She was told it was unclean to touch any leather except deer-skin. How can she start skinning dead buffalos tomorrow? Or tan leather?

(*There is a sudden chill in the air.*)

KALYANI (*tense*): Lalitakka, we are cobblers. Not skinners or tanners.

HARALAYYA (*explains*): The *holeyas* skin the carcass. The *madigas* and the *dohas* tan the hide. Only then does it come to us.

MADHUVARASA: Please, I beg of you, don't take umbrage. All this is rather unfamiliar territory to us. All these details. I'm afraid she doesn't know what she's saying. (*To Lalita*) Can't you hold your tongue?

LALITA: It's my child's life! She gets a splitting headache if she so much as smells burning camphor. She is so...so...tender.

(*She bursts into tears.*)

Each time she returns from the cobbler's street, she throws up and takes to bed.

MADHUVARASA (*thundering*): Woman, I said hold your tongue. You are insulting a *sharana*'s calling...

HARALAYYA: No, Madhuvarasa, it doesn't upset me. My wife and I became *sharanas*, gave up meat and alcohol and our ancient gods. Now when our children ask us: 'Why then are we still stitching the same old scraps of leather?' what can I answer? If my son decides to change his vocation, will the weavers accept him? Will the potters open their ranks?

LALITA: I'm sorry, Haralayya. May I tell them—about your mother?

MADHUVARASA: His mother? What about his mother? I've never seen her—

LALITA: Every full moon night, Goddess Dyamavva of the Banyan Tree speaks. Through his mother.

MADHUVARASA (*scandalized*): How do you know that?

LALITA (*defiantly*): Because I am a devotee of the goddess. I know Basavanna forbids it as blind superstition, but I am!

HARALAYYA: We became *sharanas*. But Mother refused to do so. She wept and cried that she could not forsake our family gods. So we parted. I haven't seen her since. She hasn't looked at us.

LALITA: The other day, at the full-moon fair, she prophesied—

KALYANI (*tense*): We don't believe in all that. I don't. Nor does my husband.

BASAVANNA: What was the prophecy?

LALITA: Rivers of blood will flow if the marriage takes place, she said, human limbs will rot in the streets. This is not any stranger—this is Sheela's own grandmother speaking!

MADHUVARASA (*incensed*): First you go and attend those demonic rituals in secret. Then you have the gall to make an exhibition of yourself. If you don't keep quiet, I'll give you a thrashing.

GANGAMBIKA: Shame on you, Madhuvanna. Women and cattle, they are all the same to you, aren't they?

LALITA (*bitterly*): What is a daemonic ritual and what isn't? Don't call me a termagant for railing against my own husband, Gangakka. But ten years ago he found a Pashupata Guru. For months he immersed himself in ash, shouted loudly and danced. And the family had to put up with it. Then one day he discovered the Buddha. Wanted to give away all our worldly possessions to a monastery, until I threatened to jump into a well. And now, forgive me, he is a *sharana*. And that's all that counts. The others aren't worthy of a second thought—

MADHUVARASA (*distressed*): But I have done it all in good faith, Lalita. Grant me at least my good faith!

LALITA: Such faith! Our initiation as *sharanas* was not even complete when he saw Sheelavanta and decided he was right for our daughter. But if Sheela had been a Brahmin boy, he wouldn't even have sniffed at him.

HARALAYYA: You are honest, sister—frighteningly honest. So I must tell you. When your husband proposed this alliance to me, my first thought was: 'I wasn't even allowed to dream of upper-caste girls. Now this one falls right into my son's lap!'

GANGAMBIKA: A woman is just a ripe mango on a roadside tree for all of you, isn't she? Just one more challenge to your manhood!

(*A group of* sharanas *enters. They all greet each other.* 'Sharan', 'Sharan', *etc. Much embracing and loud exchange of congratulations.*)

SHARANA ONE: The whole city is abuzz with your news.

KAKKAYYA: Oh! So the news has spread, has it?

SHARANA TWO: What do you mean? Every *sharana* home is wearing a festive air already. You've done it!

SHARANA THREE: The Brahmins are in a state of uproar. All credit to you!

SHARANA FOUR: Bravo! Excellent!

(*As the rest of the scene progresses, the hall fills up. Small groups of men and women come in, all excited, congratulating each other and joining in the debate.*)

SHARANA THREE: Just a small question, Basavanna, if you don't mind.

SHARANA TWO: You see, we heard the news and were thrilled. We knew the two families had come here to touch your feet. So we waited for them in Goolappa's shop. (*Pause.*) And they didn't come back!

SHARANA ONE: Evidently there's been a great deal of discussion.

SHARANA THREE: I wish you'd sent for us too.

KAKKAYYA: It wasn't really a meeting. They sought our blessings—

SHARANA FOUR: Precisely. That's what we heard. And—(*Pause.*)—apparently Basavanna wouldn't bless them?

HARALAYYA: Who told you that?

MADHUVARASA: No, no, that's unfair.

SHARANA FOUR: Unfair? I'm only asking a question.

HARALAYYA: Of course, he blessed them.

BASAVANNA: But I hesitated. I was—tardy.
(*Surprise all around.*)

MADHUVARASA: Anyway, all that's over and done with.

SHARANA THREE: What's done with? Why should a blessing be a problem?

BASAVANNA: I'll tell you. My immediate response was one of joy. Didn't know whether to laugh or cry. All that we'd prayed for, all that we had sought, it was there in an instant by God's grace. And yet my heart trembled.

KAKKAYYA: I too was afraid.

SHARANA ONE: Is that why you said there should be an enquiry?

BASAVANNA: Not an enquiry. (*Smiles.*) Just a bit of thinking.

SHARANA TWO: And what did you think?

SHARANA ONE: What are you afraid of, Basavanna?

BASAVANNA: We are not ready for the kind of revolution this wedding is. We haven't worked long enough or hard enough!

SHARANA THREE: So how many more generations have to roll by before a cobbler marries a Brahmin?

SHARANA FIVE: Do we mean generations? Or heads?

SHARANA FOUR (*incredulous*): You mean this marriage won't take place?

SHARANA SIX (*excited*): All these years you have been teaching us that caste and creed are phantoms. And now that people here are willing to act on your precepts, you want to turn tail? What will the world say?

SHARANA THREE: We *sharanas* will become the laughing stock of the world!

BASAVANNA: What the world thinks is immaterial. It is a question of living, breathing human beings. A question of *that* boy's life, *that* girl's safety. What matters is what *we* consider right.

SHARANA FIVE: You're a saint, a mystic, a seer. From your heights this world must look as insignificant as grass. But I have to face the orthodox tomorrow. I have to bear their gibes—

SHARANA TWO: Shall I suggest something? Let the entire congregation of *sharanas* meet tomorrow. Let's thrash the problem out.

SHARANA FOUR: That's right. There aren't enough of us here today. So tomorrow we—

BASAVANNA: No!

(*The* sharanas *are startled by his vehemence.*)

SHARANA TWO: Why not?

SHARANA ONE: You don't want to hear what the rest of us have to say? Our own brethren—

BASAVANNA: An alliance is a matter to be settled by those involved in it. Our opinion was asked. We offered it. The rest is up to the families of Haralayya and Madhuvarasa. It would be unpardonable if other pressures are brought to bear upon them.

FEMALE SHARANA: All right then. Let Haralayya answer a small doubt. Naturally he jumped at the prospect of a fair Brahmin daughter-in-law. Would he be as keen on a girl from a caste lower than his?

(*A group of boys comes running in. There's excitement. 'The King?' 'Oh, my God!' 'This is serious', etc. Everyone hurriedly stands up. Kallappa strides in, casts a cool, professional look around. Bijjala follows.*

The sharanas *bow. Bijjala acknowledges the greetings.*)

BASAVANNA: My house is honoured by the visit. And yet Your Majesty had only to send word and—

BIJJALA: You are not an officer of the court any more. And I wasn't sure my invitation would register in the delirium of communal ecstasy.

(*The* sharanas *titter obediently.*)

I want to talk to you.

BASAVANNA: We are all *sharanas* here. We have no secrets from each other.

BIJJALA: You, men of God, are truly fortunate. We kings, however, belong to the secular world. (*Pointedly.*) We are not so fortunate.

SHARANAS (*taking the hint*): It's time for the evening prayers. It's almost sun-down...

(*They disperse. Basavanna excuses himself to the King and accompanies the* sharanas *to the door. Gangambika, seeing that the King is alone, walks across to him.*)

GANGAMBIKA: I hope the Queen is well?

BIJJALA: What can one say? The various treatments go on. She seems to improve for a while. Then we are back again.

(*Lalita, avoiding her husband, rushes to Basavanna at the door.*)

LALITA (*pleading*): So what have you decided, Basavanna? I have nothing against Sheelavanta. But—his profession—can't he—can he change it?

(*Madhuvarasa and Haralayya join them.*)

HARALAYYA: I know I only have to stop this wedding and many people will heave a sigh of relief. You, also Lalitakka, Kakkayya—

LALITA: No, it's not that—

MADHUVARASA: God forbid!

HARALAYYA: But, Basavanna, you gave us hope. You told us it was possible to escape from the coils of caste. We have been snarled up in them too long. Now I am ready to face the consequences—

BASAVANNA: Promise me one thing.

HARALAYYA: Yes?

BASAVANNA: The moment the wedding is over, send the young couple away. Somewhere far away.

MADHUVARASA: But—our daughter isn't a woman yet. To send her with her husband now—

BASAVANNA: If possible, Lalitakka, you too go with them. Excuse me. The King waits...

HARALAYYA (*dubious*): All right.

(*The hall has emptied. Basavanna returns to the King, who chats with Gangambika.*)

GANGAMBIKA: Let me fetch a drink for you, Your Majesty.

BIJJALA: Nothing now, thank you.

GANGAMBIKA: This is Your Majesty's first visit to our house. You must accept a little refreshment.

(*She goes in.*)

BIJJALA (*looking around*): You know how it's in the palace. Ears— ears everywhere. And often eyes along with them. I hope you are less exposed.

BASAVANNA: Our doors, sir, are wide open.

BIJJALA: Good. Well then. I was on my way home from the court when who should confront me but a horde of howling Brahmins. It is true that normally a Brahmin does not wail or beat his breast while mourning. But let me tell you, when he sets his mind to it, no other caste can match him in the art!

BASAVANNA: What were they mourning, sir?

BIJJALA (*ignoring him*): I was tempted to rush here direct, to check if you hadn't gone off your head. But then came the next bit of news. Basavanna had refused to bless the couple, so the alliance was off. Reassuring, I thought, but one can never be certain of these *sharanas*. Let me go and confirm for myself. That's why I'm here.

BASAVANNA: Your Majesty, a *sharana* called Madhuvarasa has offered his daughter in marriage to the son of another *sharana* called Haralayya. I saw no reason to interfere. And I didn't.

BIJJALA: Of course, you didn't. How could you? After all these years of condemning the caste system, you could hardly oppose an inter-caste marriage now. That's perfectly understandable. You just held your hand back. The blessing was not completed. The wedding was called off. Correct?

BASAVANNA: I am not in charge of this wedding, sir.

BIJJALA (*a little rough*): I only hope the wedding's off. That's all I have come to hear.

BASAVANNA: It's not off as far as I know.

(*Bijjala turns on him.*)

BIJJALA (*softly*): This isn't you. Surely you aren't such a dimwit? So I can only presume that after fifteen years of being led by you, your disciples are now refusing to do your bidding.

BASAVANNA: I have no disciples, sir. No one is obliged to take my advice.

BIJJALA: Well then, I shall have to do what you evidently can't do. I shall forbid the match.

BASAVANNA (*in horror*): Sir, but that—

BIJJALA: You know perfectly well the higher castes will not take this lying down. The wedding *pandal* will turn into a slaughterhouse. The streets of Kalyan will reek of human entrails.

BASAVANNA: But who is being punished for whose crime? Are the birds to be penalized because snakes resent their ability to fly?

BIJJALA: This cursed wedding shall not take place! Do you understand? This is an order. I am not willing to discuss the matter any further.

BASAVANNA: In that event, Your Majesty, I shall go to the palace, right now, sit in the grounds there and keep on sitting till such time as the prohibition is withdrawn.

BIJJALA: Sit away! And why go alone? Take your whole congregation with you for company. You think I give a damn?

BASAVANNA (*gently*): I shall not ask anyone to come with me, sir. But they may, on their own, decide to do so.

BIJJALA: What do you mean by that?

(*Stares at Basavanna. Then—*)

Of course, that's exactly what will happen, won't it? The entire herd of *sharanas* will follow you. A simple thing like the Treasury brought tens of thousands of them out. Won't the palace bring out a hundred thousand? You are a sly fox, I admit it. A hundred and ninety-six thousand *sharanas*! They only have to lay down their implements. And market after market in the city will close down. Streets will fall empty. Trade will collapse, the economy will suffer a set-back. The question then is: will my citizens accept such losses on account of an absurd wedding? Will any jack-ass of a king agree to place himself willingly in such a mess? And would even the biggest dunderhead in the kingdom have failed to anticipate these possibilities after serving for sixteen years as the King's Treasurer?

(*Shouting.*)

But let me warn you, Basavanna, if you think I have ascended the throne merely to sit back and scratch my arse, you are in for a surprise. After sixteen years, how little you know me! You and those *sharanas* of yours! Just because the city of Kalyan has fallen into your hands, you think you can twist my arms behind my back and push me around with impunity? I am Bijjala! Know that and be on your guard. If you insist on driving me to the limits of patience, I shall stamp you all out like a cushionful of bed-bugs!

(*While he rants, Gangambika comes out with a pitcher of cool drink and three cups. Bijjala has seen her but ignored her entirely. She calmly starts filling the cups. Then, when he stops for breath.*)

GANGAMBIKA (*to Basavanna*): Shall I bring the medicine?

BASAVANNA: Eh?

GANGAMBIKA: The medicine?

BASAVANNA: What medicine?

GANGAMBIKA: For your ears. If His Majesty needs to shout even in this small house, perhaps your ears need attention.

(*Basavanna laughs. Bijjala doesn't, but glares at her balefully. Then in a hoarse whisper.*)

BIJJALA: Basavanna, I can take on the whole lot of you *sharanas* single-handed. But I swear, your women confound me!

GANGAMBIKA (*laughing as she places a cup in front of him*): Here, sir.

(*Also places cups in front of Kallappa and Basavanna, and goes out. Bijjala shouts after her.*)

BIJJALA: And listen, sister. Wherever I go, before I even sip a drop, I pour a little down Kallappa's throat to check if he won't go into convulsions and die like a sick dog. But, today, in your house, I go first—

GANGAMBIKA: Let me fetch you some more then.

(*She exits. Bijjala tosses the drink down his throat and turns to Basavanna.*)

BIJJALA: If you and those Brahmins are bent on self-destruction, go ahead. I wish you luck. I shall take my army away and entertain myself with a little warfare. When you are done, I shall return home to count your corpses.

BASAVANNA: Sir, until this day we have accepted Kalyan as our mother city. But if the *sharanas* are not to expect basic security in this land, I beg you to tell us so. We shan't bother you any further. We shall move on.

BIJJALA: Where?

BASAVANNA: Lord Shiva led us here. He'll take us to some other place. This is not a threat, Your Majesty. I speak from my heart.

BIJJALA: And you really believe your herd of a hundred and ninety-six thousand will give up home and shelter and follow you again into the wilderness?

BASAVANNA: That's for each one to decide for himself. Nevertheless, perhaps we *sharanas* have been stagnant too long—turned flaccid by the comforts of Kalyan. Perhaps we should take this as a sign and move!

(*A long pause.*)

BIJJALA: So be it. Have your wedding. I won't come in the way. Because I know I can't. You have trussed me up so I can't squirm an inch. But, Basavanna, once again you have brought home to me what I have always known: that you are the most selfish person I've ever met. Nothing matters to you—not friendship, not loyalty, not love—nothing except your society of *sharanas*. So our ways part here. I can only suggest that from now on you *sharanas* maintain your distance from me. You know how unpleasant I can be. No need to add anything more. (*Shouts.*) Good-bye, sister. Come, Kallappa!

(*He marches out. Kallappa follows him. A long silence. Jagadeva, Mallibomma, Gundanna, Kalayya, etc. enter, greet Basavanna.*)

BASAVANNA: Oh, Jagganna, Mallibomma, come. Sit down.

JAGADEVA: So, the news has already reached His Majesty's ears—

BASAVANNA: A king is expected to know what's happening in his realm.

JAGADEVA: And I suppose he refuses to let us go ahead with the wedding.

BASAVANNA: That's what he said initially—

JAGADEVA: What he says does not matter.

MALLIBOMMA: We are here. We'll see what he can do.

JAGADEVA: We'll manage everything. We've worked it all out.

MALLIBOMMA: Why don't you give Basavanna the gist of our plan?

JAGADEVA (*eagerly*): The society of *sharanas* is expanding. Rapidly. And the number of our enemies is increasing too. They won't stay put. They're bound to cook up some mischief. It's essential we anticipate their moves—

BASAVANNA: Jagganna, what's all this for?

JAGADEVA: Listen to me. We *sharanas* have several orders of minstrels spreading our message already. They wander from place to place, go door to door carrying out their vows. Now here's the plan. Each one of them can gather information by listening carefully. They can establish contact with the tribals, the shepherds, the cowherds—

BASAVANNA: His Majesty has given his consent to the wedding. (*There is stunned silence.*)

MALLI—JAGADEVA (*unbelieving*): He has?

BASAVANNA: Yes.

JAGADEVA: But can you trust him? The chances are he'll stab us in the back.

BASAVANNA: There's no reason to expect that. (*Pause.*)

JAGADEVA: You don't trust us. But you trust him.

BASAVANNA: Listen. If your're so keen to help with the wedding, why don't you do something very practical? Go and offer your services to the parents of the bride. They need all the help they can get!

JAGADEVA: Are you making fun of us?

BASAVANNA: No, Jagganna, the little problems of daily life—the ineffable demands, the pinpricks—they are the challenges a *sharana* must learn to attend to.

JAGADEVA: Then tell me. What does that vision of Allama mean?

Why the filth and the pus and the horrors with all the beautiful things?

BASAVANNA: I don't know. Things like that cannot be explained. As we go on living, we have to unravel the meaning for ourselves, strand by strand.

JAGADEVA (*looks at Mallibomma, smiles mysteriously*): So be it. *Sharan.*

BASAVANNA: *Sharan.*

JAGADEVA (*to Mallibomma as they go out*): Perhaps a lucky few live long enough to solve riddles—

(*They exit. During the above scene Gangambika has come to the door, and watched the goings-on silently.*)

BASAVANNA (*to himself*): Father, don't make me hear all day
'Whose man, whose man, whose man in this?'
Let me hear:
'This man is mine, is mine, this man is mine'.
O Lord of the Meeting Rivers, make me feel
I am a son of the house.

(*Pause.*)

GANGAMBIKA: It's late. Come in now.

BASAVANNA: All right.

(*He gets up, when a group of well-dressed merchants appears at the main door.*)

MAN: Basavanna!

(*For a minute Basavanna cannot quite place the visitors. He is too dazed, fatigued. It's dark. He cannot clearly see the man's face.*)

BASAVANNA (*slowly*): Yes?

MAN: I'm sorry we're late. It's me—Kukke Shetty.

BASAVANNA: Of course! Of course! How could I forget? Please, come in. Come in. Sit down. I've been waiting for you.

(*He looks at Gangambika, gives an apologetic smile. Then turns to the visitors.*)

What seems to be the problem?

Scene Six

A house in the Courtesans' Quarter. Damodara Bhatta enters hurriedly and bangs on the main door.

DAMODARA: Indrani...Indrani...

(A woman opens the door. He rushes in.)
　　Where is the Yuvaraj?

WOMAN: He is with Indrani...inside.

DAMODARA: Call him out, instantly. Tell him it's Damodara Bhatta...

WOMAN *(giggles)*: You don't need to introduce yourself. But I told you...he's inside. I don't think he'll like being pulled out.

DAMODARA *(starts banging on the inner door)*: Indrani...Indrani...

INDRANI *(comes out)*: Who's it? What's this? The Yuvaraj is resting. Didn't she inform you, sir?

DAMODARA *(to the woman)*: Bring a large pitcher of water.
(Ignoring Indrani's protests, Damodara Bhatta goes in, drags an inebriated Sovideva out and props him up on a chair. The woman brings a pitcher of water. Damodara Bhatta pours the water on Sovideva's head.)

INDRANI: One would think a demon had got into you—

DAMODARA: And one would be quite right.
(He slaps Sovideva repeatedly on his cheeks.)

SOVIDEVA (*waking up, groggily*): What...is it?

DAMODARA (*to Indrani*): Wipe him dry—dress him up properly. (*The two women attend to Sovideva while Damodara addresses him.*)

Is the Yuvaraj feeling any brighter or shall I order another pitcher of cold water? Now, sir, listen to me carefully. A cobbler's son is supposed to marry a Brahmin girl today...

SOVIDEVA (*snarls*): I know. So what?

DAMODARA: The whole city is like tinder—ready to ignite into flames. The citizens have vowed to stop this unnatural alliance at any cost. A hundred mercenaries arrived from Sonnalige this morning, they say. A band of fighters from Tulunadu is getting ready in Kannamma's rest house—

INDRANI: Such flexing of muscles to scare those poor *sharanas*? Isn't it a bit excessive?

DAMODARA: Our information is that the *sharanas* too are spoiling for a fight. Houses have turned into armouries. It is impossible to predict which way the wind will blow. We can only dress up and wait.

INDRANI (*laughs*): Like an ageing courtesan?

(*In the distance wedding music begins to play. They all watch. The wedding procession, with Sheelavanta and Kalavati as the bridal pair, winds down the streets of Kalyan. The sharanas are tense, almost afraid, but ready to face any consequence. Most citizens watch the procession from their roof-tops.*)

SOVIDEVA: The impudent scum! They could have had a quiet wedding in some village. Instead they have to flaunt it here—in the capital.

INDRANI: Honestly, it's beyond me why this little wedding should send the world into hysterics!

DAMODARA (*gently, sadly*): Indrani, the Rig Veda tells us that the four varnas flowed out of the Primordial Man: the Brahmin from the head, the Shudra from the feet. So what we have here in this wedding is the desecration of the body of that Purusha. How horrifying! What's worse, the person behind this crime is not an insolent Shudra or a rebellious untouchable—but a Brahmin, endowed with youth, erudition, eloquence and intelligence! What perversity drives him to this sacrilege—this profanity?

INDRANI: But the *sharanas* have done so much for the downtrodden and the destitute. For women like us—

DAMODARA (*incensed*): Nature is iniquitous. Struggle, conflict, violence—that's nature for you. But civilization has been made possible because our Vedic heritage controls and directs that self-destructive energy. How large-hearted is our dharma! To each person it says you don't have to be anyone but yourself. One's caste is like one's home—meant for one's self and one's family. It is shaped to one's needs, one's comforts, one's traditions. And that is why the Vedic tradition can absorb and accommodate all differences, from Kashmir to Kanya Kumari. And even those said to be its victims have embraced its logic of inequality.

Basavanna, on the other hand, cannot bear difference. He wants uniformity—and one that will fit his prejudices! He loves work, so to be idle is sinful. He abhors violence, so you can't eat meat. He believes in a formless, single God. So idolatry is damned.

For him the Brahmin

> is like the jackal
> who eats the vomit-nut,
> gets dizzy,
> and thinks all creation
> is whirling:
> why talk of these twice born
> who caste-mark their bodies with mud?
> If the owl blinded by day

thinks it's nightfall
does the world plunge into night,
you crazy fool?
He mocks the Shudras:
The pot is a god. The winnowing
fan is a god. The stone in the
street is a god. The comb is a
god. The bowstring is also a god.
Gods, gods, there are so many
there's no place left
for a foot.
He cannot grasp the elementary fact that a hierarchy which accommodates difference is more humane than an equality which enforces conformity.

INDRANI (*laughs*): You condemn the *sharanas*. But their poetry seems to dance on your tongue.

DAMODARA (*abashed*): To my ever-lasting shame, that's my one weakness, my indulgence in my tongue. Sanskrit is a language engraved on diamond, unchanging, austere. Eternal truths can be captured in its immutability. Kannada, our mother tongue, on the other hand, is pure flux. It changes from mouth to mouth, from caste to caste, from today to tomorrow. It is geared to the needs of squabbling couples, wheedling beggars, prostitutes spreading their saris out. It can only speak in inconstant moods. Its sensuality is addictive and the *sharanas* use it to pimp for their vulgarities.

SOVIDEVA (*wakes up*): So where is the massacre, priest? Where is the blood-letting?

DAMODARA: True enough. The wedding is over. And not a dog has barked. How can one explain it? (*Pause.*) Unless the *sharanas* were given protection—

SOVIDEVA: By whom?

DAMODARA: Protection on this scale—who else has the power to

guarantee it but the King? The baffling question is—why is
His Majesty tempting fate?

(*A knock on the door. Damodara Bhatta quickly pushes Sovideva
inside, and signals to Indrani who opens the door. Manchanna
Kramita enters, accompanied by some courtiers, tradesmen, soldiers, citizens, etc. A long pause.*
Damodara Bhatta smiles. Then starts proclaiming the titles.)

DAMODARA: *Yuvarājendra Kālanjara-Purādhīshwara Suvarṇa-
Vrishabha-dhwaja Someshwara Rājendra Bho parāk! Bho parāk!*
(*At a signal from him, Sovideva enters and stands before them.
They all bow to him.*)

Scene Seven

Front yard of the palace. It is dawn. Kallappa sits, dozing in a corner of the yard. Sovideva's voice is heard, calling him.

SOVIDEVA (*from outside*): Kallappa—Kallappa—

(*Kallappa sits up, alert and listens.*)

KALLAPPA: Is that you, young Master?

SOVIDEVA (*from outside*): Come here.

(*Kallappa is unwilling to move from his post. He looks around, half baffled, half irritated. Damodara Bhatta enters.*)

DAMODARA: Can't you hear the young Master calling you?

KALLAPPA: What is it?

DAMODARA: How should I know? I must say you would make a proper Feudal Lord. To question the Yuvaraj without even stirring from your seat. Go. I'll keep an eye on things here.

(*Kallappa looks at the door of Bijjalla's room on the first floor and moves out most unwillingly. As he steps out of the yard, he is attacked by half a dozen armed men who knock him down unconscious and drag him out.*

Damodara Bhatta signals. Several of the armed men enter the yard and spread out quietly behind the various corners of the palace. Only a young boy, Mariappa, remains with Damodara Bhatta. At a signal from Damodara Bhatta, the boy calls out in a voice shaking with fear.)

MARIAPPA: Bankanna—

(*No response. Damodara signals to Mariappa to call again.*)

Bankanna—

(*Bankanna, more or less the same age as Mariappa, appears.*)

BANKANNA: Yes?

(*Mariappa is sweating. So Bankanna asks testily.*)

What is it? And what are you doing here?

DAMODARA: Has His Majesty completed his bath?

BANKANNA: Yes. He's doing his *pooja.* (*Pointing to Mariappa.*) But what's that to him?

(*A soldier swoops upon Bankanna, gags him, lifts him up and takes him away.*)

DAMODARA (*explaining to Mariappa while keeping an eye on Bijjala's pooja room*): Mariappa, this Bankanna accompanies the King on his way to the fields in the morning. Carries the pot of water to wash His Majesty's behind. It's a time ideally suited to fill the King's ears. The King has constipation and, as his bowels lighten, he responds benignly to every suggestion. So this whipper-snapper has virtually ruled the King these last three years. Now on, you are the King's pot-bearer, you understand? Whatever the King says, the answer is: 'I don't know, sir.' Control your tongue, keep your ears open and you'll go far.

(*The effect aimed at during the above exchange is of a casual conversation going on in the immense palace yard—a normal everyday event. But the boy is stiff with fear and Damodara Bhatta's eyes are riveted to Bijjala's door. Damodara signals and a man enters carrying a silver salver, with clothes piled on it. At last Bijjala's voice is heard. Damodara pushes Mariappa away.*)

BIJJALA'S VOICE: Rudrappa, where are my robes?

(*A man rushes up the staircase and goes in. The following conversation is heard from inside.*)

BIJJALA: Who are you? And where is Rudrappa?

MAN: Rudrappa is absent today, Master...

BIJJALA: What's happening? Has my entire retinue fled the city like a pack of refugees? This one hasn't come! That one's absent!

(*A sudden roar. The man rolls down the stairs as though tossed out physically. A semi-dressed Bijjala follows him out.*)

BIJJALA: You country bumpkin, who took you on? I ask for the court robes and you leave the crown out? Your parents be—! (*Calls out.*) Rukmayya!

DAMODARA (*steps forward*): Rukmayya hasn't reported on duty today, sir.

BIJJALA: He hasn't? Blast it! Has the black plague carried away the whole city? And who are you? Ah! the priest in the Queen's Chambers, aren't you? I see you running around Sovi. But this is too early for him—

DAMODARA: A supplication, Your Majesty.

BIJJALA: Here? At this time of the day? What is it?

DAMODARA: From Raya Murari Sovideva Rajendra—

BIJJALA (*baffled*): Who? You mean our Sovi? Since when has he started sporting these ridiculous titles?

(*Suddenly he realizes what he is saying.*)

Kallappa! Where is our Kallappa? (*Calls out.*) Kallappa—

DAMODARA: Kallappa is indisposed, sir.

(*The message is clear. Bijjala rushes into his room. Bellows from inside.*)

BIJJALA: Treachery! Bloody treachery! Help...

(*He rushes out.*)

My sword! Which bastard dared touch my sword?

RAMBHAVATI (*rushes out*): What is it now?

(*She sees Damodara Bhatta.*)

What is it, sir?

(*Bijjala rushes down into the yard, runs to the main door, pushes it. It is locked from outside. He bangs on the door. Then looks through the window.*)

BIJJALA: We are surrounded by the infantry! Treason—

RAMBHAVATI: Please calm yourself. What's happened? I don't understand anything.

BIJJALA: What more can happen? It's all over. It's damnation. Your son has slit my throat. He's trapped me here...

RAMBHAVATI (*collapses*): No. It can't be true. Eeravva—Eeravva—

DAMODARA (*rushes to her*): Please, Your Majesty. There is no cause for panic. (*Orders.*) Bring Eeravva here.

BIJJALA (*bangs his head against the wall*): I was blind, Rambha. Blind! Fool! Fool! I was on the watch against the worms outside—while rearing a snake inside the house. Imbecile!

(*Eeravva comes in. She rushes to the Queen. She knows what is happening and is weeping uncontrollably. She and Bijjala help Rambha up.*

Sovideva enters wearing the crown. He is surrounded by a few courtiers, but mainly soldiers. He shakes like a leaf.)

RAMBHAVATI: What's going on, son? Say it's not your doing—

DAMODARA: Eeravva, the Queen shouldn't have been allowed to strain herself in the first place. Lead her in.

RAMBHAVATI: Aren't you ashamed to wear that thing in your father's presence? Sovi, if it's true that I have nursed you on my breasts, take off that crown. Give it to your father.

(*He doesn't move.*)

Thoo, you, you blackguard! If you don't take it off, my curse be on your head—

DAMODARA (*sternly*): Eeravva, didn't you hear me?

(*Rambhavati turns on Damodara in fury, when Bijjala restrains her.*)

BIJJALA: Go in, Rambha. The man speaks sense. They have won this throw. Nothing to be gained by making a scene now. Go in. Go.

(*Rambhavati is led in. Bijjala walks to Sovideva.*)

So! Perhaps you do have something between your legs after all—

(*Suddenly Sovideva kicks Bijjala, who, taken unawares, rolls to the ground. A chorus of surprise from those present. Damodara Bhatta rushes to the King's aid.*)

BIJJALA: Don't you dare touch me!

(*He gets up, smiling.*)

Who taught you that one? Kallappa?

(*The smile on his face disappears.*)

Where is Kallappa? Where is he?

(*No reply.*)

What have you done with him? You have killed him, haven't you?

(*Tears well up in his eyes.*)

How could you bring yourselves to do that, you bloody murderers? He was a babe—an innocent babe. You won't find another one like him in this Kaliyuga. How could you harm him?

(*He wipes his tears. Those watching are aghast to see Bijjala cry. But he makes no attempt to hide his grief.*)

You kill Kallappa but spare my life. Don't I deserve the consideration you have shown him?

DAMODARA: Sir, a throne is ringed by circles rippling out into circles; the feudatories, the flatterers, the astrologers, the courtesans, the wrestlers, the spies—Your Majesty knows. And they all survive. But a man like Kallappa disrupts the design. He lacked imagination and could not be corrupted. He was dangerous.

BIJJALA: You stretch your tongue too far, priest. Watch out lest you trip over it.

DAMODARA: Forgive us, Your Majesty. We mean no treason. We have eaten the salt of the Kalachuryas and have pledged our loyalty to the dynasty. The Empire is already ringing with proclamations—stone inscriptions are being erected. His

Majesty has decided to retire voluntarily and crown with his own hands his youngest son, Yuvaraj—

BIJJALA: Ha! Will anyone believe I would place this cadaver on the throne while four other sons are alive and kicking? Won't the whole world drown in giggles?

(*Sovideva steps out angrily. But this time Bijjala is ready, which deters him. Sovideva stands nonplussed, looking a little foolish.*)

DAMODARA (*gently*): If you please, sir—

(*Damodara Bhatta gestures to the door. Sovideva walks out, relieved.*)

BIJJALA: This game is yours. I concede that. But be under no illusion that this is the last round. If you poison me, the army in Kalyan will rise in revolt. My other sons will rush down full force. On the other hand, how long are you going to keep me alive?

DAMODARA: Each comment of His Majesty's is worthy of the *Artha Shastra*. Which only adds to our puzzlement.

BIJJALA: Yes?

DAMODARA: This marriage arranged by the *sharanas* was no trifling matter. On the one hand stands the Vedic Dharma, which has branched out in strength over the centuries and now shades the whole of Aryavarta. On the other, there is the *sharana* movement—a pestilence—but of a virulence not seen since the days of the Buddha. These two face each other in implacable hostility. The battle is without quarter. And if Your Majesty had not intervened, the *sharanas* would have met their fate on the day of that infamous wedding. But Your Majesty staunched the wrath of the people and invited disaster on his own head. Why? Why?

BIJJALA: Will you understand if I explain?

DAMODARA: I am a Brahmin, sir. It's my duty to understand.

BIJJALA: I fear this one may not be within your grasp.

(*Pause.*)

A man wandering in the desert, his throat parched, will graze on a patch of green, the size of one's palm, for its moisture. It's the same when one wanders in a godless world. The smallest—the most imperceptible—sign will do.

DAMODARA: Sign, sir?

BIJJALA (*has difficulty in using the word*): Yes...of a miracle.

DAMODARA: What miracle, sir?

BIJJALA: A Brahmin girl chooses to marry an untouchable and two hundred thousand people come out in support of it! That is the only miracle Basavanna has ever performed. But it is a miracle. Would you have stopped it?

DAMODARA: That's no miracle, sir. It's a crime against Nature—

BIJJALA (*quietly*): I knew that was beyond your reach. You need to have thirsted for a miracle to recognize one when you see it. (*Turns and calls.*) Rambha! Rambhavati!

(*He walks out.*)

Scene Eight

Basavanna's house. A conference of sharanas is going on. The atmosphere is highly charged.

BASAVANNA: The wedding of Sheelavanta-Kalavati could have turned into an unpleasant event. It didn't. For which we must give credit to the King—

(*People protest. There is an uproar.*)

HARALAYYA (*raises his hand*): Let Basavanna finish—

BASAVANNA (*more firmly*): There could have been a blood bath. Alternately, the King could have forbidden the whole affair— driven us out of this city—

SHARANA ONE: Why must you glorify the King, Basavanna? Why should he have forbidden the wedding? We were not breaking any law.

SHARANA THREE: It is no trivial matter to earn the enmity of two hundred thousand hard-working, law-abiding citizens.

SHARANA TWO: Suppose the King had said 'no'. So what? Would we have taken it lying down? We don't want to pick fights. But no one is going to push us around—

BASAVANNA: Fortunately nothing of that sort happened. But all of you know the most recent news. They say the King is being held prisoner. That's why I sent for you.

SHARANA FOUR: What would you have us do? We'll do as you say.

BASAVANNA: We should all go and gather in front of the palace—

WOMAN SHARANA: And demand to see the King. We should all sit down there and not move until the King comes out and talks to us as a free man.

BASAVANNA: It will work only if all of us go there and stand united.

SHARANA THREE: But why? It's a family squabble. A routine political event.

BASAVANNA: The King has risked his whole future for our sake. It would be rank betrayal not to stand by him now.

(*Commotion.*)

SHARANA FOUR: Betrayal is a big word. But not one to which our monarch is a stranger. Let's not forget that the palace he's now locked in once belonged to his trusting Masters.

SHARANA TWO: I'm sorry. But I can't understand you, Basavanna. Didn't you say that Bijjala himself told you he wanted nothing more to do with you—or us?

BASAVANNA: Yes.

SHARANA TWO: That he further added, 'If you *sharanas* don't stay away from me, you'll regret it—'

BASAVANNA: Something like that, yes.

SHARANA TWO: Then why are we forcing ourselves upon him?

BASAVANNA: Words spoken in anger. Whatever they were, we must stand by him—because he has nobody else but us.

MADHUVARASA: The world is awe-struck at the wedding of Sheela and Kalavati. We *sharanas* have at last shown our mettle, our indomitable spirit. And after all that, you want to lay the credit at the King's feet? I can't believe it!

SHARANA THREE: Dynasties come and go. The Chalukya is gone. The Kalachurya rules today. This one will also be gone tomorrow. But we *sharanas* have built a community which stands beyond political twists and turns. We have built our own, grounded in our own metaphysics, shaped by our practice. And it is enough that we attend to its welfare. We know you're a friend of Bijjala's. You should do as your conscience tells you. We shan't object to that. But surely, this is the moment to make the four quarters realize that the *sharanas* do not need to sit and sway in the shadow of the throne, along with you?

SHARANA FIVE: Basavanna, I don't know what's got into us these days. But something has, that's for certain. Some of us are afraid. Others lazy. Others busy rationalizing their indolence. If you want us to move—and move together—there are only two alternatives: command us to do so—

BASAVANNA: Ours is a spiritual brotherhood, a community of experience. To tell any *sharana* what to do would be to insult him.

SHARANA FIVE: Then declare that there has been a miracle, that you saw Lord Shiva in your dreams. And the whole lot will leap up and follow your lead. There's no other way.

BASAVANNA: There is. Let each *sharana* listen to his inner self and follow its dictates.

> What use
> is knowledge within
> as long as there's no action without?
> If there's no body
> would there be a shelter
> for the breath of life?
> Can one see one's face
> if there's no mirror?

And the world out there—that is the only mirror we have. What use is *bhakti* if it only hides its face?

(*Murmurs of anger, dissent.*)

SHARANA FOUR: Are you calling us escapists?

KAKKAYYA: It's past midnight. We have talked enough. Tell us what you plan to do, and each one of us will decide for himself what he should do.

BASAVANNA: Tomorrow, at dawn, after my prayers, I shall leave for the palace.

KAKKAYYA: So be it. Let's disperse now.

(*The* sharanas *disperse, fiercely arguing. Basavanna and Gangambika see them off. Basavanna comes back. Long pause.*)

BASAVANNA: I call out to you, Father.

I cry out to you, Father.

Will you not reply?

Yet I keep on calling to you.

Lord of the meeting rivers,

Why this silence?

(*A child is heard crying inside. Basavanna goes in, brings the child out and sits playing with it. Gangambika comes and sits. Silence.*)

BASAVANNA: This is the blossom of our vitals, a gift from the Lord. And yet one has no time to pick him up.

GANGAMBIKA: It's as though we have been so carried away by the excitement of building a house that we have forgotten what we came here for—to buy a few basic groceries.

(*He looks up at her, smiling.*)

BASAVANNA: Just what I was thinking, Ganga. And in the cacophony of the crowd, we have lost the Lord's voice. One needs to go back again to where there is silence—where one can again become itinerant.

GANGAMBIKA: What then about tomorrow?

BASAVANNA: Whether the others come with me or not, Ganga, this is my last night in this house.

(*Tears well up in her eyes.*)

GANGAMBIKA: Perhaps—that's best.

BASAVANNA: And once a person turns his back on his own house, does he owe the palace more? Let's hope tomorrow the King will receive his due from the *sharanas*. After that, it'll be the formless space beyond the palace. Suddenly nothingness has begun to beckon me.

> He who can turn
> space into form
> he alone is a *sharana*.
> He who can turn form into space,
> he alone can experience the *linga*.
> If these two became one,
> would there be a way
> into you, O Lord
> of the meeting rivers?

Scene Nine

Night. Jagadeva, Mallibomma, Kalayya, etc., surrounded by weapons of various sorts, are performing a private ritual.

JAGADEVA: Now we mingle our blood.

(He cuts his forearm. The others follow suit. They mix blood, wound to wound.)

So we are brothers now. Our blood flows together. *Om Namah Shivaya!*

(They repeat the chant.)

Our elders continue to debate in Basavanna's house. Enough sound and fury there to bring the roof-beams down. That's all the old fogies are good for. So it's left to us to exterminate the vermin, the enemies of Lord Shiva. Is that clear? Good. Now let's have your reports. One by one. Malli, you first.

MALLIBOMMA: For five gold coins the palace guard Rachappa is ready to show us the secret passages—

JAGADEVA: What passages?

MALLIBOMMA: —that lead into the palace.

OTHERS *(excited)*: Really? Are you sure? That's wonderful.

(Jagadeva silences the excited gathering with a wave of his hand.)

JAGADEVA: We don't need him. I could lead you to them myself.

(Exclamations of surprise.)

MALLIBOMMA: You? How do you know them?

JAGADEVA: I was a regular visitor to the palace as a child, remember? With my father. And we used to play hide-and-seek in those passages. Even Sovi was there—

MALLIBOMMA: But I don't understand! Those passages were meant for a quick get-away in the event of an enemy attack. They should be secret. You played games there?

JAGADEVA: The royal family had no need for the passages. They took to their heels at the very mention of the enemy— through the back door!

(*Laughter. Only Kalayya doesn't laugh.*)

KALAYYA: So all these days you knew about these passages and didn't let on.

JAGADEVA: I'm telling you now. Look, I'll lead you in, isn't that enough?

KALAYYA: And all along, while we were arguing and shouting and tying ourselves into knots about how to get inside the palace, you just sat there—smiling smugly—feeling superior, the solution already in your hands, didn't you? You Brahmins, you are all the same. You're only interested in having the laugh on others.

JAGADEVA: Don't you dare mention my caste, Kalayya—

MALLIBOMMA: Hey, stop it! Don't let's start squabbling now!

(*Gundanna comes in.*)

GUNDANNA: Jagganna, your wife is here to see you.

JAGADEVA: I can't see her. Tell her to go away. She knows I have sworn not to look upon a woman's face till we have achieved our goal—

GUNDANNA: This is the fourth time she's come since yesterday.

JAGADEVA: So what? I am not coming out. Tell her to go away!

GUNDANNA: I can't, I'm sorry. I can't even bear to look at her. She says your mother has taken to the mat and won't say a word.

The neighbours treat them like pariahs. Poor child! She comes, sits out there like a ghost, goes away, comes back again. All she wants is a word with you. My heart bleeds for her—

JAGADEVA: Then go and bleed somewhere else. She has to attend to her mother-in-law. She'll go back soon enough. We're not playing games here. We are here to fight for our faith and I have taken a vow of celibacy. Can't she grasp a simple thing like that? Can't any one? And why are you all staring at me— as though I have done something wrong? As though I were a criminal—a—a—

(*He chokes, goes and sits in a corner, holding his head. The others look away.*)

Scene Ten

Same as Scene Two. Rambhavati is bed-ridden. Eeravva is doing a perfunctory pooja in the adjacent sanctum. Bijjala paces up and down muttering to himself. In a corner, near the window, sits Mariappa staring vacantly out.

RAMBHAVATI: How long are you going to pace about like that? It's a wonder you haven't worn out the soles of your feet—

BIJJALA: You go to sleep.

RAMBHAVATI: What's the use of walking up and down? Will it bring our son here? Will it fetch Basavanna?

BIJJALA (*snarls*): Basavanna? What do you mean Basavanna? Why bring him into this?

RAMBHAVATI: You can't conjure him up by just—

BIJJALA: What are you talking about? Have you gone off your head? Why should he come here? I told him to stay away—not to meddle in my affairs. Why should he come? There's nothing between us now. I wasn't even thinking of him.

RAMBHAVATI: Don't lie. At least, not to me. I have shared twenty-five years with you, and I know.

BIJJALA: Woman, will you shut up? or should I...
(*Pause.*)

All right. All right! So let's suppose you're right. Let's suppose I was thinking of Basavanna. Why shouldn't I? I supported their movement. They know that. They could have stood by me. All they had to do was to get together and demand my release and my son would have come crawling to me. But no! Basavanna won't come, because I have told him not to. Those *sharanas* are obstinate—

RAMBHAVATI: Just stop pacing about. Come and sit by me.

BIJJALA: I deserve this. No point in blaming others—

(*He sits beside Rambhavati, tense and restless. Commotion outside. Servants of the palace are seen running. Mariappa addresses one of them.*)

MARIAPPA: What's it? What's happened?

WOMAN: They say Basavanna is on his way here—with lots of *sharanas*.

BIJJALA: Basavanna! He's coming? Nonsense! That's not possible. (*Jumps up.*) Didn't I tell you he'll come? How many *sharanas* are there with him? Ask her—

MARIAPPA: How many *sharanas*—

(*But the woman is gone. Others rush past the window.*)

BIJJALA: Since he would have started from his home, he will be approaching the palace from the east. That means they should be visible from that skylight in the sanctum.

(*He rushes into the sanctum.*)

Eeravva, out you go! Quick!

RAMBHAVATI: What's all this? Let her at least complete the *pooja*—

BIJJALA: Later. Later. Out now. Out!

(*He almost pushes Eeravva out.*)

Now, Mariappa, come in. Climb up to that skylight—

(*Mariappa is unwilling to step into the sanctum.*)

Don't dawdle outside, ass. I order you to step into the god's room. I permit you—anyway, nobody will know!

(*Rambhavati clicks her tongue disapprovingly. Mariappa steps in gingerly. Bijjala tries to help him climb up to the skylight. But he keeps slipping.)*

BIJJALA (*frustrated*): Where's the ladder? Ask for one—No, wait. Climb on to my shoulders. Here.

MARIAPPA (*scared*): I can't, Master—I can't!

BIJJALA: You dare say no to me, you son of a whore? I am Bijjala and I'm not dead yet. If you make any more fuss, I'll just wring your neck. So get up—

(He bends. The boy sits on his shoulder.)

That's not high enough. Stand up. Go on! I won't drop you. (*Laughs.*) I am your sovereign after all—I bear the weight of the earth on my shoulders. I won't drop you, I promise.

(Mariappa stands on Bijjala's shoulders with the support of the wall.)

Basavanna is here, Rambha. I'll show that son of yours—

RAMBHAVATI: He's been bad. But don't be hard on him—

BIJJALA: For a start, I have to return that kick of his! Other matters can follow in due course—

(To Mariappa)

What are you gawping at? Can you see anything?

MARIAPPA: Yes, Master. But they are far away—

BIJJALA: Just tell me what you see. How many?

MARIAPPA: Many, Master, so many!

BIJJALA (*roaring*): So many! So many! How many, you dolt? And where are they?

MARIAPPA: All around the temple of Ravana-Siddheswara... It's saffron...saffron...

BIJJALA: The temple of Ravana-Siddheswara? Good, continue. Beyond that is the street of washermen—by the river. And next to that is the carpenters' street. And on this side is the old excise post. You see all that?

MARIAPPA: Yes, sir.

BIJJALA: Then the streets should all be bursting with the *sharanas*—an ocean of saffron. Even a mere fifty thousand will choke that area up—

MARIAPPA: No, Master.

BIJJALA (*enraged*): What do you mean 'No, Master'?

MARIAPPA: The terraces of houses are packed with people—ordinary people—watching. But the *sharanas*—they are many—they are around the temple of Ravana-Siddheswara and then in the street of washermen. Not in the carpenters' street—

BIJJALA: Then they must by spilling over on this side, toward the old excise post—

MARIAPPA: No, sir. No one there yet.

BIJJALA: Have you lost your eyes? Look again!
(*The door opens and Damodara Bhatta steps in, smiling gently.*)

DAMODARA: Mariappa, you low-born cur, don't you know you are not to step into the sanctum? You dare pollute the royal *pooja* room? Come out instantly or else—
(*Mariappa jumps down in fright and rushes out of the sanctum.*)

BIJJALA (*trying to hide his discomfiture*): I asked him in.

DAMODARA: If Your Majesty had but commanded, I would have had the door unlocked. This way, sir. The upper terrace provides a better view of the city.

RAMBHAVATI (*unable to hold herself back*): Has he come?

DAMODARA: Yes, Your Majesty. He is on his way.

BIJJALA: It's only because he's seen Basavanna that this leech has come twitching to us—
(*Bijjala rushes out. The palace retinue which has already collected on the terrace bow to Bijjala as he rushes to the edge of the terrace and leans out eagerly. The smile disappears from his face. He stands dazed, unbelieving.
Damodara Bhatta comes behind him.*)

DAMODARA: Yes, sir. And there he is! We too were at a loss about how to meet this eventuality. The Yuvaraj couldn't sleep a wink all night. But now our accountant has carefully enumerated the *sharanas* accompanying Basavanna—there are precisely seven hundred and seventy!

(*Basavanna arrives in the yard in front of the palace, followed by his sharanas. Bijjala and Basavanna stare at each other in silence. The audience too is transfixed. A long pause.*)

BIJJALA: So you have come? Good. Good. Come. But...it's damned awkward...meeting like this.

BASAVANNA: I wanted to come. So I have. Those who wanted to come with me, they are here.

BIJJALA: I hadn't asked you to come. You hadn't said you would. But you are here. (*Pause.*) You didn't desert me.

BASAVANNA: How are you, sir?

BIJJALA: What can go wrong with me? A buffalo fatted for the Goddess Mariamma.

BASAVANNA: And Her Majesty?

BIJJALA: She's coughing again. It's...this sudden change of weather. (*Pause.*)

Well, I had better go in. She isn't too well. (*Pause.*) You'd better go too. Not much point our hanging on here. (*Pause.*) Go, Basavanna.

BASAVANNA (*nods*): I shall, sir. When we shall see each other again, I don't know. So pardon me for preaching. But let's not try and bend God's generosity to our desires. Let His will be our life. Even if He tortures us, defeats us, our triumph will be in that He has attended to us.

BIJJALA (*irritable*): There you go again! I never know what you mean. Can't you put it more simply?

BASAVANNA (*smiles*): Let me try, sir. (*Pause.*) Trust in Him.

BIJJALA (*shakes his head*): That's hard.

BASAVANNA: It is possible. If only you would believe—
(*Long pause. Suddenly—*)

BIJJALA: Do you remember? Your verse—

> He who runs is not a warrior.
> He who begs is not a devotee.
> A warrior shouldn't run.
> A devotee shouldn't beg.
> I'll not run, I'll not beg,
> O Lord of the meeting rivers.

Did I get it right?

(*Basavanna nods. Long pause.*)

BASAVANNA: Believe in Him. I too shall go now to Kappadi of the meeting rivers in search of him. May Shiva bless you. *Sharan.*

(*Bijjala nods. Basavanna and companions go away. Bijjala returns to Rambhavati's room, locks the door from inside and bursts into a mixture of sobs and laughter.*)

BIJJALA: Basavanna is here, Rambha. I shall be King again and you the Queen. A hundred and fifty thousand *sharanas* are on their way—not all of them here yet, of course. But they'll be here soon. Our son is realizing his folly. In no time at all he'll surrender...

(*He sits down by her side.*)

Don't you worry about anything now. Everything is going to be all right again—

(*She doesn't reply. He closes his eyes and leans back against the wall. In the far distance, the song sung by Basavanna and his sharanas is heard.*)

Scene Eleven

The palace. Sovideva with Manchanna Kramita and Damodara Bhatta.

DAMODARA (*bubbling with excitement*): The *sharanas* lie inert, lost, adrift in a void of their own creation. Excellent! Now we must act—

SOVIDEVA: What do we do?

DAMODARA: Arrest those responsible for the wedding. Expel the leaders of—

MANCHANNA (*gently*): What will that achieve? Basavanna is gone. But their organization continues. Money continues to flow into their coffers—

SOVIDEVA: I know. But how is that?

MANCHANNA: It's simple, sir. That inter-caste wedding shook every citizen of Kalyan. For him it meant an era in which any untouchable could ask for his daughter's hand in marriage! A nightmare! So he supported us against your father. Yet he needs the *sharanas* for his profits. It's a bond of greed—of mercantile calculation. And that has to be severed.

SOVIDEVA: So what do you advise?

MANCHANNA (*smiles*): I'm almost tempted to say, 'Let's do nothing!' The *sharanas* have lost their drive and in course of time are bound to revert to caste for sheer survival. Unfortunately Basavanna is alive and we can take nothing for granted. It is imperative that we strike—immediately.

SOVIDEVA: How do we do that?

MANCHANNA: Sir, King Mihirakula of Kashmir took care of the Buddhist menace by decimating sixteen hundred *viharas.* Our Pandya neighbour impaled eight thousand Jain scoundrels along the highway. So why are we being so circumspect?

DAMODARA: The coronation is round the corner. It's essential that the new king is seen as capable of forgiveness, generosity—

MANCHANNA: And what's a coronation, pray? The gross body is cleansed of its lowly birth and made worthy of receiving Vedic mantras and the Brahmin's salutations. The King partakes of the divine. Who dare judge the King? We are there to interpret the sacred texts. The King is there to implement our advice. That's enough.

SOVIDEVA: Bravo! That's grand! You are right. I am the King and I can now make them pay for defying me at the Treasury!

DAMODARA: Please, Your Majesty—

SOVIDEVA (*excited*): I shall strike terror in their hearts, I shall wreak havoc.

MANCHANNA: And then pay a brief visit to your father-in-law, sir? His support may come in handy—

SOVIDEVA: Yes. And see our Queen again! She is our Queen, after all, frigid bitch though she is. (*To Damodara Bhatta*) You'll accompany us?

DAMODARA: Someone is needed in the capital, sir. I suggest I stay behind.

MANCHANNA: Whenever King Bijjala went out on his campaigns, he left the city to my care.
(*To Damodara Bhatta*)

In fact, His Majesty will need someone to keep him company
in his father-in-law's house and attend to the daily rituals.
(*Damodara Bhatta reacts in anger but is silenced by Manchanna
Kramita's unctuous smile.*)
SOVIDEVA: Let's go then!
(*They all go out. Drums are heard in the distance and provide the
bridge to the next scene.*)

Scene Twelve

Jagadeva, Mallibomma, Kalayya practising the martial arts. Gundanna comes rushing in and rolls on the ground in agony.

GUNDANNA: *Ayyo...Ayyo...*Kala! Malli! I can't bear it. I can't...Mother!

OTHERS: What's it, Gundanna? What's happened? What are you screaming about?

GUNDANNA: What can I say? Mother...I'll die. I can't bear it! Haralayya—Madhuvarasa—
(*He bangs his head on the floor.*)

MALLIBOMMA: Behave yourself, Gundanna. Take hold of yourself. What's happened to Haralayya?

GUNDANNA: It's harrowing! A while ago—the King's soldiers arrested Haralayya and took him to the city square. They also brought Madhuvarasa there—And then—then—as the city watched—they plucked their eyes out—
(*A reaction of horror from those present.*)
Plucked out their eyes with iron rods—bound them hand and foot and had them dragged through the streets—tied to elephants' legs—*Ayyo!* How can I tell you?—Torn limbs along the lanes, torn entrails, flesh, bones—They died screaming!

JAGADEVA: And no one intervened? What about the *sharanas*?

GUNDANNA: They all watched, shut inside their houses. I can't stop shivering. It was horrible.

KALAYYA: Shiva! Shiva!

GUNDANNA: Now—they are impaling their bodies at the city gate—

JAGADEVA: *Thoo! Thoo! Thoo!* Our manhood be spat upon. We are not just cowards but cowards ten times over. Come on, let's tie anklets and dance like eunuchs—

KALAYYA: I told you we must act before—

JAGADEVA: You did? Always the 'I-told-you-so' Kalayya, aren't you? But suggest something, and immediately a thousand excuses—

KALAYYA: Watch it, Jagga. I won't take any more nonsense from you—

JAGADEVA: What'll you do?

MALLIBOMMA: Jagganna, Kalayya, stop it! Gundanna, what about the women of the house?

JAGADEVA: I know Kalavati's mother has gone away with the couple.

GUNDANNA: Sheela's mother saw her husband's body—a grotesque bundle of rags—and ran down the street, screaming. It froze one's blood. No one knows where she is. Perhaps a lake or a well—

JAGADEVA: We can't sit here like old women. Come on. Let's attack the palace. Sovi won't expect us to act so soon. He doesn't know I know the secret route. We'll trap him, cut the bastard into pieces.

MALLIBOMMA: But is it safe to go out armed in broad daylight?

GUNDANNA: The streets are deserted. The city is dead—like a cemetery!

JAGADEVA: Come on!

(*They rush out.*)

Scene Thirteen

The palace. Jagadeva and others rush in along with Rachappa, naked swords in their hands.

RACHAPPA: Jagganna, you've been made fools of! There's no one in the palace. They've all run away. Sovideva—Damodara Bhatta—

MALLIBOMMA: Then why didn't you let us know? It was your job—

RACHAPPA: I was waiting for you outside. I didn't know you knew the secret passages and could get into the palace without me. Besides, I sent word with Mudda—

KALAYYA: He's probably rushed straight to some whore!

JAGADEVA: We'll be the laughing stock of the world. For all our slogans of revolution, we've plunged straight into a heap of shit.

MALLIBOMMA: It's too late to worry about that now. It's dangerous to stay on here. Let's go—

JAGADEVA: And what do we do out there? Wear bangles in public?

MALLIBOMMA: No point hanging on here. He says the palace is empty—

RACHAPPA: Except for that lunatic.

KALAYYA: What lunatic?

RACHAPPA: The old King—

MALLIBOMMA: The old King?

JAGADEVA: You mean—Bijjala?

RACHAPPA: They say he's gone mad after the Queen died. He refuses to leave the palace. Refuses to step out of the Queen's chambers—

KALAYYA: Any guards there?

RACHAPPA: They too ran away—naturally.

JAGADEVA: Take us to him. Quick.

(*They rush out.*)

Scene Fourteen

Rambhavati's chamber. The same as in Scene Two. Mariappa dozes in a corner. Bijjala is sprawled in a dark corner of the sanctum. Jagadeva and others rush in. Mariappa sees them, and rushes out.

BIJJALA (*from inside*): Who's that?

JAGADEVA (*comes to the door of the sanctum*): Victory to Your Majesty.

BIJJALA: Who is that talking about my majesty?

JAGADEVA: We have come to see you, sir—

BIJJALA: Come in.

(*Jagadeva, sword in hand, is about to step into the sanctum. He beckons others to follow him. But Mallibomma stops him.*)

MALLIBOMMA (*shakes his head, and whispers, pointing to the sword*): You can't take that in.

JAGADEVA (*to Bijjala*): We have travelled a long distance, sir. Our feet are caked with mud. We don't want to dirty the temple.

BIJJALA (*laughs*): This god hasn't seen any worship for many days now. The floor hasn't even been swept.

JAGADEVA: But, sir—

BIJJALA: It's cool in here. I'm not stirring out. Say your piece from there or go away.

JAGADEVA (*suddenly*): We have come from Kappadi, sir.

BIJJALA (*walking up*): Kappadi?

JAGADEVA: —of the meeting rivers. From Basavanna.

BIJJALA: Why didn't you say so? Wait. What does he say?
(*He gets up. Mallibomma looks at Jagadeva, uncomprehending.
Jagadeva dismisses him with a wave of the hand, signals to the
others to get ready and stands poised to strike.
Bijjala steps out of the sanctum.*)

BIJJALA: What does he say?

JAGADEVA: Strike, Rachappa. Kalayya—Now!
(*He strikes Bijjala with his sword. The others too attack. Bijjala
wounded, taken by surprise, reels back. Then the warrior in him
comes awake. He pushes them back and rushes into the sanctum and
stands ready to fend off further attacks.
Mallibomma watches, stunned, uncomprehending.*)

JAGADEVA: Come, Malli! Come on, Kalayya!
(*He tries to pursue Bijjala into the sanctum but Mallibomma blocks
his way.*)

MALLIBOMMA: No, Jaggana. Nobody sheds blood in there!
(*Jagadeva ignores him, and tries to side-step him, but Mallibomma
is adamant.*)

Have you forgotten our vow? No one desecrates the Lord's
house while I am around—

JAGADEVA: So what do you want me to do?

MALLIBOMMA: Leave the swords out here.

JAGADEVA (*helpless, puts his sword down*): Come on! Let's drag him
out.

MALLIBOMMA: But why? He's no better than a patched-up piece
of leather. What's the point of all this?

JAGADEVA: He's our only chance, don't you see? If we go out
empty-handed, we'll go down in history as incompetent

clowns. Not just our enemies but our own people will laugh at us.

MALLIBOMMA: You want to kill him for that?

JAGADEVA: Don't talk too much, Malli. It's to me that Basavanna has passed on the vision of Allama. Me! No one else. He's left it to me to interpret it. You know that. Now do as I say: kill him and the meaning will take care of itself.

(*All four put their swords aside and go in. Bijjala, bleeding, is waiting for them. They grapple with him, try to pull him out but he is like a bull elephant, rooted to the earth, unyielding. Suddenly he shakes himself free and runs to the linga and embraces it. They pounce upon him and try to wrench him free. But to no avail. Bijjala gives a loud laugh.*)

BIJJALA: This, boys, is known as Bijjala's Grip! Study it! Move back now. Back.

(*They let go and move back.*)

Everyone asks the same question: Miracle? What miracle? But look here now. Basavanna couldn't make me bend before the Lord. My wife couldn't. But you young whelps have made me cling to Him. Something must be wrong with me. Whatever I reach for—wherever I crawl—I bump into miracles. Huh! All right. Let's have it. Where are you from? My son hasn't sent you—that's certain. He has more seasoned assasins. You can barely wield a knife. I could have whacked you all down like rats. But I'm tired now. Who are you? Where have you come from?

MALLIBOMMA: We are *sharanas*, sir.

BIJJALA: I see. And it's true Basavanna sent you?

JAGADEVA: Yes, sir.

MALLIBOMMA: No, sir. We came on our own.

BIJJALA: Just like that? To kill me? Go ahead. Kill me. I won't even ask why. I am sick of asking. You'll lighten my burden. But there is a condition—

MALLIBOMMA: Sir—

BIJJALA: I have a message for Basavanna. Will you deliver it to him? If you promise, I'll step out. On my own. If not, I'll stick to this *linga*: I'll be Markandeya and you play the messengers of Death—

JAGADEVA: You have our word, sir.

BIJJALA: If you fail, may the curse of Basavanna be upon your heads.

(*He gets up. He is weakening fast. He leans on the shoulders of Mallibomma, who leads him out.*)

BIJJALA: Tell Basavanna... Say! What'll you say?... Damn! I had it all clear and lucid. All these days I sat there and thrashed it out with him in detail. Things we really should have talked about when we had the time but didn't—And now, I dry up. Oh, yes! Tell Basavanna we talked of many things in our time, but we never touched upon what matters. And that is—Blast! It was on the tip of my tongue and I've lost it. Wait!—

JAGADEVA (*impatient*): Are you done, sir?

(*Bijjala looks at him in surprise. He lets go of Mallibomma and moves to Jagadeva. Leans on his shoulder.*)

BIJJALA: What's it, lad? Why are you so upset with me?

(*Jagadeva stabs him. As Bijjala collapses, he grabs Jagadeva.*)
Why, Sovi? Why—why this anger?

JAGADEVA: I am not Sovi. I am not your son.

BIJJALA (*trying to embrace him*): Sovi, son—

JAGADEVA: Let go of me! I told you—I'm not your son!

(*Jagadeva pushes Bijjala, who rolls to the floor. Then he leans against the wall and retches. Others watch.*)

MALLIBOMMA: He's dead now. Are you happy?

JAGADEVA: Go away!

MALLIBOMMA: And you?

JAGADEVA: Go. I am not coming with you.

(*All except Jagadeva leave. He stares at Bijjala's body, in a sort of delirium.*)

So this is your temple, Basavanna? These legs the pillars. This body the shrine. This head the golden cupola. And yet how easily does the moving freeze into immobility! A stab—a blow—and the river freezes. The blood clots. The body goes stiff. Look how this house of Lord Shiva shakes—rolls and pitches—and all it needs is a sprinkle of blood. And a stab—

(*As he goes into the sanctum, he sees the idol of the bull, Nandi, at the door, and addresses it.*)

You are watching, Basavanna? Good. I'm not afraid of death like my father. I am not afraid. Even of sacrilege. Watch. If you are Basavanna, I am Jagganna—the Solitary Saint.

(*Sits in front of the linga and plunges the dagger into himself.*)

Scene Fifteen

Kappadi. Basavanna with Mallibomma and Kalayya.

KALAYYA (*in tears*): The King stepped out only because he heard
   your name—

(*Mallibomma pats him on his back, calming him, while also
suggesting that he's spoken enough.*)

BASAVANNA: Go now. May Shiva be with you. *Sharan.*

(*Kalayya and Mallibomma go away.*)

   Whose name? And whose face? Whose wound and whose
   blood? This carcass is mine. And I am also the King's slayer.
   So this is the last of Allama's tableaux. The festivities are over,
   the streets deserted. The night has departed and the world is
   silent. Lord of the Meeting Rivers, absorb this inner shrine
   into the fine tip of your flame. Until all becomes light. Light
   within light. The great dawn of light.

Scene Sixteen

A messenger comes running.

MESSENGER 1: Sir! Sir!

(*Sovideva enters with a few bodyguards.*)

MESSENGER 1: Sir, Kalyan burns. People rush through its streets howling and screaming. No one to look after them, console them, protect them. Sir, you must save Kalyan—

(*He rushes out.*)

MESSENGER 2 (*enters*): The royal guards have gone on a rampage and started looting the city. Temples are sacked, trading houses torched. The city reels under gruesome tales of rape, murder and rioting. Sir, you must rush to Kalyan. (*Exits.*)

SOVIDEVA: Oh God! Why didn't anyone warn me this might happen? Why has everyone turned against me?

DAMODARA (*enters*): We should never have left Kalyan. I told you, sir, but it isn't too late yet. Let's build a new city from these ashes. A new—

SOVIDEVA: You! You are responsible for all this! I trusted you—

DAMODARA: Sir—

SOVIDEVA: Shut him up!

(*A guard strikes Damodara Bhatta with his sword. Damodara Bhatta collapses, blinking in surprise and dies.*)

For heaven's sake, I only said shut him up! Why is everybody against me? What shall I do now? The *sharanas* too are out to destroy me—that tribe of snakes! Annihilate them! Crush their progeny!

MESSENGER 3 (*enters*): News from Kappadi Sangama! Basavanna is no more. They say he merged with the elements. Nothing else is known!

MESSENGER 3 (*enters*): Sir, the *sharanas* flee Kalyan. They spread out in all eight directions. One lot has plunged into the fever-ridden jungles of Uluvi. Another heads for Andhra—

SOVIDEVA: Pursue them. Don't let them escape. Men, women, children—cut them all down. Set the hounds after them. Search each wood, each bush. Burn the houses that give them shelter. Burn their books. Yes, the books! Tear them into shreds and consign them to the wells. Their voices shall be stilled for ever—

(*Drums. Screams of women and children are heard, along with the noise of fighting.*)

With our realm in such dire straights, my brothers are marching on us. The villains! The traitors! It proves they had a hand in killing my dear father, my revered father, King Bijjala, founder of the glorious Kalachurya dynasty. Destroy them.

It is time to be wakeful, to be on guard.

The King is father to his people and the people shall love him and obey him like his offspring. No tongue shall wag against the King or his family or his retinue or his officers.

From this moment all *sharanas*, foreigners, and free thinkers are expelled from this land on pain of death. Women and the lower orders shall live within the norms prescribed by our ancient tradition, or else they'll suffer like dogs. Each citizen shall consider himself a soldier ready to lay down his life for the King. For the King is God incarnate!

(*Fire erupts in the background. Screams fill the skies. Manchanna*

*Kramita and three other Brahmins enter, seat Sovideva on a throne,
hold the 'urn of thousand holes' on his head. Water jets out in a
thousand streams and cascades on Sovideva's head.
He continues to talk through all this.
They sing Vedic chants.
The eulogies begin and drown everything else.*)

HERALDS: *Mahārājādhirāja Kālanjara-purādhishwara Go-Brāhmana-
Pratipālaka Varnāshrama-dharma-Rakshaka Dushta-shāsana
Suvarna-Vrishabhadhwaja Damaru-turya-nirghoshana
Kalachuryavamsha-Kamala-Bhāskara Triambaka-pāda-
padmamadhupa Parama-māheswara pratāpa-lankeshwara
Giridurga-malla Ripu-kari-sandoha—simha Nisshanka-malla
Bhujabalachakravarti Someshvara-Rājendra Bho parāk—Bho
parāk!*

(*Sovideva continues to gesticulate violently. The fire continues to
blaze in the background.*)

THE FIRE AND THE RAIN

The Fire and the Rain was first presented at the Chowdiah Memorial Hall, Bangalore in November 1999. The principal cast was as follows:

ANIL MENON	King
DARIUS SUNAWALA	Courtier
JAGAN DEVRAJ	Priest One/Vishwarupa
VIVEK RAO	Priest Two/Nittilai's brother
VIKRAM SHARMA	Priest Three
ASHOK MANDANNA	Paravasu
ROHIT MALKANI	Actor-Manager
VIVEK SHAH	Arvasu
PUJA CHODHA	Nittilai
JAGDISH RAJA	Andhaka
VEENA SAJNANI	Vishakha
ARORUP ACHARYA	Yavakri
PRAKASH BELAWADI	Raibhya
SANDEEP P. S.	Brahma Rakshasa
JAVINDER SINGH	Nittilai's husband
ARJUN SAJNANI	Indra
Directed by	ARJUN SAJNANI
Production Design by	JAYOO NACHIKET
Choreography by	DAKSHA SETH
Music by	DEVISSARO

Prologue

It has not rained adequately for nearly ten years. Drought grips the land. A seven-year long fire sacrifice (yajña) is being held to propitiate Indra, the god of rains.

Fire burns at the centre of step-like brick altars. There are several such altars, at all of which priests are offering oblations to the fire, while singing the prescribed hymns in unison.

The priests are all dressed in long flowing seamless pieces of cloth, and wear sacred threads. The king, who is the host, is similarly dressed but has his head covered.

Paravasu is the conducting priest (adhvaryu). He will be called the Chief Priest, since he is the most important of them all. It is his responsibility to see that there are no errors, either of omission or of commission, in the performance of the sacrifice. He is about twenty-eight.

It is an impressive panorama.

The Brahma Rakshasa, a Brahmin soul trapped in the limbo between death and rebirth, is moving around at the sacrificial precincts, though no human eye can see him.

The afternoon session is over. The priests begin to disperse.

A Courtier enters with the Actor-Manager. The latter is made to stand at a distance from the fire sacrifice since as an actor he is considered low-born. The Courtier rushes into the protected enclosure of the fire sacrifice and talks to the King. The priests surround them. There is heated discussion.

KING (*explodes*): No, impossible! It's not possible.

PRIEST ONE: But where is the troupe?

COURTIER: At the city gates. Waiting.

PRIEST TWO: Let them come, Your Majesty. Please—

KING: I am not stopping them. They can come, by all means. But I won't have that boy—

PRIEST THREE: It's three years since we saw a play.

PRIEST FOUR: And there was a time when we had four plays a month!

PRIEST THREE: These endless philosophical discussions, metaphysical speculations, debates. Every day! Surely, a sacrifice doesn't have to be so dreary.

PRIEST TWO: We need a play to freshen our minds.

PRIEST ONE: Fortunately this troupe is here—

PRIEST FOUR: Do let them perform, Your Majesty.

KING: But why do they insist on him? He is not even an actor by birth—

COURTIER: The Manager says all his actors have fled to other lands. He needs an actor. And this one, he says, is good—

KING: But the Chief Priest won't agree.

PRIEST ONE: Why don't we ask him?
(*Calls out.*)
    Sir—

PARAVASU (*entering*): Did someone call me?

KING (*to the Courtier*): You tell him.

COURTIER: Well, sir…it's like this. There's a troupe of actors at the city gates. They are keen to stage a play in honour of the fire sacrifice.

PARAVASU: I thought the famine had decimated all the troupes.

COURTIER: That's precisely it. This one has come specially for us—against all odds.

(*Points to the Actor-Manager.*)

That's the Manager of the troupe. He has come with a specific plea. He'll make his submission from a distance.

(*Paravasu nods. The Courtier shouts to the Actor-Manager.*)

You may shout out whatever you have to say, but please face away from the sacrificial enclosure so you don't pollute it.

(*The Actor-Manager stands facing away from the sacrificial enclosure and declaims theatrically.*)

ACTOR-MANAGER: Sirs, as is well known to you, Brahma, the Lord of All Creation extracted the requisite elements from the four Vedas and combined them into a fifth Veda and thus gave birth to the art of Drama. He handed it over to his son, Lord Indra, the God of the Skies. Lord Indra, in turn, passed on the art to Bharata, a human being, for the gods cannot indulge in pretence. So if Indra is to be pleased and bring to an end this long drought which ravages our land a fire sacrifice is not enough. A play has to be performed along with it. If we offer him entertainment in addition to the oblations, the god may grant us the rains we're praying for.

(*Long pause.*)

PARAVASU: Surely you don't need me to decide on this?

COURTIER (*hesitating*): The problem is...there aren't enough actors to stage a play. They want to bring a new actor with them. (*Pause.*) Your brother.

PARAVASU (*quietly*): Arvasu!

COURTIER (*hurriedly*): I told the Actor-Manager, 'Anyone but him! He's forbidden to step in here!' But the Manager says there's no play without him. Not enough of a cast!

KING: They are twisting our arms. They know the priests are desperate for some entertainment.

(*A long pause. Paravasu is silent. The priests anxiously wait for his reaction.*)

COURTIER: The Manager says that he has a special message from your brother for you. He will repeat it if permitted to do so. Your brother has taught him what to say. The exact words.

(*Paravasu nods.*)

KING (*anxious*): Is that all right with you? I mean—everyone will hear.

PARAVASU: And why shouldn't they?

COURTIER (*shouts to the Actor-Manager*): If you have anything to add, you may do so.

ACTOR-MANAGER: A message from a brother. Dear elder brother, you once said to me: 'The sons of Bharata were the first actors in the history of theatre. They were Brahmins, but lost their caste because of their profession. A curse plunged them into disrepute and disgrace. If one values one's high birth, one should not touch this profession.' And I accepted this. But today I am a criminal. I have killed my father, a noble Brahmin. I already stand tarnished. I may now become an actor. This follows from your own words. So please do not bar the way now.

(*A long pause. Everyone looks eagerly at Paravasu.*)

KING: The fire sacrifice is nearing completion. We have conducted it without a blemish for nearly seven years. And you have guided us. Let's just complete it. Let it rain. Once it rains, we can have as many plays as we like. As a sacrifice approaches completion, demons gather in the shadows. The danger of disruption increases. You said so yourself. To permit a condemned criminal in the vicinity of our sacrificial fires, to risk—at this stage—

PARAVASU: Perhaps the sacrifice needs danger.

KING: But you drove him away yourself. You called him a demon.

PARAVASU: Perhaps you can't keep demons away from the sacrifice. It's a bond we can't break. Let's have the play. We shall all watch.

(*The Courtier bows, runs to the Actor-Manager, who nods enthusiastically. They depart. The priests disperse discussing the play.*

The troupe comes on stage: It consists of only three men, the Actor-Manager, his brother, who is limping, and Arvasu, Paravasu's brother, aged about eighteen. They all carry bundles of costumes. Arvasu is also carrying a mask. A couple of women provide music, with a few wind instruments and a drum.

The King, Paravasu and the other priests sit in front. Behind them gathers the general populace.

The Actor-Manager starts singing the benedictory verse. The stage darkens, leaving Arvasu in a pool of light.)

ARVASU: He's agreed, Nittilai! He'll be there to watch the play! But where are you? Why aren't you here? Nittilai! Nittilai! I am going to act on stage! I hope you are watching. Please, please, watch. The play is about to begin. Yes, after all these years, it's going to happen. But you know, and brother knows, and I know that this isn't the real thing. This is a fiction, borrowed from the myths. The real play began somewhere else. A month ago. A month?...Was it really that recent? It seems ages and ages of darkness ago. You and I were going to get married. Begin a new life. And I had to meet the elders of your tribe.

(*Nittilai, a girl of fourteen, comes and stands next to Arvasu. Though they are obviously fond of each other, they do not touch, except when specified.*)

Act One

NITTILAI: Oh! Don't go on about it! I told you! There's nothing to worry about. The elders will gather under the big banyan tree and ask a few questions. You answer them...

ARVASU: I couldn't sleep a wink last night. Woke up in a cold sweat every time I thought of your elders...

NITTILAI: You are a fuss-pot. You've known them for years. And after all, every young man about to get married goes through it. Just declare—

ARVASU: Yes, I know. I know: Just stand there and say: 'I want to take her as my wife. I am potent. I can satisfy all her needs...'

NITTILAI (*shyly*): Yes, more or less that!

ARVASU: And in public!

NITTILAI: Of course. What's the point of saying it to yourself? (*Laughs.*)
Don't worry. It's nothing...

ARVASU: Nothing, yes. For the young men of your tribe! But I am a Brahmin. To say all that in plain, loud words to a smirking, nudging, surging multitude. No hymns to drown out one's voice. No smoke to hide behind. It's dreadful. I hope there won't be too many people there—

NITTILAI: The whole village will be there.

(*Arvasu groans.*)

And some from the neighbouring villages.

ARVASU: Are the elders brutal?

NITTILAI: Of course not. But the young men could be—

ARVASU: What young men?

NITTILAI: Your friends. My brothers. Others attending the council. They have a field day usually.

ARVASU: I am not coming!

NITTILAI: Let no evil spirit hear you. Don't be silly, Arvasu. Father has told the young men not to get carried away. He likes you. In any case, there are very few men left because of the famine. The women will be there of course. In hordes. It's not often that they get a Brahmin groom—

ARVASU: To chew upon, you mean? Your women can be more lewd than your men.

NITTILAI: It's their prerogative. Come on now, you keep bragging about how, given a chance, you could stun thousands with your wit and eloquence.

ARVASU: I was talking as an actor. But this is real—me as myself.

NITTILAI: Yes.

(*Pause.*)

And have you faced your own people? Told them yet?

(*No reply.*)

You haven't, have you? Do you feel ashamed?

ARVASU: Ashamed? Let me show you—here!

(*Grabs her hand and pulls her near.*)

NITTILAI (*scandalized*): Let go of me! Let me go! What'll everyone say?

ARVASU: Why? Don't I have my rights—?

NITTILAI: Not until we're married. Until then the girl is not supposed to touch her husband-to-be. That's our custom—

ARVASU: Mother of mine! I'm about to jettison my caste, my people, my whole heritage for you. Can't you forget a minor custom for my sake?

NITTILAI: It's a nice custom. Sensible. Worth observing.

ARVASU: All these days I couldn't touch you because Brahmins don't touch other castes. Now you can't touch me because among hunters, girls don't touch their betrothed. Are you sure someone won't think of something else once we're married? (*She stops him and points. They are at some distance from the hermitage of Yavakri's father. A blind man, called Andhaka, who is a Sudra by caste, is sitting by the gate. Arvasu nods, signals to her to watch. Then proceeds toward the hermitage, moving zig-zag, trying to camouflage his walk.*)

ANDHAKA: Who's that? Arvasu?

(*Nittilai doubles up with laughter. Arvasu jumps up and down in mock frustration, but is actually quite annoyed with himself.*)

ARVASU: Curse your ears! *Curse your ears!*

NITTILAI (*to Andhaka*): He was trying to walk so you wouldn't guess who it was.

ANDHAKA: They all try that. But I can always tell. Just as you can recognize a man by his face—I can recognize him by the sound of his steps—

ARVASU: I'll fool you yet, old man!

ANDHAKA: I wish you luck. But in the meantime you two have cheered my heart, children. Made my ears happy...

NITTILAI: You mean you already know?

ARVASU: We thought we'd surprise you.

NITTILAI: You never move out of here. Yet you hear of everything...

ANDHAKA: You two are brave. It's one thing to frolic together as children. But you're not children any longer. You're old enough to know that the world can be cruel and ruthless.

NITTILAI: Even now he hasn't told his family.

ANDHAKA: Fair enough! 'You must always extract the honey without ruffling the bees.'

ARVASU: I keep telling her, no one cares! The one advantage of this famine—

NITTILAI: Don't say that! That's not nice—

ARVASU: I know. Nevertheless. The famine has sent my relatives fleeing to the city. The last thing they want is to send a daughter back to this cursed land. So they couldn't care less whom I marry—

ANDHAKA (*not unkindly*): Besides—you're not known to be bright. You are not in demand. That's an advantage.

(*Arvasu makes a wry face. Nittilai giggles silently.*)

ARVASU: Actually, I did have some moments of panic. But then the other day as I sat thinking—

(*For Andhaka's benefit*)

'trying hard' to think, if you like—it suddenly occurred to me how stupid I was being. I'll never be learned like father or uncle. I shan't ever conduct the royal sacrifice like Paravasu or perform penance like cousin Yavakri. All I want is to dance and sing and act. And be with Nittilai. It doesn't matter a flake of cowdung to my father whether I'm alive or dead. My sister-in-law lives wrapped up in a world of her own. That leaves only my brother—

ANDHAKA: A hard man...who will not be crossed...

ARVASU: Hard? Never to me. To me he's been a mother, father, brother, nurse, teacher—everything rolled into one. He taught me to win at marbles and play tunes on reeds. I owe everything to him—

ANDHAKA: And what if he forbids you now?

ARVASU: I'll tell him: 'I can't give up Nittilai. She is my life. I can't live without her—I would rather be an outcaste—'

ANDHAKA: Beautiful! Beautiful! Such moving words.

(*Nittilai laughs happily.*)

But Paravasu is not one to be easily moved, I warn you.

ARVASU: You'll see. The only reason I haven't told him yet is that the sacrifice is about to end. And he *is* the Chief Priest. It's important that he is not disturbed—

(*Nittilai nods in agreement.*)

ANDHAKA: But surely he'll hear about your meeting with her tribal elders this afternoon?

ARVASU: How was I to know her father would call this Council so suddenly? He never asked me.

NITTILAI: So Father's to blame? Do you know why Father called the elders in such haste? He always says: 'These high-caste men are glad enough to bed our women but not to wed them.'

ARVASU: All right! Now I'll wed you so you can—

NITTILAI (*screams*): Shut up!

(*They all laugh.*)

ANDHAKA: Your cousin Yavakri will be so happy—

ARVASU: Is he in?

ANDHAKA: No. In fact he said he was heading in the direction of your hermitage.

ARVASU: We are on our way there too. He's sent word asking me to meet him there.

NITTILAI: It would have been so convenient if you could have finished talking to him here. We could have gone directly to our village—

ANDHAKA: Yavakri gets no peace here. It's this endless stream of visitors. Morning to night. Ceaseless. Learned men, ascetics, pundits, all dying to find out how he talked to the god…What Lord Indra said…the details of his austerities…what hymns he chanted…

ARVASU (*to Nittilai*): You see? It's no small matter. Don't joke about it...

ANDHAKA: She joked about it? What did she say?

(*Nittilai glares at Arvasu as though to say, 'There! You've done it!' Andhaka is getting more and more agitated.*)

Speak up, child. You joked about what?

NITTILAI: I only said I didn't know why Yavakri had to spend ten years in the jungle—

ANDHAKA: He was seeking God so he could ask for Universal Knowledge! And gods don't yield to men so easily. He had to mortify himself, practise austerities, fast, meditate, pray.

NITTILAI: I know but—

ANDHAKA: Ten years of rigorous penance. And still Lord Indra would not oblige. Finally, Yavakri stood in the middle of a circle of fire and started offering his limbs to the fire—first his fingers, then his eyes, then his entrails, his tongue, and at last, his heart—that's when the god appeared to him, restored him limbs, and granted him the boon.

NITTILAI (*simply, with no offence meant*): Did he tell you all this, Grandfather?

ARVASU: Don't be silly. A man of his stature wouldn't talk about himself—

NITTILAI: Then how does everyone know what happened in a remote corner of the jungle—miles away from the nearest prying eye?

ANDHAKA: Every Brahmin on the face of this earth wants to gain spiritual powers. But few succeed. In my lifetime I have known only two who did. Your uncle and your father, Arvasu. But they got their knowledge from human gurus. By diligent study. Yavakri has gone beyond even them. He received his knowledge from the gods, direct! Your uncle was sure he would fail. How he tried to dissuade the boy from taking on this ordeal. But I said to him, 'Master, let him go to the jungle. You don't know your son. I do. I brought him up on this lap of mine. He will succeed in anything he tries, you mark my words!' If my Master had listened to me, he would be alive today. But he died of a broken heart.

(*Pause.*)

I waited. Right here. For ten years. I took care of this hermitage for the day when my Yavakri would return home. And now he has come back. In triumph. The whole world is at his feet.

NITTILAI: But what I want to know is why are the Brahmins so secretive about everything?

ARVASU: Oh God! She's got into one of her argumentative moods! (*Walks off a little distance. Stands concentrating.*)

NITTILAI (*continuing*): You know, their fire sacrifices are conducted in covered enclosures. They mortify themselves in the dark of the jungle. Even their gods appear so secretly. Why? What are they afraid of? Look at my people. Everything is done in public view there. The priest announces that he'll invoke the deity at such and such a time on such and such a day. And then there, right in front of the whole tribe, he gets possessed. And the spirit answers your questions. You can feel it come and go. You *know* it's there. Not mere hearsay—

ANDHAKA: Take care, child. The gods that their priests seek are far mightier than yours. Don't talk of the two in the same breath.

NITTILAI: My point is since Lord Indra appeared to Yavakri and Indra is their God of Rains, why didn't Yavakri ask for a couple of good showers? You should see the region around our village. Parched. Every morning, women with babes on their hips, shrunken children, shrivelled old men and women gather in front of my father's house—for the gruel he distributes. No young people. They have all disappeared! And

Father says all the land needs is a couple of heavy downpours. That'll revive the earth. Not too much to ask of a god, is it?

ANDHAKA (*half agreeing*): But they say that such powers shouldn't be used to solve day-to-day problems. They are meant to lead one to—to—inner knowledge.

NITTILAI: What's that?

ANDHAKA: I don't know. That's what Yavakri's father used to say.

NITTILAI: Then what's the use of all these powers?

ANDHAKA: Ask Yavakri, when you meet him. He won't mind. In fact, he'll like it. He's a gentle soul.

NITTILAI: Actually, I want to ask Yavakri *two* questions. Can he make it rain? And then, can he tell when he is going to die?...Just two. What is the point of any knowledge, if you can't save dying children and if you can't predict your moment of death.

ARVASU (*from far*): Now, guess what animal this is!

NITTILAI: He can't think of anything else!
(*But closes her eyes and listens.*)
    All right.
(*Arvasu charges, pretending to be a wild animal.*)

ANDHAKA (*listens*): A wild horse...No! A boar? I know. A bison!

NITTILAI: Yes. A bison. That was good.

ARVASU (*ecstatic*): Triumph! They say one shouldn't imitate! One should embody the essence. Only the essence! It means I have captured the essence of a bison—

NITTILAI: You don't need to try. You were born with it.

ARVASU: That's why the hunters love me!
(*They all laugh.*)

NITTILAI: Let's go.

ANDHAKA: Wait, child. I know you're restless to reach your village. But Yavakri wants you to meet him when the sun's overhead, doesn't he?

ARVASU: 'Exactly.'...I don't know why. But his message said
  'exactly'. Neither earlier. Nor later. Exactly when the sun's
  overhead...

ANDHAKA: So you've time. Stay and chat. Listening to you makes
  me feel happy.

ARVASU: The question is how do you capture the essence of the
  gods in your footsteps, since a god's feet never touch the earth?
(*The stage darkens.*

*Lights come up in another part of the stage, representing the
hermitage of Raibhya, father of Arvasu. Vishakha, aged about
twenty-six, is filling water in a metal urn. She has scooped out water
from holes dug in the wet sand and collected it in the pot. She must
have been an attractive person once, but now looks sullen and
haggard. She looks around furtively. There's no one around. She
picks up the pot, puts it on her waist and starts for home. Yavakri
is standing right in the middle of her path. She stops but avoids
looking at him. A long pause.*)

VISHAKHA (*without looking at him*): Please...

YAVAKRI: At last, a word! After waiting for four days—I practically
  had to wrench it out of you by blocking your path.

(*As he moves aside and sits down on a rock, she takes a few steps
towards her house.*)

  Stay, Vishakha—Please. There's no one there in your house.
  Your father-in-law has gone out. Your brother-in-law is never
  home. What's the hurry?

VISHAKHA: My father-in-law will be back tomorrow. Speak to him
  then.

YAVAKRI: It's not the need to speak to him that brings me here.

VISHAKHA: I can't stay here chatting with a stranger.

YAVAKRI: A stranger!
(*Laughs.*)
  That's good.

VISHAKHA: I am a married woman.

YAVAKRI: I know you are. The first piece of news to greet me on my return was that you had married Paravasu. And I was shattered. But it was silly of me not to have expected it. Ten years is a long time. Ten years of silence is longer still. Can't we just talk?

(*Pause.*)

Ten years ago I swore to you that I would not look at another woman. I kept my word.

VISHAKHA: That's over and done with now.

YAVAKRI: Don't think I regret it. No, not for a moment. But doesn't that give me some right to say: 'Please put the pot down for a few minutes and talk to me?'

(*Vishakha makes a move to go.*)

Vishakha, after ten years in solitude, I am hungry for words.

(*Startled, Vishakha looks up at him for the first time.*)

VISHAKHA: They say that pleased with your rigorous penance, Lord Indra has granted you Universal Knowledge. I don't feel equal to the task of—

YAVAKRI: Universal Knowledge! What a phrase! It makes me laugh now. But do you know it was in order to win some such grandiose prize that I went into the jungle? You put it so simply in that one sentence. So beautifully. You go into the jungle. You perform austerities in the name of some god. You stand in a circle of fire. The pressure of your austerities forces the god to grant you your wish. And you get 'Universal knowledge'. Victory!

(*Pause.*)

It wasn't at all like that, you know.

VISHAKHA (*gently*): Why?

YAVAKRI: For a start, life in the jungle is sheer hell. Flies, giant ants, beetles, pests, leeches attacking at the suspicion of moisture, vipers lurking in bowls of dust. The relentless heat. Not demons but mosquitoes to torture you—

VISHAKHA: Perhaps that's how the gods test one.

YAVAKRI: One would expect the appearance of a god to be a shattering experience. Concrete. Indubitable. Almost physical. But though I think Indra came to me several times, I was never certain. The first time he appeared he said, 'No, Yavakri, you can't master knowledge through austerities. It must come with experience. Knowledge is time. It is space. You must move through these dimensions.' I said, 'No, I must have it. Grant me all knowledge.' He laughed and said: 'You are being silly.' That's it! Common dialogue. Not very profound. And when the god disappeared, nothing was left behind to prove he had ever been there. I looked around. The same old black scorpion. The same horned chameleon. The shower of bird-shit around me. So was it all a hallucination caused by something I'd eaten that morning? Or was it fever working on my brain? So I go on. Another year. Or perhaps two. Then the god comes again. 'Why are you being so stubborn?' He chides. 'You can't cross a full stream on a bridge of sand.' I insist that my demands are met—another trite exchange of words—

VISHAKHA: But you did win in the end?

YAVAKRI: Yes, one day I decided I had won. So I have come back. I have no clear recollection how I arrived at that conclusion.

(*Laughs.*)

Some knowledge, but probably little wisdom. I know now what *can't* be achieved. That itself is wisdom, isn't it? But I mustn't complain. I think I have some mystical powers I hadn't before. Mastered a few secret arts. Got a few *mantras* at my finger-tips. You'll see for yourself soon—

VISHAKHA: Me? No, thank you.

YAVAKRI: The strangest thing however is that I've discovered a corner within me—left untouched by those ten years! Undisturbed by all that self-lashing! So if you feel insulted by what I am going to tell you, go away. I won't see you again. In that case, let these be the last words I speak to you.

(*Pause.*)

The day I decided my penance was over I fell down in a dead faint. I don't know how long I was in that state. It was terrible exhaustion, the pain of sheer relief. And when I opened my eyes, do you know the first thing that I thought of? Ten years ago I had come to your house to bid you goodbye. And you led me quickly to the jack-fruit grove behind your house. You opened the knot of your blouse, pressed my face to your breasts, then turned and fled. I stood there stunned. The trees were loaded with fruit. Many were ripe and had split open and the rich golden segments poured out. The sweet sick smell of the jack-fruit, the maddening hum of a fly. The smell of your body. Ten years later I opened my eyes and I knew I was hungry for that moment.

VISHAKHA: I can't believe it! The whole world may be singing your praises. But you haven't grown up! These ten years have not made any difference to your teenage fantasies. That's all gone, Yavakri. Indra may be immortal. But... my breasts hang loose now.

(*Laughs.*)

YAVAKRI: Why are you laughing?

VISHAKHA: I have been trembling at the sight of you these last three days. Now, I only feel sorry.

YAVAKRI: Good. I told you you could go home if you were angry. But you are not angry. My tale only makes you feel sorry for me. So you can stay?

VISHAKHA: The moment I heard you say you were hungry for words, I knew it was too late to go. I couldn't walk out on you after that. I had lost the initiative—missed the moment of decision. Because I know that hunger well, Yavakri. That's why I should have gone back without saying a word to you.

YAVAKRI: Don't go, Vishakha!

VISHAKHA: Have I gone? I am still here. You are a fool, Yavakri.
And you talk like one.

(*Yavakri goes to her. There's a pause. She looks at him steadily,
smiling. He embraces her. She pushes him away, puts the pot down
on the ground.*)

YAVAKRI: You want to hit me? Go ahead—

VISHAKHA: It's not you I am worried about. It's the water. I have
dug it out like precious gold... You are hungry for words. And
so am I. So let's talk. Sit down.

YAVAKRI: You and Indra. That's right. The presiding deities of my
life. It's because of you two that I have avoided women
altogether until now. Conserved my seed like you conserve
your water. Now as I sit in front of you, I want to betray
Indra—he left me ignorant...

VISHAKHA: They say Indra has a thousand 'eyes'—or whatever.
(*Laughs.*)

He could have opened at least one for you
(*Yavakri tries to kiss her.*)

YAVAKRI: Shush now.

VISHAKHA: What do you mean 'Shush'? What you have done is to
rekindle my need to talk. I thought it was dead and gone.
Gently! Don't rush. Oh, Yavakri! The pleasure of calling
someone a fool. Of the desire welling up inside one to protect
him. I live in this hermitage, parched and wordless, like a she-
devil. And words are like water—precious. I was afraid to
bathe. Now I want to drown. Listen to me. You went away.
I was married off—

YAVAKRI: Your father must have felt relieved that I went away.
Paravasu was a better match. I was only his miserable cousin.

VISHAKHA: Yes, Father was happy. I was married off to Paravasu.
I didn't want to, but that didn't matter. The night of the

wedding, my husband said to me: 'I know you didn't want to marry me. But don't worry. I'll make you happy for a year.' And he did. Exactly for one year. He plunged me into a kind of bliss I didn't know existed. It was heaven—here and now—at the tip of all my senses. Then on the first day of the second year of our marriage, he said: 'Enough of that. We now start on our search.' And then—it wasn't that I was not happy. But the question of happiness receded into the background. He used my body, and his own body, like an experimenter, an explorer. As instruments in a search. Search for what? I never knew. But I knew he knew. Nothing was too shameful, too degrading, even too painful. Shame died in me. And I yielded. I let my body be turned inside out as he did his own. I had a sense he was leading me to something. Mystical? Spiritual? We never talked. Only the sense pervaded the air. You're still lost in the fragrance of the jack-fruit, Yavakri. I have known what it is to grow heavy, burst open, drip and rot, to fill the world with one's innards. Then one day he received the invitation from the King. To be the Chief Priest of the fire sacrifice. And he left. The site of the fire sacrifice is only a couple of hours away from here. But in all these seven years he hasn't come back. I know he can't. But I look forward to having him home once the seven years are over. Alone, I have become dry like tinder. Ready to burst into flames at a breath. To burn things around me down at the slightest chance—

YAVAKRI (*looks up*): Soon the sun will be overhead.

VISHAKHA: My husband and you! He left no pore in my body alone. And you—you think a woman is only a pair of half-formed breasts.

YAVAKRI: Enough now.

VISHAKHA: I'll give you the knowledge Indra couldn't give you. My body—it's light with speech now.

(*They go behind a dry champak tree on the bank. Long pause. Nittilai and Arvasu enter.*)

NITTILAI: He's going to settle down here now, isn't he? So why can't you see him tomorrow? Surely a day isn't going to make a difference. If we are late, the elders will be angry with us and...

ARVASU: Let's give him five minutes. That's all, Nittilai. Please. You know there's always been a lot of bitterness between us cousins. Verging on hatred. Now he's made the gesture of asking me to meet him. Let me reciprocate. I'll touch his feet. Ask for his blessings. Then we go on.

NITTILAI: All right. But there's no one here. I hope he doesn't make us wait.

(*Goes toward the stream. Stops. Suddenly she is transformed, from an innocent young girl into a consummate huntress. Silently, she beckons Arvasu. He goes near her. She points to something in the dry bed of the river. It is Vishakha's pot.*)

ARVASU (*in a low voice*): Our water pot! What's it doing here? Has sister-in-law forgotten to take it back?

NITTILAI: No one leaves a full pot of water behind.

ARVASU: That's true.

(*Scared.*)

They say a panther has strayed into these parts. If he was thirsty and—

NITTILAI (*inspects the river bed*): No. Tracks of the barking deer. A couple of porcupines. A family of mongooses. No sign of a panther—or anything that big—not within the last three days.

ARVASU (*picks up a stick*): Shall I go in and see?

NITTILAI (*smiles at the sight of the stick*): No need. It's all here. Those footprints are obviously your sister-in-law's. She didn't drop the pot. She set it down, carefully. So as not to spill the water. And then—

(*She freezes. Stares at the ground. Looks in the direction in which Vishakha and Yavakri have gone.*)

NITTILAI: Is your brother back?

ARVASU: Paravasu? Of course not. He can't leave the sacrifice—

NITTILAI (*gets up*): Come, Arvasu. Let's go.

ARVASU: Where?

NITTILAI: Let's go. Please. To my village.

ARVASU: And leave sister-in-law to her fate?—

NITTILAI: Listen to me. Nothing's happened to her.

ARVASU: I can't do that! I must know—I'll be back in a minute—
(*He goes behind the champak tree into the bushes. Suddenly exclamations, etc. Arvasu rushes out, followed by Vishakha. Her clothes are torn. Her back is covered with mud. She runs to the hermitage without even glancing at Nittilai. Arvasu stares uncomprehending. Then he sees the pot. Lifts it to his shoulder.*)
    I'd better take it home. I'll be back—
(*She nods. At this moment Yavakri steps out. He picks up a small metal pot with a snout and a handle—called a kamandalu—which he has hidden behind a tree. He looks at the two, calmly walks to Arvasu, tips the pot on his shoulder to fill his kamandalu. Arvasu watches helplessly.*)

NITTILAI (*angry*): Some people put the treacherous viper to shame.

YAVAKRI (*turns to her*): Aren't you the whelp who was asking my old servant if I knew my moment of death?

NITTILAI (*taken aback*): How did you know that?

YAVAKRI (*ignoring her question*): I don't know when I'll die. But I promise you this—you'll be dead within the month.
(*Nittilai recoils, shocked.*)

NITTILAI: Oh—I—I'm going home—

ARVASU: Nittilai—wait—I'll follow you—
(*But she disappears. He, with the pot on his shoulder, stands unable to follow.*)

YAVAKRI (*calmly*): And you, Arvasu, you'll find me under the banyan tree, next to the black cliff.

(*Exits. Arvasu, confused, walks to his father's hermitage.*
Vishakha has gone to the hermitage ahead of Arvasu. She is about to enter the house when her father-in-law, Raibhya, steps out. He is thin and emaciated, but physically active. Vishakha is horrified to see him. He scowls at her.)

RAIBHYA: Where were you all this while?

VISHAKHA: I—I'd gone—to fetch water.

(*She has no pot with her.*)

RAIBHYA: Really?

(*Arvasu comes in with the pot of water and is startled to see Raibhya.*)

ARVASU: Father! I didn't know you were returning home today—

RAIBHYA: I didn't either. But perhaps I should give the two of you more such surprises.

(*Arvasu puts the pot down in a corner and retreats.*)

RAIBHYA: Wait!

(*To Vishakha*)

You go to fetch water. And your brother-in-law carries it back for you. Strange! What *is* happening here? Why are you so filthy? You look like a buffalo that's been rolling in mud.

VISHAKHA: I suddenly felt faint. And fell down.

RAIBHYA: And he turned up, just at that moment to help you! Isn't that convenient! And you two have been taking a long time for just that—what were you up to?

ARVASU (*hurriedly*): Nittilai was there too—

RAIBHYA: Who?

ARVASU: Nittilai. The hunter girl.

RAIBHYA: A savage! Was there anybody else?

(*Arvasu, taken unawares by the question, looks at Vishakha. Raibhya notices the look.*)

RAIBHYA: So there was someone else there, wasn't there? Who was it?

ARVASU (*finds it hard to lie*): No one, Father. Nittilai and I went there—

RAIBHYA (*pointing to Vishakha*): Was she alone? Or was there anybody else with her?

ARVASU: No, there was no one else. She was feeling faint—and fell down—so I helped her. I must go—

RAIBHYA: You want to run away, do you? All right. Go. But where will she go?
(*To Vishakha*)
Tell me who was there. Tell me.

(*He grabs her by her hair and starts beating her. Kicks her. Arvasu can't bear to see it. He rushes to her help. Holds Raibhya back.*)

ARVASU: Stop it, Father. Please. Go away, Sister-in-law. Go—please—

RAIBHYA: Where can she go? I want the truth and I'll kill her if necessary. Let me go! I know how to handle her—
(*Struggles to get out of Arvasu's hold.*)

VISHAKHA: Let him go, Arvasu.
(*Calmly*)
Yes, there was somebody else there. Yavakri! And he had come to see me. Alone.

(*Long pause. They stare at each other.*)

RAIBHYA: You whore—you roving whore! I could reduce you to ashes—turn you into a fistful of dust—with a simple curse. But let that husband of yours handle you. Paravasu, Chief Priest of the sacrifice! Let him clean up his own shit! Yavakri—So this is what ten years of austerities amount to! So be it. So Yavakri, now it's between you and me. Where's that pot of water? Bring it here—

VISHAKHA: No. Please! Don't do anything to him. It's my fault.

Please, don't harm Yavakri. I'm willing to face the consequences—punish me. Not him. Please.

RAIBHYA: Bring the water!

(*Raibhya sits cross-legged and sinks into deep meditation. Vishakha
and Arvasu watch him horrified, fascinated. Raibhya opens his eyes.
Suddenly, he is calm. There is no trace of anger in him.*)

VISHAKHA: Vishakha, go and tell your lover I accept his challenge.
I shall invoke the *kritya* and send a Brahma Rakshasa, a
demon soul, after him. Let Yavakri save himself. He need only
go and hide in his father's hermitage. I loved my brother and
will not desecrate his altar. Let Yavakri cower in there like a
dog. If he steps out, he will be dead. Tell him this, too—that
if he can manage to stay alive for another twenty-four hours,
I, Raibhya, shall accept defeat and enter fire.

(*Sinks back into meditation.*)

VISHAKHA (*wakes up*): Arvasu, we must warn Yavakri. Instantly.
Go to your uncle's hermitage.

ARVASU: But Yavakri said he would be under the banyan tree near
the black cliff—

VISHAKHA: I'll run there. It's nearby. You go to the hermitage in
case he's there—

ARVASU: But—but—

VISHAKHA: Run, please. I've never asked anything of you till now.
Just this once. Go. Run.

(*They run in opposite directions. Raibhya opens his eyes, pulls out
a strand of hair from his head and throws it to the ground. The
Brahma Rakshasa appears. He is thin, almost naked and holds a
trident. He runs in the direction of Yavakri as the lights fade out.
Andhaka, the blind man, is sitting at the gate of Yavakri's hermitage.
He hears footsteps.*)

ANDHAKA: Ah, Arvasu!

(*Arvasu arrives.*)

Haven't you gone to the meeting—

ARVASU: I'm on my way. But has Yavakri come here?

ANDHAKA: Not since you and Nittilai left.

ARVASU: If he comes, tell him to stay inside the hermitage. Not to step out. Don't let him even peep out. His life's in danger.

ANDHAKA: What? How?

ARVASU: You don't move from here either. Wait for him—you must warn him.

ANDHAKA: I will—but—

ARVASU: I have to go—Nittilai's waiting.

ANDHAKA: Listen, boy—
(*Arvasu runs away. Andhaka sits down, all ears.*
Vishakha arrives at the banyan tree next to the black cliff. Yavakri is murmuring incantations, sitting cross-legged, with his kamandalu in front of him. Vishakha runs in, panting, sweating profusely and heaves a sigh of relief when she sees Yavakri. He briefly looks at her, nods encouragingly and carries on meditating.)

VISHAKHA: You mustn't stay here, Yavakri. Go to your father's hermitage. Immediately. Please!
(*No reply.*)
My father-in-law has found out everything—and he is bent on destroying you.
(*Pause.*)
Yavakri, he is calling up the *kritya*—

YAVAKRI: He is? I am flattered. To invoke the *kritya* spell is to engage one's full powers. That he should choose this instrument of death for me, it's certainly an honour.

VISHAKHA: Go to your place, Yavakri. Father-in-law said you would be safe there. Please. Hurry.

YAVAKRI: Don't be afraid, Vishakha, I was expecting something like this. You see this water...I have consecrated it.
(*He points to the water in the* kamandalu.)

A drop of this water. And the Brahma Rakshasa will become numb. Powerless. Uncle's entire threat will turn into a farce. You needn't have bothered—but now that you're here, stay and see for yourself.

VISHAKHA: But you don't need any of this. You only have to be in your father's hermitage—the Brahma Rakshasa can't touch you *there*! Once you are safe, I'll happily watch that living corpse burn—

YAVAKRI: Oh Vishakha! It's so wonderful to have you here. Because *you* used to console me—don't you remember—when we were young? I cried at the humiliations piled on my father. He was one of the most learned men in the land. Probably the most brilliant mind. But he was scorned while this unscrupulous brother of his grabbed all the honours.

VISHAKHA: Why are you bringing up all those grievances now, Yavakri? It's hardly the time—

YAVAKRI: Grievances! You don't even flatter me with the word 'hatred'. But it doesn't matter. What matters is that I hate your husband's family. My father deserved to be invited as the Chief Priest of the sacrifice. But that too went to Paravasu, your husband. Even in the midst of my austerities I wept when I heard the news. For I knew Father would refuse to take offence. I knew he would go and congratulate Paravasu on the honour, embrace and bless him—

VISHAKHA: Yes, he did that.

YAVAKRI (*enraged*): Why? I despised him for it. *He* was one of the reasons I fled to the jungle.

VISHAKHA: Do we have to talk about it now? The past is gone.

YAVAKRI: The past *isn't* gone. It's here inside me. The time has come to show the world what my father's son is capable of. This is my moment.

VISHAKHA: But today your name's on every tongue in the land and they pronounce it with awe. Why do you need to—

YAVAKRI: The others don't matter, except as witnesses.
(*Looks out.*)

Where is that demon? Why is he late?

(*To Vishakha.*)

One night in the jungle, Indra came to me and said: 'You are ready now to receive knowledge. But knowledge involves control of passions, serenity, objectivity.' And I shouted back: 'No, that's not the knowledge I want. That's not knowledge. That's suicide! This obsession. This hatred. This venom. All this is me. I'll not deny anything of myself. I want knowledge so I can be vicious, destructive!'

VISHAKHA: If anything happens to you, I'll never forgive myself. Go, go to your home altar. Please.

YAVAKRI (*incensed*): Don't you understand anything? You want me to run away after issuing my challenge?

VISHAKHA: Challenge?

YAVAKRI: Do you think all this happened accidentally? You think I would leave anything to chance? How do you think Arvasu happened to arrive at the river-bank at the right moment? Who called your father-in-law back?

VISHAKHA (*scared*): Enough, Yavakri. Don't say anything more. I don't want to know. It's my fault. I shouldn't have yielded to you—I—

YAVAKRI: It was fortunate that you yielded. If you hadn't I would have had to take you by force.

(*Vishakha stares at him in horror.*)

This is the moment toward which my entire life has rushed headlong. I will not let anything stand in its way. Your father-in-law will die, Vishakha. Let's see what your husband does then. Will he continue to hide like a bandicoot in his ritual world? Or will he commit sacrilege by stepping out to face me? Look, I am trembling. I am drenched in sweat. Because everything has worked out just right.

VISHAKHA (*under her breath*): Oh, my God!...Yavakri!

YAVAKRI: Try to understand. They would have turned their backsides on me with contempt if I'd let them—as they did with Father! There was only one way to force them to confront me. Catch Paravasu by his scrotum. Squeeze it so that he couldn't even squirm—

(*She is numbly staring at him.*)

I love you, Vishakha. I have not looked at another woman in my whole life. But that you happened to marry Paravasu is not my fault!

(*Pause. Yavakri paces restlessly, waiting for the Brahma Rakshasa.*)

VISHAKHA (*quietly*): I was so happy this morning. You were so good. So warm. I wanted to envelope you in everything I could give. It was more as a mother that I offered my breasts to you—

(*He is pacing restlessly, looking eagerly in the direction of Raibhya's hermitage. Quietly, she goes to the* kamandalu *and picks it up.*)

Why is life so contrary, Yavakri? One thinks one has stepped on to a bit of solid ground—a little haven—and the earth gives way—

YAVAKRI: Where's that shadow puppet?

(*Slowly, calmly, Vishakha starts pouring the water out. He looks at her and for a moment cannot comprehend what she is doing. He suddenly screams.*)

Oh God! What are you doing? The water—the sanctified water! My life! What are you doing?

(*He grabs the* kamandalu *from her hand. It's empty. He starts banging it on the ground.*)

Water, please! Just a drop. Oh gods! Only a drop... You devil. I trusted you... A drop of water.

(*Suddenly a very strange wail is heard from the distance, unearthly, terrifying and evil. Vishakha is frightened.*)

VISHAKHA: Yavakri, hurry. Go to your father's hermitage.

YAVAKRI: A drop—only a drop.

VISHAKHA (*pushing him*): Go! Run!

YAVAKRI: I'm not here to run away—I've triumphed over Indra, the Lord of Gods. Who are you to order me around?

VISHAKHA: Go!

(*She pushes him. Suddenly Yavakri wakes up and starts to run.*) Don't stop till you reach your father's house.

(*Yavakri runs. Vishakha stares after him, then heaves a sigh and turns. The Brahma Rakshasa has entered and is standing behind her. She sees him, gasps, and falls down in a faint. The Brahma Rakshasa runs after Yavakri. Yavakri stops now and then, desperately digs for water, then not finding any, runs on.*

He comes to the hermitage, which is still being guarded by Andhaka. As Yavakri comes running and is about to step into the hermitage, Andhaka jumps up and grabs him. Doesn't let him move.)

ANDHAKA: Who's that? Who—

YAVAKRI: Let me go! Let me—

(*The Brahma Rakshasa comes and spears him. Yavakri collapses in Andhaka's arms. The demon pulls out the trident and goes away.*)

ANDHAKA: Who—Yavakri—? Yavakri—Son.

(*He lowers Yavakri's body to the ground. Shakes him furiously as though to wake him up. Arvasu comes running, stands frozen with horror.*)

Yavakri! Child! What happened to you? I didn't recognize your steps—Why, why couldn't I recognize your steps?

(*It gets dark on stage.*)

Act Two

Evening. The village square. Nittilai's brother and a couple of his friends are waiting under a tree. They talk in low tones. The brother looks up and sees Arvasu in the distance.

BROTHER: He's come!

FRIENDS: Oh God! Now?—

(*They fall silent as Arvasu comes running. He is sweating, panting. They do not greet him. He tries to regain his breath. Looks around.*)

ARVASU: Hello! Isn't the Council of the Elders meeting here?
(*The brother nods.*)
     Then where—where is everybody?

BROTHER: Everyone's gone home.

ARVASU: Home? Oh God! But—but—the Elders—

BROTHER: The Elders waited for you all day. You did not come.

ARVASU: I know. I'm sorry. But I couldn't help it. What happened was—

BROTHER: It doesn't matter.

ARVASU: It does. It does. Please. I would like to explain to the Elders and apologize.

BROTHER: It's no—

ARVASU (*suppressing the mounting panic*): You judge for yourself.

I was on my way here when I saw Yavakri running. He was scared. I knew his life was in danger. I ran after him. When I got to his hermitage, he was lying there. Dead.

BROTHER: Dead?

ARVASU: Blood was still spurting from his back. Andhaka was there too—but had gone stone-deaf. He couldn't hear anything I said to him. Blind. Stunned. How could I leave the dead body with him there and come away?

(*The brother listens intently.*)

The blood was fresh. It was gushing out. And wild animals had already started appearing in the bushes. Hyenas. Wolves. Ready to tear into Yavakri—into the old man, too. I had to cremate the body on the spot... What would you have done?

BROTHER (*guarded*): You were perfectly right.

ARVASU: I knew you would understand. I know the Elders will too. I—

BROTHER: The Elders have all gone home.

ARVASU: I'll go to each one's house and explain. I'll touch their feet. I'll ask their forgiveness. Perhaps the Elders can meet again tomorrow—

BROTHER: Meet again? To do what?

ARVASU: To bless me and Nittilai!

BROTHER: Arvasu, since you failed to attend the Council meeting, the Elders decreed that Nittilai will marry another boy—of our own tribe.

(*Arvasu stares, stunned.*)

ARVASU: What? Oh, no! No! No! No! That can't be—

BROTHER: That'll have to be, Arvasu. It's the decision of the Elders.

ARVASU: But it's not sunset yet! Nittilai said the Council would go on till sundown—I'm here well before then—

BROTHER: I agree. I'm afraid my father was a little hasty. But he was tired of waiting. He felt angry, humiliated. 'This daughter of mine has made me a laughing stock in the eyes of the world', he said, 'I'm willing to marry her off to anyone who'll take her.' Fortunately, it was a nice young man, one of our relatives, who stepped forward. Nittilai will be happy. Console yourself with that thought.

ARVASU: No, no, you're making fun of me. I know you are—tell me you're making—

BROTHER: Nothing can be changed now. If only you'd come half an hour earlier.

ARVASU: Half an hour! Half an hour! Don't say that. Please, can I see the young man? I'll explain to him. Plead with him. I'll debase myself in front of him. Please, let me meet your father and the Elders. I'll go right now—I'll explain—It can't be—

BROTHER: Go home, Arvasu.

ARVASU: I'll offer chunks of my flesh to your gods as a penance—

BROTHER: It's no use.

ARVASU (*shouts*): But I want my Nittilai—I—
(*In one quick movement, the brother knocks him down and plants his foot on his chest.*)

BROTHER: You've caused enough trouble, Brahmin. Nittilai is to be married in the next couple of days. People are already sniggering about the two of you. Don't shame her further by shouting her name in public.

ARVASU: Can I—can I talk to her?

BROTHER (*withdrawing*): No, you can't. Not till the wedding's over.

ARVASU: And after that?

BROTHER: That's up to her and her husband.

ARVASU: Please, tell me. How's she taken it?

BROTHER: It's been a terrible day for her. She is exhausted. Even now she is crying her heart out. You'll only make it worse for her by hanging around here. Go away.

ARVASU (*starts to go, turns*): But listen. It's not my fault.
(*The brother grabs him by the scruff of his neck.*)

BROTHER: Go!

(*Arvasu stumbles home. Raibhya is still awake in the hermitage. Arvasu throws himself down in a corner of the veranda.
Footsteps. Paravasu enters in the dark. He is covered in a black rug. He carries a bow and quiver of arrows slung on his back.*)

RAIBHYA: Who's that? Who's that coming in the dead of the night?

PARAVASU: It's me, Father. Paravasu.

RAIBHYA (*taken aback*): Paravasu?
(*Runs out of the house to make sure.*)
    Paravasu? It's not possible!

PARAVASU (*gently*): Your blessings be on my head, Father.
(*Prostrates himself in front of Raibhya.*)

RAIBHYA (*horrified*): You? Here? What are you doing here? There's still a month left to go before the sacrifice ends. You are—you can't—you have broken the rules! You are *deliberately defying* the gods!

PARAVASU: I felt like coming home.

RAIBHYA: Felt? And just walked out? With the ritual bracelet on? As though the sacrifice were a market place?... Or have they thrown you out? Your wife's reputation must have reached there by now—

(*By now Arvasu and Vishakha have got up and are listening from a distance.*)

PARAVASU (*gently*): Of course, they've heard the news. But they haven't chased me out.

RAIBHYA: So this is your usual insolence. Wilful transgression of the rules—

PARAVASU: If I am back there before dawn, no one need know.

RAIBHYA (*explodes*): No one need know? The Chief Priest of the royal sacrifice sneaks out at night, crawls home, his face covered like a leper, and you think the gods won't know? They won't retaliate? How could I have fathered two such imbeciles? I told the King, 'Mark my words, my son defecates wherever he goes. And he will defecate in your sacrifice—'

PARAVASU: The King often says he would have preferred you to be the Chief Priest. But it was a seven-year rite. They thought...a younger man safer.

RAIBHYA: I see. So you measured my life-span, did you—you and your King? Tested the strength of my life-line? Well, the sacrifice is almost over and I'm still here. Still here. Alive and kicking. Tell the King I shall outlive my sons. I shall live long enough to feed their dead souls. Tell him the swarm of dogs sniffing around my daughter-in-law's bottom keeps me in good shape.

PARAVASU: I thought with your permission I would have a word with my wife.

RAIBHYA: You disgust me. You and that bitch of yours. I am going out—

PARAVASU: At this time of night, Father? Isn't it dangerous in the jungle?

(*Calls*)

Arvasu—

ARVASU: Yes—

(*Steps out.*)

RAIBHYA: If you want to be alone with your wife, send that fool somewhere else. I don't need him. It's not the wild beasts one has to watch out for—it's the human beings—

(*Paravasu bows to his father. Raibhya walks off. Paravasu turns to Arvasu.*)

PARAVASU: How are you?

ARVASU: I'm all right.

PARAVASU (*pause*): Your eyes are blood-shot. I'm sorry if I've disturbed your sleep.

ARVASU: No, no.

PARAVASU: With your love of theatre, I should have thought you would be quite used to late nights.

ARVASU: There haven't been any plays for ages... what with this famine.

(*Paravasu senses something is wrong but doesn't say anything. Arvasu is confused and tries to hide his confusion.*)
I tell everyone—let brother's sacrifice conclude. It will rain. The players will come back.

PARAVASU (*smiles*): And then you'll be able to act on stage again.

ARVASU: Me? I never act. I haven't done so since you asked me not to—

PARAVASU: I told you not to act?

ARVASU: Don't you remember? Long ago—before you left for the sacrifice—I was dancing with the hunters and you said: 'Bharata's sons lost caste because of the stage.' I haven't acted on stage since then.

PARAVASU: Arvasu! How silly of you to have taken me at my word. You shouldn't have obeyed me!

ARVASU: I couldn't *disobey* you—

PARAVASU: Then you should have asked me again!

ARVASU: Again? How would that have helped?

PARAVASU: You asked a question. It evoked an answer. Suppose, you repeated the same question—precisely—in the same words. You would get the same answer. You ask again. Would that have helped? Yes, certainly. Each time the question and the answer were repeated, a new nuance would have arisen.

Do you know, you could repeat a question and an answer without altering a syllable, endlessly, and create a whole new universe of meanings, more acceptable to you.

(*Arvasu looks at Paravasu, uncomprehending. Then.*)

ARVASU: I'll be on the tamarind hill. Call me if you need me.

(*Arvasu runs away. Paravasu puts away his bow and arrows. Vishakha brings a pot of water and silently places it near Paravasu, who washes his hands and feet in total silence. He sits down. Long pause.*)

VISHAKHA (*in a low voice*): How are you, Husband?

(*No reply.*)

Only occasional bits of news about you. When someone from here goes to the city and attends the sacrifice—

(*No response.*)

Are you well? Or do you still drive yourself to the point of illness—like a demon?

(*No reply.*)

I was sure you wouldn't come home even if I were on my deathbed.

(*No reply.*)

But my fornication was reason enough, wasn't it?

(*No reply.*)

Whatever you heard about Yavakri and me...was no rumour.

(*No reply.*)

Yavakri and you. How much you resemble each other. You both go away when you feel like it. Come back without an explanation. As though Indra is explanation enough! He isn't. Not for me. Why did you go away like that?

PARAVASU: One can practise austerities like your fool, Yavakri, to coerce the gods to bend to one's will. Stand in a circle of fire. Torture oneself. So many techniques, all equally crass, to make the gods appear. And when they give in, what do you do? Extend the begging bowl: 'Give us rains. Cattle. Sons. Wealth.' As though one defined human beings by their begging—I despise it. I went because the fire sacrifice is a formal rite. Structured. It involves no emotional acrobatics from the participants. The process itself will bring Indra to me. And if anything goes wrong, there's nothing the gods can do about it. It has to be set right by a man. By me. That's why when the moment comes I shall confront Indra in silence. As an equal. For that, it is essential that one shed all human weakness. Be alone. Absolutely on one's own to face that moment. Become a diamond. Unscratchable.

VISHAKHA: And become immortal?

PARAVASU: At least for that moment, yes.

VISHAKHA: And for that you must break all the rules?

PARAVASU: To say 'all' is to make a rule.
(*He gets up.*)

VISHAKHA: Will you come home once the fire sacrifice is over?
(*No answer.*)

I suppose that would be too human. But what's wrong with being human? What's wrong with being happy, as we were before you got Indra into you?
(*No answer.*)

I shouldn't ask. I should be silent. And you, in any case, will be silent. My silence again followed by yours. Silences endlessly repeated. Perhaps they too will describe a whole universe. But I am sick of silence.
(*No answer.*)

All right. Then do me a favour before you go back. Please.
(*She takes his bow and arrow, puts them in his hands with the arrow pointing to herself. Then lies down on her back in front of him.*)

I'll lay myself open to you as a devoted wife.

PARAVASU: You want me to kill you?

VISHAKHA: At last, a question from you.
(*Pause.*)

We're three of us here. Your brother's never home. That leaves
me and your father.

(*Pause.*)

Something died inside your father the day the King invited
you to be the Chief Priest. He's been drying up like a dead
tree since then. No sap runs in him.

(*Pause.*)

On the one hand, there's his sense of being humiliated by you.
On the other, there's lust. It consumes him. An old man's
curdled lust. And there's no one else here to take his rage out
on but me.

(*Pause.*)

At least Yavakri was warm, gentle. For a few minutes, he made
me forget the wizened body, the scratchy claws, and the
blood, cold as ice. And he paid for it with his life.

(*Raibhya's steps are heard in the distance, as he returns.*)

Here it comes. The crab! Scuttling back to make sure I don't
defile the Chief Priest as I did Yavakri. Grant me this favour,
please. Kill me. For all your experiments you haven't yet tried
the ultimate. Human sacrifice! You could now.

PARAVASU: You're right. I must.

(*Pause.*)

You are still my guru.

(*He aims his arrow at her. A long silence as they wait. Then a low
cough is heard from Raibhya. Instantly Paravasu moves the arrow
around so that it points in the direction of Raibhya, and shoots.
Raibhya collapses without a sound. Vishakha gasps. Pause.*)

VISHAKHA: Now you'll never know if I told you a lie.

(*Pause.*)

PARAVASU: You didn't need to. He deserved to die. He killed
Yavakri to disturb me in the last stages of the sacrifice. Not
to punish Yavakri, but to be even with me. I had to attend
to him before he went any farther.

(*Pause.*)

VISHAKHA: What's worrying you then?

(*No answer.*)

Something is, isn't it? I knew it the moment I saw you this evening. And it wasn't just your father. Something else you've come looking for.

(*No answer.*)

Yavakri would have poured out his woes. But you'd rather let the poison burn your insides than speak out.

(*Takes his hand in her hand.*)

Look at your hand. It's so tense. Your sinews are twisted like ropes—ready to snap. Tell me. What's bothering you?

PARAVASU (*looks in the direction of Raibhya*): We must attend to the old man.

VISHAKHA: He's had a long life. Why should he be in a hurry now?

(*They look at each other. The stage darkens on them. We see Arvasu on the tamarind hill talking to himself.*)

ARVASU: Thorns! The wind has thorns now. The light too is nettled. Words—even your name, Nittilai—has fangs that rip the skin off my mind and make it bleed. How can I punish myself enough? Half an hour! Half an hour! But I stopped to bathe on my way to your village—to dig for water so I could wash myself before coming to you. I knew it was getting late, but I had just cremated a dead body. I couldn't bear the thought of touching you with those unclean hands. An untouchable wouldn't have cared. An outcaste wouldn't have cared. But my cursed caste wouldn't let me go... To think you would have been mine. Half an hour!

PARAVASU'S VOICE: Arvasu—Arvasu—

(*Arvasu gets up. Runs to the hermitage. He sees Paravasu and Vishakha bending over something near a thicket.*)

PARAVASU: Arvasu—here!

(*Plucks the arrow from Raibhya's body.*)

ARVASU: Where are you?

PARAVASU: Here, near the neem tree.

ARVASU: What are you doing there?

(*He goes and finds Paravasu and Vishakha kneeling over Raibhya's body.*)

> What is it? What's happened? Is that Father? What happened to him? Oh God! Blood! Blood—what's happened? Oh my God—I can't—

PARAVASU: In the dark, I—I mistook him for a wild animal—

ARVASU (*almost hysterical*): Is he all right? We must do something. He may still be alive. There. His eyelids—they're moving. Let's move him to—

PARAVASU: Take hold of yourself, Arvasu. He is dead—

(*Arvasu starts crying. Paravasu slaps him.*)

> Stop it. Don't be a child. There's no time to howl and wail now. I have to get back before I'm missed.

(*Arvasu and Vishakha react.*)

> If anyone gets wind of what's happened here, the fire sacrifice is ruined. Do you follow me?

ARVASU: But—after all this—do you mean to go back? To the sacrifice?

PARAVASU: Yes, the sacrifice must go on. You know that. And only I can ensure that—

ARVASU: But the blood—on your hands—

PARAVASU: Yes, that has to be washed. We must atone for Father's death. I know I should perform the rites of penitence. But I have to return. Immediately. So there's only one person who can do that. You. As his son, it's your prerogative and your duty.

(*Vishakha and Arvasu react in horror.*)

> Cremate the body right now. And then concentrate on the penitential rites.

ARVASU: But, Brother—

PARAVASU: But? What do you mean 'but'? Can't you see what is at stake? You must do it.

(*He starts to leave.*)

VISHAKHA: Say 'No', Arvasu.

ARVASU: Sister-in-law—

VISHAKHA: Refuse. He killed his father. Let him atone for it. Don't get involved in it.

ARVASU: But then—what about the sacrifice?

VISHAKHA: Let it go to ruin. Does it matter? There has been enough bloodshed already. Enough tears. Live your own life.

PARAVASU (*as though she hasn't spoken*): Don't rush through the rites. Perform them with care. Every detail has to be right.

ARVASU (*lost*): Bless me, Brother.

(*Paravasu blesses him by placing his right palm on his head and walks away. Vishakha stares dumbly after him and then walks mechanically back into the hermitage. Arvasu starts piling wood for the funeral pyre.*

Paravasu walks back through the jungle when a figure jumps out of the shadows and stands in his path. Paravasu and the Brahma Rakshasa stare at each other for a brief moment.)

PARAVASU: Ah! Not the Brahma Rakshasa himself! What a pleasure.

BRAHMA RAKSHASA: How did you recognize me?

PARAVASU: I was expecting you. Where else could you possibly go?

BRAHMA RAKSHASA: Help me. Please.

PARAVASU: Don't ask me. I don't help anyone.

BRAHMA RAKSHASA: Please, don't say that. I beg of you. You are my only hope.

PARAVASU: Hope of what?

BRAHMA RAKSHASA: I admire you. You aren't scared of me. You are tough. Your father gave me a new birth. We two are brothers.

PARAVASU: I don't need any more brothers.

BRAHMA RAKSHASA: You have no choice. Look, when I lived my 'human life', I—how shall I put it—I was bad. I'll spare you the details. But the result was that after my death I was not reborn, as any ordinary mortal would do. I became a Brahma Rakshasa. A soul locked in nothingness like a foetus stitched up inside its mother's sac. You can't imagine the horror of that existence. Nothing to look forward to: no birth, no death; nothingness stretching endlessly. Your father plucked me out and put me back in time, in order to kill Yavakri. I didn't want to, but I obeyed. And as a result, now I have something new. Hope. Of release—from this state—

PARAVASU: You should have asked Father—

BRAHMA RAKSHASA: I would have. But you killed him before he'd recovered from his ordeal. *You* killed him. Now you have taken on his inheritance. Not that I mind. You may be more capable of getting me what I want—

PARAVASU: What do you want?

BRAHMA RAKSHASA: Free me from this pain. Liberate me. I want to fade away. To become nothing—

PARAVASU (*laughs*): Yavakri asked for 'all knowledge' in a begging bowl. You ask for the final release. Moksha! The demands seem to be escalating! I am not interested in your final release. I am not even interested in *my* final release.

(*Mocking.*)

'Liberate' you! How's one supposed to do that?

BRAHMA RAKSHASA: I wish I knew. I can only beg. Ask the gods when you face them.

PARAVASU: I will ask them for nothing.

BRAHMA RAKSHASA: You talk of immortality. Look, I have been immortal! And I long for death. Release me. You owe it to me.

PARAVASU: I don't owe anyone anything. Don't pester me. You'll get nothing.

(*They have reached the sacrificial site.*)

I must go in. Remember the sacrificial enclosures are protected against all unnatural spirits.

(*Goes in. The Brahma Rakshasa watches him.*)

BRAHMA RAKSHASA: It's not so easy to get rid of a brother— Brother!

(*Disappears.*

Arvasu completes the funeral rites. Comes home. Calls out to his sister-in-law. No reply. He goes in. The hermitage is empty. In a corner he sees the water pot, covered with cobwebs. He walks out of the house.

Arvasu comes to the sacrificial area. The fire sacrifice is going on. He enters the enclosure and goes and sits among the Brahmins watching the rituals. Paravasu, initially engrossed in his work, notices him and suddenly freezes. His face turns pale. Words fail him. His unexpected silence draws everyone's attention. The hymns come to a stop. They all stare, uncomprehending, at Paravasu first and then at Arvasu. Arvasu is baffled and embarrassed.)

PARAVASU: You!

(*Points to Arvasu, who gets up, puzzled, scared.*)

ARVASU: Me?

PARAVASU: Yes, you! Who are you?

ARVASU: Me? I—

PARAVASU: Yes, Tell us.

ARVASU: I'm Arvasu, son of Raibhya.

PARAVASU: And where have you come from?

ARVASU: My father died. I've just completed his obsequies—and the expiation.

PARAVASU: Why the expiation? Tell us. Why?

ARVASU: He was killed—

(*Consternation in the assembly. Paravasu silences the crowds.*)

PARAVASU: At whose hands?

(*Long pause.*)

ARVASU: At the hands of his son.

(*The gathering breaks out into commotion.*)

PARAVASU: Patricide—patricide! What is he doing in these sanctified precincts? Throw him out—out! Out! Demon!

ARVASU: But—but—

(*Three or four Brahmins pounce on Arvasu and drag him out.
Dazed, Arvasu lets himself be dragged and pushed out of the
sacrificial enclosure. Suddenly, he starts shouting.*)

ARVASU: But why, Brother, why?...Why?

(*A couple of soldiers get hold of him and drag him away as he keeps
shouting.*)

   Why? Why? Tell me why—please.

(*Paravasu looks at the assembly of priests and watchers.*)

PARAVASU: As the sacrifice approaches its completion, the demons
come out. Rakshasas. Their sole aim is to disrupt the sacrifice.
We must be on our guard.

(*At a sign from him, the rites begin again. The stage darkens.*)

Act Three

Night. The outskirts of the city. The stage is filled with bodies of people sleeping. Nittilai sleeps next to Arvasu.

Arvasu wakes up. Sits up. Looks around, and as though frightened by the night, begins to crawl across the sleeping bodies. Nittilai stretches her hand out in her sleep to make sure Arvasu is next to her. He is not there. She sits up with a start, looks around, sees him and goes to him.

NITTILAI: Arvasu—

(Arvasu gasps and turns to her.)

Where are you going?

(He stares.)

It's me, Nittilai—

(She feels his forehead.)

The fever has gone down. Thank God!

(Feels his clothes.)

You are soaking wet.

ARVASU *(unbelieving)*: Nittilai! You—?

It can't be—it isn't—

NITTILAI *(laughing)*: Yes, it is.

(Suddenly Arvasu laughs happily like a child.)

ARVASU: Nittilai! Nittilai! Am I dreaming? Or are you really here? You won't disappear again, will you? Nittilai! Where have you

come from, Nittilai! You *are* Nittilai, aren't you? Don't melt
away. Please. Nittilai—stay, now that you're here.
(*Grabs her hand.*)
    I'll hold on to Nittilai now. I won't let Nittilai go.

NITTILAI: Ssh! You'll wake them up!

ARVASU (*laughing*): How did you come here?

NITTILAI: We can't talk in this place. Let's go there.
(*Helps him up. He is light-headed and almost falls down again. She
supports him. She also carries a bundle of fruit with her. They move
a little distance away.*)
    Be careful! You're still light-headed.

ARVASU (*laughing*): Light-headed. Light-footed. I'm flying—I'm
    floating—I'm flowing down a torrent of wind—I feel happy.
    You are here! It's beautiful.
(*Tries to stand by himself. Reels. Clings to her. They both laugh.*)

NITTILAI: Wait! Don't be a child. Here. Let me tie your *dhoti*
    properly.
(*Unselfconsciously, she reties his* dhoti, *as though he were a child.
Then leads him along.*)
    Sit down here.
(*She rekindles a dying fire as they talk.*)

ARVASU: Where are we?

NITTILAI: Outside the city gates.

ARVASU: And these people?

NITTILAI: Mostly starving villagers. They are here for the end of
    the fire sacrifice. They are waiting for the concluding feast.

ARVASU: The fire sacrifice. Yes, I remember.
(*He looks at her attentively.*)
    You look so lovely. All those patterns on your hands and face.
    You're like a bride.
(*Suddenly.*)
    But—didn't you go home to sleep last night?

NITTILAI (*puts a fruit in his hand*): Here. Eat this. I don't know when you had a proper meal last.

ARVASU: How is it that you're here, Nittilai?

NITTILAI: I've run away.

ARVASU: From your husband?

NITTILAI: From my husband. From my family. From everything. (*Pause.*)

ARVASU: Oh!
(*Pause.*)
Why? Didn't you like him? Did he beat you?

NITTILAI: I liked him. Very much. He's always smiling. I might have been happy with him.
(*Pause.*)
If any other girl had done what I have done, I'd be the first to thrash her in the village square. But when I heard what'd happened to you—

ARVASU: What?

NITTILAI: We heard terrible stories.

ARVASU (*remembering*): Yes, yes.

NITTILAI: I almost died when I heard they'd beaten you up. I got up and...ran all the way here.

ARVASU (*pause*): And how did you find me—

NITTILAI: It didn't take much searching. Every stray pup here knows about you.
(*Long pause.*)

ARVASU: I went back to meet Paravasu.
(*Excited.*)
That night. I had to know why. What had I done? I thought he might tell me if I went to him secretly. So I went back at night. But he never came out—

NITTILAI: Arvasu, it's all right. All that's done with—

ARVASU: Soldiers pounced on me. Kicked me. Dragged me to some cemetery. Tore my sacred thread. I kept calling out to him. 'Why, Brother, why?' They beat me.

NITTILAI: There now—don't excite yourself. Lie down.

ARVASU: Did he think I was married to you? Did he think I had become a low-caste actor? No, no. I remember. He clearly said 'Out! Out! Demon... Away with you!'

NITTILAI: Quiet now. Come, sleep for a while. It's still dark.
(*She makes him lie down with his head on her lap.*)

ARVASU: I had such nightmares. And whenever I woke up I saw these bodies. Lying about, inert in the dark. I thought I was in the land of the dead. But I didn't see *you*. I wish I had.
(*Stares at her.*)
I worshipped my brother. And he betrayed me. I let you down and you risk everything for my sake.

NITTILAI (*simply*): I like you.
(*Gives him another fruit.*)
Here, I hid these for you. There are three children in the actor's family. Poor things! They're eternally famished—

ARVASU: Actors?

NITTILAI: Yes, it was they who saved your life.

ARVASU (*suddenly*): Nittilai, how long is it since you left home?

NITTILAI: Three days.

ARVASU (*excited*): Three days! Three days, she says calmly! And you've been moving around in this city for three days! Are you crazed?

NITTILAI (*lightly*): I was only waiting for you to gain some strength.

ARVASU (*angry*): Woman, have you no brains? You only think of others! I know your people. Hunters. Once they decide on vengeance... We must leave immediately.

NITTILAI: Let's. If your legs have gained as much strength as your voice, we should be able to cover a fair distance today!

(*Suddenly they both burst out laughing. Then in a serious voice.*)

Arvasu, when I say we should go together—I don't mean we have to live together—like lovers or like husband and wife. I have been vicious enough to my husband. I don't want to disgrace him further. Let's be together—like brother and sister. You marry any girl you like. Only please, Arvasu—spare a corner for me.

ARVASU: I won't marry. Ever. It's enough that you are there with me.

NITTILAI (*gets up*): Take a little rest. I'll see you soon.

ARVASU: Where are you going?

NITTILAI: Let me arrange for something to eat on the way. Some meat. Fruit. The actor's family wants to go with us. Those poor starving babies—

ARVASU (*gently*): Nittilai—

(*Nittilai stops.*)

While you're away I think I'll make another attempt.

NITTILAI: Attempt?

ARVASU: To see my brother.

NITTILAI: How will you do that? Will he let you come anywhere near him?

ARVASU: No, he won't. But how can I go away without knowing why he acted as he did? I have to find out—I must—

NITTILAI: Will he tell you?

ARVASU: I don't think so.

(*Pause.*)

No—he won't.

NITTILAI: And suppose he did tell you? What will that do for you? Haven't you suffered enough?

ARVASU: If he can't justify his act—I'll—I'll push his face in it. I'll make him pay—I'll revenge myself on him—

NITTILAI: Arvasu!

ARVASU: I can't help it. I want to make them all pay. Yavakri. Father. Paravasu. It's a conspiracy, don't you see, it's all planned—because I wanted to marry you. Because I was ready to reject my caste, my birth. Can't you see it? I wanted to strike out on my own. So, first a corpse curls itself round my ankles. Yavakri. Then it's Father. Bodies drenched in blood. Like rats that pour out during the plague and die vomiting blood.

NITTILAI: Arvasu—

ARVASU: Listen. It's clear to me. Yavakri is dead. Father is dead—and Paravasu is alive. So he must know. He must be behind it all—my brother knew I would marry you even if he forbade it. So he—and his wife—and all those priests—yes, they planted those corpses in my way.

NITTILAI: You are talking nonsense.

ARVASU: You don't understand. You hunters—you only know minor spells and witchcrafts—spirits slithering in shallow caves or dangling on trees. But Yavakri and Father and Brother can bring out the terrors from the womb of the earth and play with them. They can set this foul nature against you. Can't you see the design in it all? Corpses pursuing me—evil, like a stink emanating from that sacrifice—

NITTILAI: Suppose you are right. What are you going to do about it?

ARVASU: I don't know. I don't know anything. Don't confuse me with questions. But if such an evil man continues as the Chief Priest of the sacrifice, it'll rain blood at the end—

NITTILAI: Leave that to the gods, Arvasu. Look at your family. Yavakri avenges his father's shame by attacking your sister-in-law. Your father avenges her by killing Yavakri. Your brother kills your father. And now you in your turn want vengeance—where will it all end?

ARVASU: So what do I do? Sit in a corner with my hands crossed, like an eunuch?

NITTILAI: Do that, Better that than become the man you hate.

ARVASU: Become? What's there left for me to become? I am an unregenerate sinner in the eyes of the world, a killer.

NITTILAI: Then kick that world aside, Arvasu. Your hands are clean. Even I have wounded—betrayed—my husband. You have remained good. Stay that way. We don't need this world. We can find our own.

(*He doesn't answer. A long tense pause. Nittilai gets up.*)

All right, let's go.

ARVASU: Go? Where?

NITTILAI: Let's go and face your brother. I don't want you to feel I'm depriving you.

ARVASU (*calms down*): You are right. He won't let me get anywhere near him. I knew that from the beginning, didn't I? So what was I making such a fuss about? Do you think I'm going mad?

NITTILAI: You've been through so much, I'm surprised you're not worse.

(*The Actor-Manager comes.*)

ACTOR-MANAGER: Ahha! So the patient is better today?

NITTILAI: Yes, thank you.

(*To Arvasu*)

He saved your life, Arvasu.

ARVASU: Thank you—

ACTOR-MANAGER: Hardly 'saved'. Our old man died. We went to bury him. And there you were in the burial grounds—stretched out stiff. Except that you weren't cold. You were burning hot. The bamboos we'd taken him out on served to carry you back. And you almost burned through them.

NITTILAI: I'm sorry your old man had to go. But it's lucky for us he chose that day. How's your brother?

ACTOR-MANAGER: His foot's much better, thank you. He can hobble about. Your magic touch again!

NITTILAI (*pleased*): Good. I'll get him some fresh herbs.

ACTOR-MANAGER (*pointing to Arvasu*): Now that he's well, do we start today?

NITTILAI: Within the next couple of hours. Let me go and arrange provisions for the trip.

(*Nittilai goes.*)

ACTOR-MANAGER: What an extraordinary girl!

ARVASU (*distracted*): Hm.

ACTOR-MANAGER: Lucky for you that she's here. Don't you ever forget that.

ARVASU (*startled*): Why... why should I?

ACTOR-MANAGER: Listen, son. We actors are always on the move. Never stationary. And often along the way we see a scene. A bit of life. Only a tiny bit as we pass by. But enough to give us a sense of the rest of the story.

ARVASU: What do you mean?

ACTOR-MANAGER: I don't know what you are to her. Not that I want to know. Any fool can see you two belong to different worlds. Anything's possible in these troubled times. So I won't comment. But your name's on every tongue in this town and they are mostly trying to spit it out. I didn't save your life. She did. I only found you. You were lucky that she turned up soon after and it's she who's been nursing you. Mopping up your vomit, wiping your bottom. Like a baby. I'm grateful to her because my babies were starving when she came and now they get a bite to eat every day. Where she gets the food from I don't know—but she knows the woods. We would have moved out of this town the day the old man died, except that we've become dependent on her. For food. For nursing. For laughter. We're just waiting to leave with her but she won't budge till you're better.

(*Pause.*)

Something about you worries me. She's a good girl. Don't hurt her.

ARVASU (*quietly*): I won't hurt her.

(*While this scene is going on, in the background, Nittilai's brother and husband enter, make a fire and sit near it, silent and immobile. Nittilai enters, sees them, freezes and flees in panic. They haven't seen her. Long pause. The Actor-Manager hums a song.*)

ARVASU: You said you'd gone to bury your old man when you found me? You bury your dead? Not cremate them?

ACTOR-MANAGER: No, we are actors. We have been actors since the Lord of Creation entrusted the job to my ancestors. The earth gave us the body. When we are done, we hand over the job to our children and hand back the body to the earth.

ARVASU: But the body will rot in the earth, surely...

ACTOR-MANAGER: What were we in our mother's womb? Floating bits of flesh? Squiggly worms? To burn is to destroy. Neither the earth gets it. Nor the wind. Well, to each his beliefs! My ancestors were actors and—

ARVASU: Then why are you leaving town?

ACTOR-MANAGER: We came here to perform a play for the sacrifice, but this town hasn't been good for us. The old man died. My brother's foot got infected—

ARVASU (*excited*): How can you give up so easily? Surely you have a duty to your art.

ACTOR-MANAGER: Couldn't agree more. But a body needs to be fed before it can act. In fact, even the gods, who are bodiless, need to be fed before they will act. Hence all these oblations. But there are no oblations without a performance, and there's no performance without actors. I don't have enough actors, it's as simple as that.

ARVASU (*shyly*): May I—may I—ask you something?

ACTOR-MANAGER: Go ahead.

ARVASU: You don't mind?

ACTOR-MANAGER: What is it?

ARVASU: Will you watch me?

ACTOR-MANAGER: Watch you?

ARVASU: I like dancing. If I dance now—will you tell me if I am any good?

ACTOR-MANAGER: You?

ARVASU: I realize—it sounds absurd—

ACTOR-MANAGER: But you are not an actor. You are a high-caste—

ARVASU: I used to be with the hunters most of the time. Dancing. Singing. I like dancing.

ACTOR-MANAGER: Well, some other time. We'll be travelling together, after all. I have other worries at the moment...

(*But Arvasu has started dancing. Initially the Actor-Manager is only half interested. But slowly as Arvasu dances, his eyes light up. He keeps the beat.*)

ACTOR-MANAGER: Not bad—not bad at all.

(*He too stands up and starts dancing. Slowly first, then faster. He leads. Arvasu follows. The Actor-Manager occasionally tries to trick Arvasu with a complicated step. But Arvasu accepts the challenge.*)
    Where did you learn all that?

(*Arvasu, increasingly confident, laughs and taps his own skull in reply. He dances faster.*)
    Enough. Enough now. Don't tire yourself. You've just got up from the sick-bed. Sit down.

(*They both sit.*)

ARVASU: So—I'm not too bad then?

ACTOR-MANAGER: Bad? You're excellent. And that's what makes my stomach burn. It's just my cursed luck—

ARVASU: Why?

ACTOR-MANAGER: The fire sacrifice will be completed in the next few days. That's long enough for you to pick up a few bits of dialogue and half a dozen steps. We could have a show ready to celebrate the completion—but my evil stars have made sure that the one actor I could use can't go anywhere near the sacrificial precincts.

ARVASU: Actually, I don't think that would be a problem.

ACTOR-MANAGER: What do you mean?

ARVASU: I don't think Brother will stop me from acting. The problem is—I won't act—I can't.

ACTOR-MANAGER: But why not?

ARVASU: Nittilai and I must go away today.

ACTOR-MANAGER: We could all leave together—later—

ARVASU: No, we must leave—today.

ACTOR-MANAGER (*disappointed*): Oh!
(*Hopefully.*)
Perhaps we can have a show in some other town—on the way?

ARVASU: Perhaps.
(*Pause.*)
In a land far, far away!
(*Pause.*)

ACTOR-MANAGER: Let me warn you. I never give up.
(*Nittilai comes rushing in. She is frightened.*)

NITTILAI: Arvasu, Arvasu—

ARVASU: Nittilai!

ACTOR-MANAGER: What's happened?

NITTILAI: I was on my way—and I saw them. They were sitting round a fire… They didn't see me—in the dark—

ARVASU: Who?

NITTILAI: My brother. And husband.

ARVASU: Oh my God!

ACTOR-MANAGER: Ah!

NITTILAI: I just turned round and ran back—

ARVASU (*excited*): We must leave then—immediately. Before it dawns, we must get out of the city—

NITTILAI (*desperate*): No, no, we can't. Not now. Don't you see? It's too late—

ARVASU: Too late? Why?

NITTILAI: They don't know I'm here. That's why it's taken them three days to get here. They must have been searching among friends and relatives—

ARVASU: So?

NITTILAI: But everyone knows you're here. In this city. If you disappear now, they'll instantly realize we're together. Then they'll chase us—

ARVASU: So what do we do?

NITTILAI: I don't know!

ACTOR-MANAGER: Is this why you have been acting so mysterious, girl? Why didn't you tell me? I'm a wizard at disguise. With a little bit of make-up, I would have changed your entire appearance. Made you as good as invisible—

ARVASU (*exasperated*): They are hunters. They don't need to see a quarry. They can smell it out. And once they are on the track, they'll run it to the ground.

NITTILAI: One thing's certain. Arvasu. You'll have to stay on in the city—be visible! Only that will throw them off the scent.

ACTOR-MANAGER: But won't they harm him?

ARVASU: No, I am an outsider.

(*Bitterly*)

Everywhere.

NITTILAI: They're after me.

ARVASU: So what will you do?

NITTILAI: I'll disappear. Go and hide in the jungle.

ARVASU (*enraged*): Hide? What do you mean hide? Are we playing games here? You there. Me here. No, I won't let you go.

NITTILAI (*flying into a temper*): Do you think I want to die? You think I want to be hunted down by my brother and my husband? If they had come separately, it might have meant anything. But they're here—together! And they sat there by the fire—still. Alert. Listening. We never talk when we are on a hunt. We only listen. And my husband wasn't smiling. He looked—so sad. That scares me, Arvasu. I'm still young. I don't want to die.

(*She starts weeping.*)

ARVASU: Don't cry. Please. It'll soon be light. And if you have to go you must. But what am I to do?

NITTILAI (*angry*): Why do you keep asking me? Why don't you decide? Don't push everything on to my shoulders—

ARVASU (*quietly*): I only meant—staying here in the city won't be easy—being spat upon, sneered at—

NITTILAI: Is that all you can think of when—

ACTOR-MANAGER: Act in my show.

ARVASU (*annoyed*): Please, don't try to be funny—

ACTOR-MANAGER: I'm quite serious. If you are going to be here till the sacrifice is over, you might as well take part in my play.

ARVASU: Listen now—

NITTILAI: What's that?

ACTOR-MANAGER: A moment ago he danced. He dances like a

celestial being. With him I could stage a show in honour of the festival. But he won't agree—

NITTILAI: Paravasu will never let him—

ARVASU (*defiant*): Paravasu himself has ostracized me. I'm an outcaste now. He can't stop me from acting...but how can I sing and dance while you're in mortal danger?

NITTILAI: I'll be safe enough. The jungle's like a home to me.

ACTOR-MANAGER: I am a selfish man. If this performance takes place, I'll be rich. We'll all be rich. My children will sleep on a full stomach for another two months. But that's not all. Think of yourself. If Arvasu has to be 'visible', what better than rehearsing in the open, getting ready for a stage performance with the whole town in attendance?

(*Pause. He waits for his words to sink in.*)

NITTILAI: Are you sure he'll be able to carry it off? He's never faced an audience before.

ACTOR-MANAGER: I am a professional, Sister. Do you think I would knowingly risk a failure? I even have a play ready. We'd just decided on it when the old man died. A perfect choice for this fire sacrifice. *The Triumph of Lord Indra.* A play about the struggle between Lord Indra and the demon Vritra.

(*She laughs.*)

NITTILAI: Then Arvasu will want to play the demon.

(*To Arvasu*)

Aren't I right?

(*To the Actor-Manager*)

He loves all that ghoulish make-up, the roaring and thumping, the acrobatics.

ARVASU: I never know whether you're going to laugh or cry.

ACTOR-MANAGER: He'll have to play Vritra. I, needless to say, will play the main role, Indra. The actor playing Vritra basically needs to dance. And my brother is in no state to dance. And the few speeches that are there won't be a problem to a Brahmin.

ARVASU: I am not a Brahmin—

ACTOR-MANAGER: Quite! Quite! But you won't need to be taught basic pronunciation.

(*Pause.*)

Think about it. I'll go and get the costumes for Vritra. If you're willing, we might as well start rehearsals right away.

(*Exits.*)

ARVASU: What shall I do, Nittilai?

NITTILAI: I don't know. What do you want to do?

ARVASU: What he said made good sense. But—

NITTILAI: You've always wanted to act. As long as I can remember. What will you do otherwise? Brood over Paravasu? Whip yourself into a frenzy of anxiety over me?

ARVASU: I'm afraid.

NITTILAI: What's there to fear?

ARVASU: It's the nightmare I told you about. I am dying of thirst. But there's no water. Then I peer into a huge well. There's water there, but it has my reflection in it. I stare at it. And the reflection snarls: 'Why are you staring, wretch? Go away.' So I say: 'You exist because I stare. You wouldn't be there if I went away.' It says: 'You think so, do you, you swollen-headed doll of flesh? I'll show you.' And the reflection leaps out of the water. Gouges my eyes out. Chews up my face in its jaws. I scream, but I have no face... It keeps on returning, that nightmare, so that now I'm not at all sure it's me standing here and not my reflection, all ready to attack—

NITTILAI: How long are you going to turn your face away from it then? Face it. Face your brother as you wanted to.

(*He looks at her in surprise.*)

Not in hate, Arvasu. In the play. Show him how good you are.
I'm sure the play will wash off the fear—the anger—

(*He nods.*)

ARVASU: All right.

NITTILAI: I'd better go. It's almost dawn.

ARVASU: Nittilai—

NITTILAI: What is it?

ARVASU: Isn't there any way you could watch the play that day?
It would give me so much courage—

NITTILAI: I wish I could! But it's too dangerous. Come here after
the play is over. At night. There'll be enormous crowds. We'll
meet at this point—and fade away—

(*She stands reluctant to go.*)

I'm glad you're not playing Indra. I don't like that god of
yours.

ARVASU: Why?

NITTILAI: He is immortal. When someone doesn't die, can't die,
what can he know about anything? He can't change himself.
He can't—can't *create* anything. I like Vritra because even
when he's triumphant he chooses death. I always wonder—
if flowers didn't know they were to fade and die, would they
ever blossom?

(*Gets up.*)

I must leave.

ARVASU: Nittilai, I wish you could hide here—in the city
somewhere.

NITTILAI: No. It's better that even you don't know where I am.

(*Moves to go.*)

ARVASU: Don't I—

NITTILAI: Concentrate on your rehearsals. Learn. I am sure you'll
be marvellous. I'm sure your dancing will bring the rains—
Goodbye—

ARVASU: Nittilai—

(*She smiles and disappears. He stares dumbly after her. The Actor-Manager who's been waiting at a distance enters with the costumes and the mask of Vritra.*)

ACTOR-MANAGER: Here. This is the mask of Vritra the demon. Now surrender to the mask. Surrender and pour life into it. But remember, once you bring a mask to life you have to keep a tight control over it, otherwise it'll try to take over. It'll begin to dictate terms to you and you must never let that happen. Prostrate yourself before it. Pray to it. Enter it. Then control it.

(*Arvasu opens the bundle of clothes and dresses, almost in a trance. The stage darkens. Nittilai's brother and husband melt away in the darkness. The audience, including Paravasu and the King, occupy their places and watch.*)

The Epilogue

Slowly, Arvasu puts on the mask. There is a roar of drums and then a sudden silence. Arvasu gives a wild roar and jumps up. He dances violently. The audience responds with enthusiasm. The play is on. The Actor-Manager dressed up as Indra enters from one side. The Actor playing Vishwarupa enters from the other. Vishwarupa and Vritra rush to each other, embrace.

VISHWARUPA: Dear Brother Vritra—

VRITRA: Dear Brother Vishwarupa—

(Since Vishwarupa is limping, Vritra dances, holding Vishwarupa's hands, emphasizing their affection for each other. The audience reacts with pleasure. Indra watches from a distance, then talks to the audience.)

INDRA: ...After all, I am Indra, the King of the Gods. Should I then not be Supreme in the three worlds? Should not Brahma, the Father of All Creation, who gave me birth, have ensured that I stood unrivalled in all these domains? But alas! He fell in love with a mortal and produced a son by human womb, whom he crowned the King of Men. Vishwarupa! Everyone admires Vishwarupa. Everyone sings his praises. His wisdom and gentleness and mastery of the lores inspires a love which makes me feel like the eclipsed moon. It threatens my sovereignty of the worlds. But how can I destroy him?

For my father mated with a woman from the nether world and created a third son, a demon, Vritra. He made him the King of the Nether World and told him: 'Vritra, protect your brother Vishwarupa, the King of Men, if necessary with your own life. For Indra is bound to try and harm him!'

And the two are inseparable. I sent, as you saw, the most enchanting of my celestial beauties to lure Vishwarupa to a lonely place. But he will not leave that infernal demon behind. How can I separate them? How can I isolate Vishwarupa?

(*He reflects.*)

Aha! I have it. I shall organize a fire sacrifice in honour of our father, Brahma, the Lord of All Creation...

(*He adds with a wink.*)

whom incidentally I have already destroyed. I shall invite all the gods and men to this sacrifice.

(*Goes round the stage and comes to Vishwarupa.*)

Vishwarupa, my dear brother—

VISHWARUPA: I bow to you, Brother Indra—

INDRA: Vishwarupa, I am conducting a fire sacrifice in our father's memory. All the gods and the best of men have been invited. You must come too—

VISHWARUPA: Indeed, I shall. You are my elder brother. I don't need an invitation to attend a sacrifice conducted by you, I would have come on my own the moment I heard the news.

INDRA: Your love for me is beyond description. Come, enter this sacrificial enclosure.

(*Vishwarupa tries to enter, followed by Vritra.*)

No, Vishwarupa. You are most welcome, but Vritra, who is accompanying you, may not enter the sacrificial precincts.

VISHWARUPA: And why is that?

INDRA: Because he is demon, a Rakshasa.

VISHWARUPA: But, Brother, he is our father's son. Hence he is our

brother and like our father, a Brahmin. Surely you will not
forbid him entry?

INDRA: His mother was a demoness and demon blood flows in
his veins. A demon may not be permitted near the altar lest
he is tempted to desecrate it. The rules are more ancient
that us. We cannot tamper with them.

VISHWARUPA: So be it.

(*To Vritra*)

Dear Vritra, you have heard what Indra has to say. So please,
you wait here outside the enclosure while I go in.

VRITRA: Brother, my father gave me life so I could protect you.
Let me come in with you. This Indra is treacherous.

VISHWARUPA: But, Vritra, you know that I have extracted from
him a promise not to hurt me.

VRITRA: They say gods should never be trusted.

(*Laughter from the audience.*)

Indeed, it's said that when the gods speak to us, the meaning
they attach to each word is quite different from the meaning
we humans attach to it. Thus *their* side of their speech often
denies what *our* side of their speech promises.

(*Applause.*)

Even their silences have double meanings. Hence the saying,
that the thirty-three gods occupying the heavens make for
sixty-six silences.

(*Laughter.*)

At least.

(*Thunderous applause and laughter.*)

VISHWARUPA: But, dear Vritra, one must obey one's brother. So
let me go.

VRITRA: Brother, I love you. But you'll not listen to me. So be
it. I'll wait for you here outside.

(*Vritra stamps in exasperation, goes and strikes a worried pose.
The audience loves it. Applause. Vishwarupa goes round the stage
to indicate that he is covering a long distance.*)

ARVASU (*aside*): Nittilai, I hadn't known it would be like this. I can feel the audience reaching out to me—their warmth coming in wave after wave, lapping against me. I'm good! Yet suddenly I don't care for this sea of smiling faces. I want yours. Where are you? Are you safe? My heart trembles to think of you.

(*Vishwarupa finishes the round and arrives at Indra's fire sacrifice.*)

VISHWARUPA: Brother Indra, now I enter your sacrificial pavilion.

INDRA (*laughs*): Come, come. I shall welcome you properly. Come and sit by the altar and offer oblations to the gods.

(*Vishwarupa mimes sitting down and pouring oblations in the fire. Indra laughing silently, moves behind him, takes up his thunderbolt, takes aim and plunges it into Vishwarupa's back. Vishwarupa screams. Paravasu, who has been watching impassively until now, jumps to his feet. The Brahma Rakshasa appears next to him. The rest of the people on stage freeze.*)

PARAVASU: No. No. Wrong! That's wrong!

BRAHMA RAKSHASA: What's wrong?

PARAVASU: They understand nothing, the fools. Indra didn't mean to kill him—

BRAHMA RAKSHASA: Then what happened?

PARAVASU: He was panic-stricken.

BRAHMA RAKSHASA: Why?

PARAVASU: He saw a face by the altar. Whose face was it? The face of my dead father? Or of my brother, who is a simpleton, yet knows everything? Or was it my own face? Cold fear tore through him. He stood paralysed. When he came to, he heard a voice asking: 'Who are you?' His own voice. There was no choice now but to go on, to strike. But to think that the fear had lain coiled inside him and he wasn't even aware—

BRAHMA RAKSHASA: I see. Well, then. I must go.

PARAVASU (*startled*): Go? Where?

BRAHMA RAKSHASA: I had better look elsewhere for help. You've enough problems of your own, Brother.

PARAVASU: I'll help you. I can.

BRAHMA RAKSHASA: Goodbye.

PARAVASU: Trust me. I'll help you—

(*The Brahma Rakshasa disappears. Paravasu shouts.*)

Come back—come back, Demon!

(*The stage, frozen till then, leaps to life. The audience, startled by Paravasu's shout, looks at him. Arvasu reacts to his brother's voice. Vishwarupa screams continuing his earlier scream. Rolls back. Indra strikes again.*)

VISHWARUPA: You, Brother? Why? I trusted you—

VRITRA: Whose voice is that? Familiar words!

(*Indra gives a villainous laugh.*)

VISHWARUPA: Brother, why this treachery?

VRITRA: Why, Brother? Why, why, why? Brother, why? Why? Indra's laughter—And why are the vultures, sparrows, kites and eagles reeling in such frenzy over the sacrificial sanctum? Why are they ripping the skies with their shrill screams? Why is a wave of blood breaking out of the sacrificial enclosure like a flock of fear-crazed jungle fowl?

(*He mimes entering the enclosure. Vishwarupa is dying.*)

Another treachery! Another filthy death! How long will this go on? How long will these rats crawl around my feet vomiting blood? I must put an end to this conspiracy—wait, Indra—

(*Attacks Indra with a ferocity which takes the Actor-Manager by surprise. They fight. The Actor-Manager is agile and well trained. But Vritra's violence shakes him. He runs. Vritra chases him.*)

You can elude me, Indra. But you can't escape me. Even if you fly like a falcon across ninety-nine rivers I'll find you. I'll destroy you. I'll raze your befouled sacrifice to the ground.

(He pounces on a guard standing nearby and grabs a torch from his hand and rushes toward the real sacrificial enclosure.)

I'll burn down the sacrifice—

ACTOR-MANAGER: No, no! Not *that*—stop him! Stop him, for God's sake—

(Two or three guards try to stop Arvasu but he is uncontrollable. He swings his torch about and in a swift move, pulls out a dagger from a guard's belt. The guards, half scared, step back.)

ARVASU: I am a Brahmin. If you try to stop me, I'll kill myself. And the sin of killing a Brahmin will be on your heads. I am a Rakshasa! And I'll kill anyone who tries to stop me—

(He rushes into the sacrificial pavilion. The guards rush in after him. There is commotion.)

ACTOR-MANAGER: It's the mask—it's the mask come alive. Restrain him—or there'll be chaos.

KING: Stop him! Stop him!

GUARD *(rushes out of the sacrificial enclosure)*: But he is not human, Sir. His feet don't touch the ground. He flies in the smoke like a Rakshasa—he disappears in the flames—

(Suddenly the weak and hungry villagers watching the scene from the crowds get up and start rushing into the burning pavilion. There is a stampede.)

BRAHMINS: It's the tribals—the savages—they're desecrating the sacrifice—Oh God! This is madness. The doomsday—they are eating and drinking the food kept for the gods. They're levelling the sacrifice to the ground—

KING: Chief Priest! Sir! What shall we do?

(Paravasu has been watching the chaos, without so much as moving a muscle. He gets up and without a word calmly walks into the blazing enclosure.

Nittilai comes running.)

NITTILAI: Arvasu!

(She rushes into the burning structure. The crowds mill around. The

structure, made of dry bamboo and wood bursts into flames.
Nittilai comes out, supporting Arvasu. She takes off his mask,
throws it away.)

NITTILAI: It's all right. Don't worry now—

ARVASU: I don't know what came over me, Nittilai.

NITTILAI: It's all over. Thank God, you aren't hurt—

ARVASU: I lost, Nittilai. And Paravasu won. He went and sat
    there in front of the altar, unafraid and carried on with the
    sacrifice. I couldn't destroy him...

NITTILAI: You didn't mean to, Arvasu.

ARVASU: He went up in flames while I stood watching, untouched.

NITTILAI: It doesn't matter! Let's just go away from all this.

ARVASU: Yes, let us. Don't let go of me—please—

NITTILAI: Of course, I won't, silly boy. Come.
(Suddenly Nittilai's brother and husband step out of the crowd
and bar their way. She screams.)

ARVASU: No! Listen—listen to me—

NITTILAI: Please, Brother—Husband—please, don't—
(The brother knocks Arvasu down and pins him to the ground. The
husband pulls out a knife, grabs Nittilai by her hair and slashes
her throat in one swift motion. He then lets her drop. The two
go away. Arvasu gets up, rushes to her, takes her in his arms. She
lies there, her eyes open, bleeding, dying like a sacrificial animal.
The commotion dies away as Arvasu stares numbly at Nittilai.)

ARVASU (*softly*): Serves you right! Who asked you to meddle with
    this world? You plunge in—like a lamp into a hurricane.
    What do you expect? No one'll weep for you, Nittilai. Not
    even me. I'll sing no lullaby of grief for you. But I'll come
    with you. Where nothing matters, not your goodness, nor
    my stupidity, nor this world's evil. Where the fire will have
    reduced everything to ashes.
(He lifts up her corpse, puts it on his shoulder and goes into the

sacrificial pavilion which is still burning. The crowds watch in
silence. He goes and stands inside the burning structure. The fire
slowly dies out.

Melodious music. The sunlight becomes soft and gentle. The en-
tire atmosphere gets an ethereal hue. The voice of Indra is heard
from the skies.)

INDRA: Arvasu, Son, do not grieve. We are pleased with you.
Ask for any boon and it shall be granted.

ARVASU (*baffled*): Who's that? Who's that?

INDRA: I am Indra, the Lord of Gods. Know that all the gods
are pleased with you.

ARVASU: Indra? But what do I have to do with Indra? I didn't
seek Indra, or any other god. Yavakri did. Paravasu did. I
seek only Death. Why are you here?

INDRA (*laughs*): You question the gods? Other mortals would
be happy to receive—

ARVASU: But—what have I done to deserve this visit?

INDRA: We loved the way you challenged Indra and then pursued
him...in the play. But it could also be because of Paravasu's sacrifice or Nittilai's humanity. You humans are free to
construe the acts of gods as you wish. The point is we are
here and you can ask for anything you want—

CROWDS: Rain! Arvasu, ask for the rains! Water—

ARVASU (*slowly*): Lord Indra, I want Nittilai back. Alive. That's
all I want in my life. Grant me that. Nittilai—my gentle
Nittilai—I killed her. I want her back—

CROWDS: Water, Arvasu, ask for the rains!

INDRA: It's no great matter to bring Nittilai back to life. But
once the wheel of Time starts rolling back, there's no saying
where it'll stop. Along with Nittilai, others too may return
to life—your brother Paravasu, your father, even Yavakri—

ARVASU: Yes, let them. Let them.

(*Strange music fills the air. The souls of Nittilai, Paravasu, Ra-ibhya, Yavakri, Andhaka as well as a host of other dead people enter the stage silently and come close to Arvasu. He looks at them and calls out.*)

ARVASU (*happily*): Nittilai! Nittilai! Brother! Father—and who are all the others, Lord?

INDRA: Those who died all over the earth at the same time as your family. If the wheel of Time rolls back they come back to life too—

ARVASU: Yes. Yes. Let the world be as it was—

INDRA: But then, won't the entire tragedy repeat itself, Arvasu? How will it help anyone to go through all that suffering again?

ARVASU: No, it won't. Lord, I have been a benighted creature all my life. My blindness contributed to that tragedy—fuelled it on. But after all that I have been through, I'm wiser. I can now stop the tragedy from repeating itself. I can provide the missing sense to our lives—

INDRA: Are you sure?

ARVASU: Yes, I am.

INDRA: Well then—

(*As this moment a shout is heard from afar. It is the voice of the Brahma Rakshasa.*)

BRAHMA RAKSHASA: Arvasu—

ARVASU: Who's that?

BRAHMA RAKSHASA: It's me. The Brahma Rakshasa. Your father invoked me. He ordered me to kill Yavakri and I did. I have done my duty and now I wander lost, and in torment. Help me, Arvasu.

ARVASU: What do you want?

BRAHMA RAKSHASA: I want release—release from this bondage. Your father gave me this life. We are brothers. So you must complete what your father couldn't—I want to melt away—

I want peace—eternal peace—I beg of you—intercede on my behalf with the gods—

ARVASU: Lord Indra, you heard that. Could you—

INDRA: Arvasu, the wheel of Time must roll back if Nittilai is to return to life. It must roll forward for the Brahma Rakshasa to be released. You can't have it both ways. Choose—

ARVASU (*helplessly to the Brahma Rakshasa*): You see, there's nothing I can do.

BRAHMA RAKSHASA: You can, Arvasu. You can. Don't abandon me.

INDRA: There's another consideration, Arvasu. Not even the gods can guarantee a soul the ultimate release. That is a law beyond us. I may grant his release from birth and death because you ask for it. But there is every chance it may not work. In that case, his situation will remain unchanged and you'll lose Nittilai.

ARVASU: You heard that, Brahma Rakshasa. So forgive me—

(*The souls draw closer to Arvasu, their eyes pleading with him.*)

BRAHMA RAKSHASA: I don't forgive. I can't. But you are a human being. You are capable of mercy. You can understand pain and suffering as the gods can't—

ARVASU: I don't want to listen to you. Go away! Go away!

BRAHMA RAKSHASA: And when Nittilai comes back what will you tell her? Will you tell her that because of her a soul writhes in pain—

ARVASU: Shut up! She is not at fault—

BRAHMA RAKSHASA: Nittilai came to help you because she cared for you. She would have cared for me. Wept at the thought of my endless life in death. If you bring her back, you'll have destroyed what made her such a beautiful person—

ARVASU: That's not true.

BRAHMA RAKSHASA: Remember, Arvasu. If Nittilai lives again, she'll live a life as tormented as mine—tormented by the knowledge that her resurrection condemned me beyond salvation. And every moment of her life, she'll hear my screams. What you are asking for is not a boon. You are asking Indra to condemn Nittilai to a hell-hole much worse than the one I'm in. Think, Arvasu, you're wiser now—

(*Arvasu is silent. The souls make a strange moaning noise.*)

INDRA: Arvasu, have you decided?

ARVASU: Lord Indra—

INDRA: Yes—

ARVASU: Grant this Brahma Rakshasa his release. Let him go.

INDRA: You're sure you want that?

ARVASU: Nittilai would have wanted it so.

INDRA: Well then, so be it!

(*The Brahma Rakshasa cries out in triumph. A long pause. The crowd of souls gives a long, mournful sigh of disappointment and begins to withdraw. Nittilai's soul too goes away with them.*)

ARVASU: Nittilai!

(*Sits down and clutches Nittilai's corpse. The Brahma Rakshasa waits impatiently but nothing happens. He looks around baffled, scared. The world seems to stand still.*

The crowds begin to whisper.)

CROWDS: What's that?—You smell that?—Yes. Yes. The smell of wet earth. Of fresh rains. It's raining. Somewhere. Nearby. The air is blossoming with the fragrance of earth. It's raining—It's raining—Rain! The rain!

(*Wind blows. Lightening. Thunder. People shout 'Rain! It's raining!' Suddenly the Brahma Rakshasa roars with laughter and melts away. Only his laughter can be heard for a few moments, reverberating, mixed with the rolling thunder. It pours. People dance with joy. They roll in the mud. Arvasu sits clutching Nittilai's body.*)

ARVASU: It's raining, Nittilai! It's raining!

THE DREAMS OF TIPU SULTAN

NOTE

Those who wish to stage the play should kindly resist the temptation of using masks, special lighting or costumes for the dream scenes. It is essential for the total impact of the play that the dreams are staged absolutely realistically, and that the scenes follow each other in rapid succession. As this rapidity can be best achieved by quick shifts of location on stage and of lighting, exits and entrances of characters have not always been indicated in the text in the traditional fashion.

The Dreams of Tipu Sultan was first presented by the Madras Players at the YMCA Amphitheatre, Chennai, on 17 February 2000. The principal cast was as follows:

TONY PICKFORD	Colin Mackenzie
HARSHA SUBRAMANIAM	Hussain Ali Kirmani
RAVI KATARI	Mark Wilks
P. VENKAT	Zafer
JASPER UTLEY	Arthur Wellesley
VIKRAM GOPALAKRISHNAN	Nadeem Khan
ASIM SHARMA	Tipu Sultan
T. T. SRINATH	Poornaiya
RUPA BOSE	Female Idols
MALA GOVIAS	
P. VENKAT	Old Men
BRIAN PAPALLI	
GAUTHAM ADITHYA	Mir Sadiq
PAUL MATHEW	Ghulam Ali Khan
EJJI UMAMAHESH	Osman Khan
P. VENKAT	
SIDDHARTH CHOUDHRY	Fath Haidar
SUKRIT CHOUDHRY	Muizuddin
MADHULICA SUNDARAM	Abdul Khaliq
ANURADHA ANANTH	Young Man

JIM HODGETTS	Charles Malet
ARYAMA SUNDARAM	Nana Phadnavis
SRIYA CHARI	Ruqayya Banu
SUMIKA MUKERJI	Hasina
RANJAN DE	Lord Cornwallis
JAGAN R.	Qamaruddin
VENKY NAIK	Haidar Ali
ARUN MANI	Hari Pant
TONY PICKFORD	Lord Mornington (Richard Wellesley)
JIM HODGETTS	William Kirkpatrick
Directed by	N. S. YAMUNA
Sets and lights by	M. NATESH

Act One

1803. The house of the historian, Mir Hussain Ali Khan Kirmani, in the city of Mysore. Colonel Colin Mackenzie, the Oriental scholar, is taking off his shoes, as though he has just arrived. He looks around at the notes, books, and manuscripts littering the floor. Kirmani enters with a jug of water and a tumbler, and places them next to Mackenzie.

MACKENZIE: How's the work progressing?

KIRMANI: Not at all well.

MACKENZIE: Why not?

KIRMANI: It's not easy. It hurts.

MACKENZIE: That's what you keep saying, Janaab Kirmani. But come now—after all these years—

KIRMANI: There's no healing. True, the blood and the tears dried up a long time ago. But the wound remains fresh.

MACKENZIE: That's understandable. I mean, you *were* close to him. But you are also a historian. You need to develop a certain objectivity—

KIRMANI: Yes, that's what you keep telling me, Mackenzie Sahib. Objectivity. Dispassionate distance. Is that even possible?

MACKENZIE: Essential, I'd say. A must.

KIRMANI: Then perhaps you should dismiss me. You pay me to write history while I malinger and mope...

MACKENZIE: I didn't mean that. In any case, you know you are irreplaceable, you old rascal! One can't buy genuine court historians in the bazaar.

KIRMANI: Perhaps you think malingering is a courtier's disease?

MACKENZIE: No, I don't. I think you're far too obsessed with his death.

KIRMANI: Not his death. The way he was destroyed.

MACKENZIE: Surely you're being melodramatic now. Every bit of evidence we've gathered proves he asked for it.

KIRMANI: Yes. For you, he's made up of bits of evidence, bits of argument that prove that your side was right. And that's what I don't understand. You have your version of history, all worked out. Why do you want my side? Why do you care?

MACKENZIE: I am interested in the other side. You could say that's how we Europeans are brought up...to be interested in the other side as well. That I suppose is our strength.

KIRMANI: I find a lifetime insufficient to understand my own. Besides I spent my life serving him and his father. And now I work for you, his enemies. What does that make me? A traitor? Am I trustworthy any more? Doesn't that worry you? It worries me.

MACKENZIE: Our loyalty is to history, Kirmaniji. Keep emotion out. Stick to the facts.

KIRMANI: You mean, memories. But that's where the real betrayal lies. Do you know I was just trying to remember what he looked like on that last day and I just couldn't.

MACKENZIE: That's another thing you have avoided writing about. His last day.

KIRMANI: I remember it vividly. But the crucial detail still eludes me. He was staying in the caravanserai on the northern ramparts. He'd been there for a couple of days, with the soldiers, watching the English noose tighten. It was sweltering hot. We had been praying for a downpour, for then the moats would have been flooded and the English attack delayed. But the clouds had hung ominously, inert, neutral. We were halfway through our lunch, our sweat streaming into our plates, when the skies exploded. The English had launched their assault. The Sultan washed his fingers and got up. He buckled on his sword belt, took out an envelope from his pocket, sealed it and gave it to me: 'Keep it till I come back,' he said. At that moment, news came that Syed Gaffar had been killed by a cannonball. He mumbled a prayer and left. I remember thinking, I'll never forget that expression on his face. But I have. For the life of me, I can't remember his face at that moment. It's such...such betrayal!

MACKENZIE: And then?

KIRMANI: I forgot all about the letter. Naturally, with all that followed. Next day, I found it in my pocket. Reluctantly, I broke open the seal. Inside was a paper on which he had recorded the dream he had had the previous night. His last dream. With that my history ends. Yours begins. (*Pause.*)

MACKENZIE: I saw him first in the flickering light of a torch. Still warm. We thought he was alive, buried deep under a pile of corpses. Near the water gate of the fort. The night of the fourth of May, 1799.

(*Ramparts of the Seringapatam—or Srirangapatna—fort. Midnight. There has been savage fighting and the ground is thick with the bodies of the dead and the dying. British soldiers are searching through the piles of bodies for Tipu's corpse. Tipu's servants, brought in to help identify his body, squat around, dozing.*)

SOLDIER 1: Is that him?

SOLDIER 2: Could be. No way one can be certain.

CAPT. WILKS: Corpulent, with big twirly moustaches, round face...

SOLDIER 2: Yes, sir. We know that by heart now. But the description seems to fit most of these bastards.

WILKS: Ask that black there.

SOLDIER 3: Look, sir, I'm sure we're wasting our time. I'm sure the bird's flown. He would be stupid not to—

WILKS (*ignores him*): Ask him.

SOLDIER 2: Is there any point, sir? These swine have already identified a dozen corpses as the Sultan's—they're making fools of us.

WILKS: Ask the one huddled in the right corner of the group. We haven't tried him.

SOLDIER 2: *Arre suno—Tum naheen—Han! Tum!* (You there! Not you—Yes, you!)

ZAFER: *Jee Huzoor.*

SOLDIER 2: *Yehan aao.* (Come here.)

ZAFER: *Jee.*

SOLDIER 2: *Naam kya hai?* (Name?)

ZAFER: Zafer.

SOLDIER 2: *Yeh murdah. Kya yeh tumhare Sultan ka hai?* (This corpse. Is it your Sultan's?)

ZAFER: *Dikhai naheen de rahaa... Andhera.* (Can't see... It's dark.)

SOLDIER 2: He says he can't see in the dark.

WILKS: True enough. Why haven't the torches arrived? Halloo—Ricketts—

VOICE (*distant*): Sah!

WILKS: Where are the torches? We can't see a damn thing here.

VOICE: On their way I suppose, sah—

WILKS: You suppose, do you? Thanks. Send your torch here.

VOICE: A moment, sah. We may have something here.

WILKS: So may we. So send it here. On the double.

SOLDIER 3: It's bloody ridiculous. We fight and kill these devils through the day. Then sift their rotting bodies through the night. Like scavengers.

SOLDIER 1: A dozen teams scavenging and three torches between them.

VOICE: More torches and flares coming, sah. And it's Colonel Wellesley, sah.

WELLESLEY (*from a distance*): Hello! Captain Wilks—

WILKS: Here, sir.

WELLESLEY (*from a distance*): Where are you, Mark?

WILKS: Near the water gate, sir. Could you bring some torches and flares with you, sir?

(*Colonel Arthur Wellesley enters with a group of soldiers carrying torches. The torches are distributed.*)

WELLESLEY: This surely is what hell is like!

WILKS: It's Tipu's men, sir. They wouldn't yield. It was carnage.

SOLDIER 1: It's hot as hell too.

WILKS: We've had it if it rains now.

WELLESLEY: Even without the rains, it should not take long before they begin to stink. And the city must be getting restive. They'll want their dead. Let's hope we find him soon. Apparently he was last seen around here.

SOLDIER 3: If I may say so, sir, if the bastard's really lying dead somewhere here, we should let him rot in the sun—feed him to the dogs!

WELLESLEY: I understand how you feel. But we can't leave any corpse unturned, you understand.

WILKS (*laughs*): Of course not, sir.

WELLESLEY: We've got to decide whether Tipu is dead or in hiding or has run away before we can take the next step. Colonel Mackenzie should be here soon with the Manager of the Fort. But we must carry on in the meantime.

WILKS: Would you like to see some fun, sir?

(*Pointing to Zafer*)

Ask him, Jones.

SOLDIER 2: *Aao, dekho. Inko pehchante ho?* (Come and look. Do you recognize him?)

(*Holds a torch to a dead body. Zafer looks and begins to wail.*)

ZAFER: *Han! Han! Yehee hain hamare padshah! Yehi hain—Allah! Ab kya hoga?*

SOLDIER 2 (*resigned*): He says, yes. It's the Sultan.

WILKS: While the others sit on their haunches and watch calmly from a distance?

SOLDIER 3: Why don't we kick the bastards? They aren't even trying to fool us!

WELLESLEY: Can't blame them.

WILKS: All right. Pile that body along with the others.

SOLDIER 3: I'll take any bet Tipu's run away, his tail between his legs.

SOLDIER 2 (*laughs*): We'll take bets when we're done with the city. You'll have something to bet with then.

SOLDIER 3: I can barely wait to lay my hands on it. I was a prisoner here. I've seen the city. Plated with gold, it is.

WILKS: Stop counting your chickens and get on with the bloody job.

VOICE (*distant*): Halloo—Is Colonel Wellesley there?

WELLESLEY (*shouts back*): Here! Near the water gate. Is that you, Colin?

MACKENZIE (*entering along with Nadeem Khan*): This is Qilledar Nadeem Khan, Manager of the Fort. Colonel Wellesley.

WELLESLEY: Delighted to meet you, sir. I wish the circumstances were more pleasant.

NADEEM: It's God's will.

WELLESLEY: We'd be grateful for your assistance.

NADEEM: It's my duty to the Sultan. I saw him last here, fighting like a man possessed.

WELLESLEY: Is it likely that Tipu Sultan might have escaped?

NADEEM: That wouldn't be like him. Besides, all the gates of the fort were closed.

(*Pause.*)

I had seen to that.

(*Neither Wellesley nor Mackenzie react.*)

If you'll permit me—

(*He starts looking for Tipu's body.*)

WELLESLEY: What news of the palace, Colin? All well, I presume.

MACKENZIE: They surrendered all right. There was no resistance. The princes took their time coming out; they were shaking with fright. General Baird became a little impatient—

WELLESLEY: Let me guess the rest.

MACKENZIE: Nothing serious. He cooled down soon enough.

WELLESLEY: Hm! Any trace of the Sultan?

MACKENZIE: He's not in the palace. They say he left two days ago. Has been camping out with the soldiers, somewhere on the ramparts.

NADEEM: Sahib—*Yeh hain*—Raja Khan—

SOLDIER 2 (*excited*): Nadeem Khan's found Raja Khan, the Sultan's personal assistant.

(*They run.*)

MACKENZIE: That means Tipu's body must be somewhere around? Where, Qilledar Sahib? There? Move these bodies. The lot. Look sharp.

SOLDIER 2: *Jaldi—Jaldi*—(Quick! Quick!)

NADEEM: *Thehro*! *Yeh hain*—(Stop. That's him!)

MACKENZIE: I think we've found him. Careful. That one with the gold buckle on his belt. Lift him out.

WILKS (*shouts*): We have found him. Bring all the torches here.

VOICES (*distant*): You have?—That's bloody marvellous—They've found him—Where?
(*Commotion. Soldiers come running and crowd around the body.*)

WELLESLEY: Steady now. Form a circle and hold your torches close to him. Is that Tipu Sultan, Qilledar Sahib?

NADEEM (*broken voice*): Jee han.

WELLESLEY: So that's the Tiger of Mysore.

SOLDIER 2: He's warm.

WELLESLEY: Is he alive?
(*Feels Tipu's temperature.*)

MACKENZIE: Is he?

WELLESLEY: He is warm, but that wound on his temple. Couldn't have survived that.
(*A chorus of voices, mainly female, is heard wailing in the far distance. They listen.*)

WELLESLEY (*listening*): But what's that?

MACKENZIE: That's from the palace—The harem—

WELLESLEY: The ladies of the palace mourning!

MACKENZIE: But how could they have known so soon? The palace is a mile away.

WILKS: Some secret signal.

WELLESLEY: In this dark?

MACKENZIE: It's eerie.

WELLESLEY: If we were looking for confirmation, I suppose that's it—
(*The wailing gets louder and spreads. The entire city is soon wailing.*)

SOLDIER 3 (*eagerly*): Is the city ours then, sir?

WELLESLEY: I suppose I can't stop you.

(*The soldiers rush out, hurrahing, eager to plunder the city.*)
   The only thing more melancholy than losing a battle is winning it. Mark—

WILKS: Yes, sir.

WELLESLEY: Get the body moved to the palace. And keep watch.

WILKS: Yes, sir.

(*They move away discussing the details.*)

SOLDIER 1: Excuse me, sir.

MACKENZIE: Yes?

SOLDIER 1: May I borrow your penknife, sir? I lost mine in the action.

MACKENZIE: Penknife? Certainly. Here.

SOLDIER 1: Thank you, sir. Before the body is taken away, I mean. I'd promised my friend Dr Cruso of our Establishment a present—

(*Chops off one of Tipu's moustaches.*)

MACKENZIE (*shouts*): What are you doing, man? What in the name of the Devil are you doing? Stop that lunatic—

(*Exclamations of horror, not too loud, in Urdu and Kannada. 'Arre—Roko—Ayyo! Ayyo! Yeh kya kiya?'*)

SOLDIER 1: The tiger's own whiskers. A prize booty.

MACKENZIE: Arrest that damned fool!

(*The sounds of wailing grow louder and merge with the shouts and screams of the city being pillaged. The sound track is entirely taken over by the latter. We are back in Kirmani's house.*)

KIRMANI: So the Tiger of Mysore had at last been hunted down. And the first salutation he received from the hunters was to have his whiskers chopped off.

MACKENZIE: That act of vandalism will not be forgotten.

KIRMANI: How could it be? It was a perfect prelude to a night of unprecedented rapacity.

MACKENZIE: I had never seen British soldiers go berserk like that!

KIRMANI: Every house looted. Every available woman raped. Soldiers throwing away precious jewellery because they could not carry any more.

MACKENZIE: Wellesley had to hang three soldiers before the pillage died down. Dreadful! Well, I'd better get back to my Sanskrit. The *Arthasastra*. The Science of Governance. A cynical piece of writing, if there ever was one. Get over your despondency, old man, and get on with your writing.

KIRMANI: I'll try. But I don't know what to write.

MACKENZIE: For the hundredth time, Kirmaniji, I wish you would write about Tipu's embassy to Mauritius—the Malarctic adventure. It proved to be his undoing and yet we don't have enough details.

KIRMANI: It never happened.

MACKENZIE: There! I can't understand it! It wasn't half as bad as the other things he did. Like trying to befriend Napoleon. Governor Malarctic is insignificant, an eminently forgettable Frenchman, if he hadn't caused Tipu's downfall. Yet you keep denying the whole thing. Why?

KIRMANI: Colonel Sahib, what you call the Malarctic Deal never happened.

MACKENZIE (*resigned*): If you insist. But Lord Mornington had absolute proof of Tipu's mischief.

KIRMANI: Perhaps His Lordship was dreaming.

MACKENZIE: I beg your pardon, Kirmaniji. Are you accusing the Governor General of India of lying?

KIRMANI: How could I, Colonel Sahib? I am employed by the Honourable John Company. But dreaming is not dishonourable. My master, Tipu Sultan, dreamt.

MACKENZIE: I know. And kept a record! By the way, what happened to his last dream?

KIRMANI: The night he was buried, a thunderstorm burst over Seringapatam.

MACKENZIE: Ah, yes! I remember. A deluge of extraordinary violence—two of our men were killed—

KIRMANI: Doors and windows in the city had already been torn down by the British soldiers. Most houses were roofless. And now, through the night, the rain lashed with a fury that made the soldiers' rampage seem like child's play. It destroyed all my papers. Wiped away every word written in ink. Within a night, all my recorded facts became memory.

MACKENZIE: Pity!

KIRMANI: Nature did with *that* dream what Munshi Habibullah should have done with the rest.

MACKENZIE: What do you mean?

KIRMANI: Munshi Habibullah was a fool. He should have destroyed the diary, when he found it.

MACKENZIE: There was no harm in it.

KIRMANI: It was a diary in which my master had recorded his dreams. He had kept it concealed from his closest confidants. I didn't know of its existence. None of us did. I couldn't believe my eyes when I saw the words written on its first page, in the Sultan's own hand.

(*Suddenly Tipu's voice is heard. But only Kirmani reacts to it.*)

TIPU'S VOICE: In this register are recorded the dreams I've had and am having.

KIRMANI: The Sultan had hidden the diary under his pillow and there it had lain after his death...until that idiot Munshi stumbled on it. It was sacred, personal.

MACKENZIE: I'm afraid we merely saw it as an odd little book. A pleasantly inconsequential conversation piece. (*Ironic.*) An ideal gift for the Chairman of the Court of Directors of the Honourable East India Company.

KIRMANI (*almost to himself*): There were blank pages in the diary. What dreams Tipu meant to record there and why he didn't will never be known.

MACKENZIE: Blank pages in a secret record of dreams—that's Tipu for you.

KIRMANI: Evidently, Colonel Colin Mackenzie Sahib, he recorded the dreams that spoke to him.

(*Pause.*)

And some probably didn't.

MACKENZIE (*laughs*): Janaab Hussain Ali Kirmani Sahib. I am interested in the people who spoke to him and the ones he spoke to. You keep the dreams to yourself.

KIRMANI (*smiling*): I will too.

(*From now on, Kirmani and Mackenzie act as choric characters, commenting on the action, as indicated. The stage darkens. Tipu enters, accompanied by Poornaiya.*)

TIPU: On the 3rd day of the month of Thamari, the last night of the month of Ramzan followed next morning by Idd in the year of Dalw 1213 from the birth of the Prophet, I was returning with my army from Farrukhi near Salamabad when I had the following dream. I had been on an elephant shikar and on my way back was walking with Poornaiya, the Finance Minister, when we saw a big temple. It was in a dilapidated state, and I said: 'Poornaiya, look at that structure. It looks quite mysterious.'

POORNAIYA: Yes, Your Majesty. It does indeed.

TIPU: Let's go in and have a look.

(*Lights come on to show a strange building with several human images.*)

Poornaiya, what idols are these? Are they some gods you recognize?

POORNAIYA: No, Your Majesty. I don't think they are gods.

TIPU: They don't seem to belong to any religion I know.

POORNAIYA: They are strange. I have never seen such figures before.

TIPU: Look, Poornaiya—look—their eyes! They are moving. These stone images are moving their eyes!

POORNAIYA: Let's go back, sir. This darkness has a malevolence about it. We'd better get out—

TIPU: No, let's go on. Let's inspect them more closely.

POORNAIYA: Be careful, sir. Those two. They are getting up. Look out!

(*Two women in the last row stand up. They are wearing nine-yard saris. One of them pulls her sari up between her knees.*)

TIPU: Who are you? Are you human or are you some spirits?

WOMAN: Your Majesty, we are living women. The rest of us, these men here, are merely images. We have been here for many centuries now, praying to God and seeking our salvation.

TIPU: Good. I'm sorry then we've disturbed you. Do you need any help?

WOMAN: None at all except for total isolation.

TIPU: So be it. Ladies, keep yourselves occupied with thoughts of God. Come, Poornaiya. Let's go. We'll have the temple repaired, the walls rebuilt so that these seekers after God are not disturbed.

POORNAIYA: As Your Majesty wishes.

(*They walk out of the temple when two old men, with long beards, in flowing silk gowns, approach them. Beside them are two elephants and several footmen carrying spears and guns.*)

OLD MAN: Greetings to Your Majesty.

TIPU: Greetings! Who are you? You seem to have come from a long distance.

OLD MAN: We are the envoys of the Emperor of China.

TIPU: Please enter and take a seat in the Diwan-i-Aam. What is the object of your visit?

OLD MAN: We wish nothing but the promotion of greater friendship. The Emperor of China sends you a white elephant and these horses as a token of his friendship and affection for you.

TIPU: The elephants and horses are indeed beautiful. I am deeply touched. I am also eager to know how you capture and train elephants in China. Besides, I know from Hadrat Nizami's book, *Sikandar-namah*, that the Emperor of China had sent a present of a white elephant, a horse, and a female slave to the Great Alexander.

OLD MAN: Yes indeed. The Emperor has never sent a white elephant to anyone except the Great Alexander and now to Your Presence.

(*Tipu addresses the audience while the others on stage are enveloped in darkness.*)

TIPU: In the meantime morning dawned and I rose. My interpretation of the dream is that God Almighty and our Prophet will make me another Alexander...

(*He moves to the Diwan-i-khas and holds a conference with Mir Sadiq and Poornaiya.*)

...and the many faiths in my Kingdom will depend upon me for protection and succour.

POORNAIYA: As indeed they do.

TIPU: Have another kebab, Mir Sadiq.

MIR SADIQ: No, thank you, Your Majesty. The kebabs are delicious, which I have already proved by my enormous appetite.

TIPU: Poornaiya, another apple?

POORNAIYA: Your Majesty is most generous. But I must decline.

TIPU: From Kashmir, as you know. A rare delicacy in south India. You shouldn't refuse—

POORNAIYA: Its texture is so exquisite and the colouring so delicate that it is a supreme pleasure just to look at it.

TIPU: Like a woman's...

(*Pause.*)

...cheeks?

(*Laughter.*)

So where were we? Ah, yes! To the list drawn up for our delegation, add silkworms and eggs from the island of Jezeriah Diraz near Muscat—

MIR SADIQ: But the ones we got from China are doing very well, sir. Do we need—

TIPU: Of course we need others. These may be better. I'm told they are better suited to our climatic conditions. Five or six men who know the proper mode of rearing the worms will need to be brought along with them. All right, what next?

MIR SADIQ: The letter from Raja Ramchander.

TIPU: Oh, that one! He is an ass.

MIR SADIQ: Your Majesty, I think he has a point. He says the idea of shops and warehouses owned by the Government is scaring the traders off. They are actually moving to customers who are poorer—

TIPU (*impatient*): Oh, will none of you ever learn? If profits are only seven pagodas while the expenses on clerks and accountants come to ten, how can anyone survive in business? How long will these traders be able to carry their bullion to other places? Don't you worry! They'll come back to us—crawling.

POORNAIYA: What the Honourable Mir Sadiq means, I think, is that it's not the economics that scares the traders. It's the idea of dealing with the Government, particularly the idea of the Government turning into a trading agency.

TIPU (*exploding*): Then they'd better like it. And both of you too! We need glass. We need guns. We need cannons. Shall we keep buying them from abroad? Even for that we need money. And shall we be content with the pittance we get by taxing our businessmen when we have ivory and sandalwood freely available? Can an individual trader deal in sandalwood? For centuries we begged and borrowed silk from the Chinese. And everyone predicted disaster when I got a few eggs from China. And now we have a flourishing industry of our own. Shall we sit back like the stupid Nizam and the Marathas who continue as though the English never existed—indeed, as though the Europeans never existed? Any other mail?

MIR SADIQ: None of importance.

TIPU: Good. Have the Honourable Ghulam Ali Khan and others arrived?

MIR SADIQ: They wait in the audience chamber.

TIPU: That's the Noble Ghulam Ali for you. Always on time—like a European. Send them in. And where are my sons?

MIR SADIQ: Their Persian teacher must be here.

TIPU: Would you please send for them? The teacher can wait. I want my sons to be present when I talk to the delegation. It's time they started learning about the world.

(Mir Sadiq signals to a servant who departs to fetch the children. Ghulam Ali Khan and Osman Khan enter.)

OSMAN KHAN: May the Lord protect Your Majesty.

TIPU: Welcome, welcome, Honourable Osman Khan, Ghulam Ali Khan. I hope your families are well.

GHULAM ALI KHAN: God's mercy and your diligence look after them.

(Fath Haidar, aged around ten, Muizuddin and Abdul Khaliq, just short of six, enter and bow to those present.)

TIPU: Ah, Fath Haidar, Muizuddin, Abdul Khaliq! Come and sit down and listen carefully. Pay attention to everything. You know these noblemen.

PRINCES: Yes, Father. We bow to you, Uncles.

OSMAN KHAN: May God's grace be on you.

TIPU: Let me come to the point without further ado. We wish to send a delegation to France. You know Monsieur Pierre Monneron, from Pondicherry. Through his good offices we have arranged with the French Governor General of Mauritius for a visit by a royal delegation of Mysore to France. The Governor General has agreed to talk to the King of France and arrange an audience. Gentlemen, I want you to go on that delegation. Honourable Osman Khan, you'll lead it.

OSMAN KHAN: This is indeed an honour—

GHULAM ALI KHAN: We shall be the envy of the world.

TIPU: Actually, how I wish I could go with you. I envy you!

OSMAN KHAN: Your Majesty would certainly have proved a better leader of the delegation than I and the King of France would have been happier to deal with a quicker intelligence.

TIPU: Go on, go on. Make fun of me. What else am I here for? But they say in the sea off Mauritius, you can actually see the seven colours of the rainbow. Then Paris, Versailles! You are going on a fairy-tale voyage. I envy you. But unlike you, I am not a free man.

(*Laughter. Roar of tigers is heard in the background.*)

TIPU: Why are the tigers restless? Have they been fed?

SERVANT: Yes, Your Majesty. It's that Bahadur Khan—he's noisy.

TIPU: He is growing up. He needs more food than the others. Tell that to the zoo-keeper.

SERVANT: Yes, Your Majesty.

(*The children suppress their laughter.*)

TIPU: What's funny?

(*The children fall suddenly silent.*)

What's so funny?

FATH: The tigers become restless this time every day. And every day you give the same instruction.

(*Laughter. Tipu playfully growls at his children. Then turns to the delegation.*)

Your main objective is to explain to the King of France the situation in India. Particularly the state of the French here.

OSMAN KHAN: Yes, Your Majesty.

TIPU: I'll give you a letter for King Louis the XVI. But a letter is no substitute for direct persuasion. You must convince the King that if the French don't wake up, the English will gobble up the whole of India. The French here have become listless. The King must prod them, kick them if necessary into activity. Louis and I could sign a Treaty of Perpetual Alliance. Then if ten thousand French soldiers could march under me—under me, make that clear, no separate treaties with the British or the other Indian princes, I give the orders—if the King could give me that little, we could change the face of India. Do you understand?

GHULAM ALI KHAN: We do, Your Majesty.

TIPU: When you return, bring with you, not just the ten thousand soldiers, but French craftsmen who could make guns, cannons, pistols.

OSMAN KHAN: Yes, Your Majesty.

TIPU: You know that the delegation we sent to Istanbul last year to His Holiness the Caliph of All Islamic Nations proved a sensational success. Turkey, Arabia, Iran—they are all clamouring for our products.

MIR SADIQ: The Imam of Muscat has fallen in love with the sandalwood and spices of our land and permitted us to build a factory for our products there.

TIPU: So that's what you've got to look for—opportunities for business! It'll benefit them and of course us. Soldiers, yes, but trade, industry, money. I've made a provisional list of professionals we'll need. Poornaiya, read out the list so they can think about it.

POORNAIYA: A doctor, a surgeon, a smelter, a carpenter, a weaver, a blacksmith, a locksmith, a cutter...

MUIZ: And a watch-maker, Father.

TIPU: It's there, son. It's there.

POORNAIYA: A dyer. A watch-maker.

FATH: And a gardener, Father?

TIPU (*delighted*): You see, I have geniuses for sons. And they know what I've in mind. Do you think I would have forgotten a gardener?

POORNAIYA: I have not included a gardener, Your Majesty. We have many of our own.

TIPU: No, no, no. We must have someone from there. We need new ideas. Two gardeners. From the garden of Versailles. They'll work in our Lal Bagh.

FATH: They should bring new varieties of trees, flowers and bushes.

OSMAN: We shall endeavour to bring every item of interest we come across, Your Highness.

TIPU: You must, you must indeed. That's what makes Europe so wonderful—it's full of new ideas—inventions—all kinds of machines—bursting with energy. Why don't we in our country think like them? I've just read about something called a ther-mo-meter. You must bring me one.

GHULAM ALI KHAN: I beg your pardon, sir?

TIPU: Ther-mo-meter! It is quicksilver in a glass tube. When placed in the hands of a sick man, the quicksilver rises to a certain number of degrees and indicates the height of his disorder. That helps the *hakim* decide on the treatment.

POORNAIYA: Pardon me, sir. But can such a thing be possible?

TIPU: Ah! Poornaiya, the sceptic! He believes his ancestors knew everything that could possibly be known and that there's nothing new left to discover.

POORNAIYA: I look forward to seeing this wonderful instrument, Your Majesty.

TIPU: Which means, my dear princes, that he doesn't believe my word. Well, I'm told there's a whole book on that subject. We should get it translated into Persian.

MIR SADIQ: It'll be done the moment I receive a copy.

TIPU: But no self-indulgence. No slacking. This is not a picnic. Please bear that in mind. I'm told the city of Paris enchants people like a woman, and they forget themselves in its embrace. Whenever you feel lazy or despondent, think of the John Company—how they came to this country, poor, cringing, and what they have become in a mere fifty years. They threaten us today. It's all because of their passion for trade.

OSMAN KHAN: We shall do our best, Your Majesty.

TIPU: Good then. Start preparing for your journey. The Chief Astrologer of Chennapatna has chosen four days within the next three months on which the stars are propitious. We've sent the dates to Pondicherry and the French will let us know on which of those days a ship of theirs is scheduled to sail for Mauritius.

GHULAM ALI KHAN: This is like a dream come true, Your Majesty.

OSMAN KHAN: We can barely wait for that day.

TIPU: Be with your families till then. Be affectionate to your children, loving to your wives. You'll not see them for a couple of years.

(*Laughter.*)

May God be with you.

OSMAN KHAN: With your permission, Your Majesty.

(*The delegation withdraws.*)

TIPU: So what do you think of that, Sons?

FATH: What a marvellous idea, Father! We'll stun the world! Father—

TIPU: Yes?

FATH: Can't I join the delegation?

TIPU: And what about your studies here?

FATH: I'll learn on the way. Uncles will teach me. Besides you always say grandfather couldn't even read and write and yet—

TIPU: And was therefore foul-mouthed. You have to prepare for a different world. Go now. Your teacher must be waiting.

MUIZ: How long will it take the French troops to come, Father? Can I march with them into battle?

TIPU: Let's hope they don't take that long.
(*Laughter.*)

Off you go!
(*The children bow and go out.*)

POORNAIYA: If they come at all, Your Majesty. Forgive me for saying so but the English and the French have signed a treaty in Versailles, by which neither is allowed to enter into the local affairs in India.

TIPU (*thoughtful*): You may be right. But I keep hoping. After all, the French and the English are neighbours—they can't be friends for ever. They are bound to start quarrelling. We can't live from moment to moment, without a plan of action, Poornaiya, although the Nizam has proved that even that can be done.

MIR SADIQ: But the recent reports from Madras suggest that the English may be in a friendlier mood now.

TIPU: They have puppets in Madras. We need to keep our ears tuned to Calcutta. That's the Capital, after all.

POORNAIYA: The new Governor General, one gathers, has been

specially instructed by the Board of Control not to get into trouble with us.

TIPU: Ah! Pitt's India Act! The 'Leave-India-alone' Act! Do you believe a word of it? Do you think if the English wanted peace they would have appointed Lord Cornwallis as the Governor General?

POORNAIYA: We're told he is a wise, upright man—

TIPU: And a defeated General! Poornaiya, you are a Brahmin. You ride a horse and lead a battalion, but you think like a pedant. You do not understand a soldier. This man Cornwallis—he led the English armies in the Americas and he lost the war! To a farmer called Washington! And his Government sends him to India—

POORNAIYA: Let's pray that he understands Peace, Your Majesty.

TIPU: He understands nothing but the ignominy of defeat, of surrender. Can't you imagine the whispers, the sly smiles, the nudges that must have greeted the Lord in London? Even if no slights were intended, he would have imagined them. He must, if he is a soldier! Can't you see him tossing and turning in bed, thinking only of refurbishing his honour? And he knows—and I know—that to get the stain off his reputation he needs to vanquish one man in India—only one—Tipu Sultan!

(*Pause.*)

His appointment is as sure a pointer as the conjuction of Saturn and Mars in the third sector of Aries. We'll soon have the shadow of the English falling across our doorstep.

(*The stage darkens. Tipu turns to the audience.*)

TIPU: On the sixth day of the Khusrawi month in the year of Busd, as I was preparing for a night attack on the Maratha armies of Hari Pant Phadke at Shahnur near Devgiri, I had a dream.

(*A young man, turbaned like a Maratha, enters.*)

A handsome young man, fair-skinned and light-eyed, approached me and I said: 'Who are you, young man? Why don't you speak?'

YOUNG MAN (*female voice*): You are very handsome, Your Majesty.

TIPU: Thank you. Come. Come and sit by me.

YOUNG MAN: But I'm not telling you anything you don't already know.

TIPU: Well, it's always nice to be reminded. When one spends as much time on horseback as I do, there's no time to look into mirrors.

YOUNG MAN: But surely your *begums* tell you. Specially Ruqayya Banu, your favourite queen—

TIPU: Beware! You're being impertinent.

YOUNG MAN: It's my intense admiration for you that makes me so bold—

TIPU: Look, I'm not given to entering into such conversation with just anyone.

YOUNG MAN: But I'm not just anyone.

TIPU: Then who are you?

YOUNG MAN: Doesn't anything strike you as unusual about me?

TIPU: Oh! Several things. You're delicate looking. And you have a woman's voice.

(*The young man bows in front of Tipu.*)

YOUNG MAN: Will the Sarkar-e-Khudadad kindly take off my turban?

(*Tipu takes off the turban and a cascade of long hair comes tumbling down on the shoulders of the youth. He then stands with his back to the audience, facing Tipu.*)

YOUNG MAN: Will you unbutton my blouse, Your Majesty?
(*Pause.*)

You're blushing. You have gone red. I didn't realize Your Majesty is such a shy man. Let me do that for you, sir... Here!

(*Unbuttons the blouse. Tipu reacts.*)

TIPU: You are a woman! Why are you in this disguise?

YOUNG MAN: I didn't know whether you would admit a strange woman into your presence.

TIPU (*angry*): You've tricked me. You've inveigled the Padshah into giving you audience, into talking to you. Get out of here! Out!

(*The young visitor runs out. Tipu turns to the audience.*)

After consulting my closest advisers, I interpret this dream in the following fashion. May it please God, though these Marathas are dressed in male attire, they will in fact prove to be women.

(*The Maratha court in Pune. Nana Phadnavis, the Maratha statesman, with Charles Malet, representative of Lord Cornwallis.*)

MALET: Nana Sahib, Our Governor-General-in-Council, Lord Cornwallis, would like to reassure the Maratha court at Pune that we have no intention of entering into confrontation with any of the Indian princes. Our Board of Control in London has advised our Governor General explicitly to adopt a pacific and defensive system since we, the Honourable East India Company, are completely satisfied with the possessions we already have.

NANA: That's good news! But then tell me, Malet Sahib, why are you here?

MALET: We wish to assure the Maratha rulers that we are good friends who can be relied upon in moments of crisis.

NANA: Ah! That raises two questions. First, is there a crisis?

MALET: That's for our friends to decide for themselves. The Company recognizes, sir, your right to assess your own political situation. Article XVI of the Treaty of Versailles states—at the insistence of the English, I might add—that neither the French nor the English shall get involved in what we would consider differences of opinion between Indian princes.

NANA: Very kind of you. That leads us to the second question. Are we your friends?

MALET: Surely the great Nana Sahib is jesting. Need the question be asked?

NANA: Who *are* your friends?

MALET: Apart from your honourable court at Pune, sir, there's the Scindia, the other Maratha Chiefs, the Nizam of Hyderabad, the Nawabs of Carnatic and Oudh, the Rajahs of Travancore and Cochin.

NANA: A dreary lot. I can't stand Shinde or the Nizam and I mean to give them a good hiding soon. The others are beneath contempt.

MALET: In view of what I've already said we have nothing to say on that.

NANA: I see Tipu Sultan Khan Sahib of Mysore is conspicuously missing from your list.

MALET: As you know, Nana Sahib, we are having a little trouble with him.

NANA: I see. So signing a Treaty of Perpetual Peace with someone does not constitute a gesture of friendship for the English.

MALET: Oh, but it does. And I'm sorry if I gave the impression that it does not.

NANA: You signed a treaty of friendship with Tipu Sultan Khan Sahib not so long ago at Mangalore.

MALET: The Treaty of Mangalore was forced on us.

NANA (*warming up*): Treaties are always forced upon the losing side, Malet Saheb. I'm sorry, but your 'friends' are a bunch of nincompoops. Tipu is worth a hundred of the Nizam, who is nothing but a whining little limpet. I must accuse you English of duplicity—

MALET: Surely not, sir—

NANA: We Marathas too have signed a Treaty of Perpetual Peace with Tipu Sultan and we have more regard for our word than the English seem to have for theirs. I would prefer to deal with the *vakils* of Tipu Sultan who are waiting outside the door this minute. They at least do not take me for a brainless weather vane.

MALET: I urge you, sir, there's no cause for that feeling. The moment he arrived in India, Lord Cornwallis assured our Board of Control that we neither wish to indulge in a breach of the Treaty of Mangalore nor contravene the solemn injunction in Pitt's India Act—

NANA: Mis-sterr Malet, your mind swarms with documents. Please do not try to confuse me with conflicting quotations. I am a Brahmin. I am an expert at it.

MALET: May we then stick to facts, Your Honour?

NANA: That's better. Yes, the facts.

MALET: Of which there's only one that matters to us. Tipu has attacked the Rajah of Travancore, who as I said before, is one of our friends.

NANA: The Raja of Tiruvidankoor is a mischievous little rat who would have kept a respectful distance from Tipu Sultan had he not been certain that Cornwallis would support his antics.

MALET: We cannot watch while our friends are harassed.

NANA: Then you go ahead and fight Tipu Sultan. I have nothing against him.

MALET: Except for the vast Maratha territories which his father grabbed unjustly and which Tipu still retains.

(*Pause.*)

May we point out that when Tipu made his peace with the Marathas, he returned all his recent acquisitions but not his father's? While the bravery of the Marathas is known the world over, so, sir, is Tipu's. If the Marathas ever face Tipu alone, it's likely to be a stalemate again. If you'll permit a rash observation, sir, it's unlikely that you will subdue him enough to make him surrender those territories. I'm sorry but that's a fact which I'm sure the wise Nana Sahib will not deny.

NANA: Nor will Nana Sahib deny the infinite cunning of your stratagem. The world will see instantly that even the Marathas needed the help of the English?

MALET: Sir, Lord Cornwallis is aware that such a misapprehension may be created and is most anxious to prevent it. He therefore suggests that the Marathas, the Nizam and the Honourable Company declare war on Tipu independently of each other. There will be no open collaboration. We shall attack from three different directions—separately.

(*Pause.*)

The Marathas have been robbed. The Nizam has been robbed. The Rajah of Travancore has been attacked. To be honest, sir, we, the English, do not like his repeated attempts to join hands with the villainous French, though of course they are our friends after the recent treaty. The Governor General hopes that the Maratha Chief will use this opportunity to obtain reparation and recover the territories seized unjustly by Tipu Sultan's father, Haider Ali, and will join us in punishing a man who we believe is the enemy of all mankind.

(*Pause.*)

NANA (*thoughtful*): Uh hum!

(*The inner chamber of Tipu's palace. Tipu is sitting alone, next to Queen Ruqayya Banu's bed, watching, with an affectionate smile, the rumpus going on. Off-stage, we hear the almost life-like growls of a mechanical tiger and the equally life-like screams of a human doll. It all sounds real at the start. But soon peals of laughter from the children dispel any sense of real violence.*)

RUQAYYA BANU (*laughing off-stage*): What will they think of next!

MUIZ (*off-stage*): Shall I play it again?

RUQAYYA (*off-stage*): Enough now, Muizuddin. It's a dreadful toy.

MUIZ (*off-stage*): Just once, please.

TIPU: Let them. Why are you stopping them?

(*More growls and screams again along with the screams of relish from the princes. Ruqayya Banu enters and reclines on the bed. She is obviously not too well. Abdul Khaliq comes and sits, almost clinging to her. Muizuddin and Fath Haidar continue off-stage.*)

MUIZ: It's so real...terrifying!

FATH: I wish there was a little blood! That would have made it even more frightening.

RUQAYYA: Be quiet, Fath Haidar. Come here, both of you. The toy is violent enough as it is. I don't like it. Why do you bring such awful things for our children?

TIPU: At their age I had to deal with real blood and gore. You've brought them up to be too soft!

ABDUL KHALIQ: Mother, you've been laughing at it too.

TIPU: And how!

RUQAYYA: That's what I don't like. I wouldn't care to be present when a man is being mauled by a tiger. So why should I enjoy it when a toy tiger tears up a man? It's unnatural.

(*Fath Haidar and Muizuddin come in, excited.*)

FATH: But, Mother, the mechanism—it's so ingenious—so life-like—

TIPU: The French are just superb at that kind of thing.

FATH: Father, can't our craftsmen produce something like this?

TIPU: Actually I asked the toy-makers of Chennapatna before ordering it from the French. And do you know what they said? 'Oh sir, our ancient tradition is dedicated to things beautiful. Let the foreigners handle these cruel toys!'

(*Ruqayya Banu laughs along with Tipu.*)

Imagine their gall! I built that wretched village into a centre for glassware, musical instruments, and toys. And they give me a lecture on the morality of aesthetics.

RUQAYYA: Good for them. Truly, I wish there were more like them around you.

MUIZ: Father, that man being attacked by the tiger...he's an Englishman, isn't he?

TIPU: Yes, he is.

MUIZ: Is that because the French don't like the English?

TIPU: Yes, and I don't like them either.

RUQAYYA: And they don't like you.

TIPU: Fair enough. (*To the children*) But let me tell you, I've had two teachers in my life. My father, who taught me war, and the English, who taught me trade. They taught me that the era of the camel is over, that it is now the age of the sailing ship. And they dislike me for being so adept a pupil.

RUQAYYA: Why are they after you now?

TIPU: No idea. I actually asked the English Governor in Madras to send a delegation to Seringapatam so we could sort our differences out. But he declined. It would reduce them in the eyes of the other Indian princes!

RUQAYYA: You can hardly expect them to love a man who plays with a toy like that—

TIPU: The English have better reasons than that. I have refused to have their Resident at my court.

MUIZ: Can I play it again?

RUQAYYA: No, you can't. I want to lie down. I feel tired.

TIPU: Do, yes. Hasina, give her another pillow. Good. Fath Haidar, have the tiger removed to the Diwan-i-Aam, before your mother shoots it down.

FATH (*laughs*): Yes, Father.
(*Exits.*)

TIPU: Abdul Khaliq, can't you sit up like a prince? Your mother's trying to rest. You don't have to crawl into her bed every time—

RUQAYYA: Let him be. He's my baby.

TIPU: And he's remained one. Look at Muizuddin. He isn't cuddling up to you all the time. And he's younger.

RUQAYYA: Enough, please. You spend so little time with them. And then you are forever reprimanding them. Sit down, please. Relax. Be their father, not their Sarkar-e-Khudadad. Why do you drive yourself like this? Please, slow down a bit—

TIPU: This land is *ours* and it's rich, overflowing with goods the world hungers for, and we let foreigners come in and rob us of our wealth! Today the Indian princes are all comatose, wrapped in their opium dreams. But some day they'll wake up and throw out the Europeans. So the only way the Europeans can ensure their profits for all time to come is by becoming rulers themselves. You see? It's them or us. Now you rest. The hakims say you must take care of yourself and not get excited over trifles. There are enough people to look after palace chores...

RUQAYYA: They don't bother me. You know what worries me— You!

TIPU: I'll give the English and the Nizam a drubbing they'll remember till the end of time.

RUQAYYA: You're worried about the Marathas.

TIPU: Yes, I am. Only Mahadji Shinde understands the English. The Marathas of Pune are coy, flirtatious, unreliable. But I need their help, so I've made peace with them. So long as they keep out of this conflict—and I have returned the territories I had conquered from them—I've nothing to worry about.

HASINA (*enters*): May the Lord protect Your Majesty. The Honourable Mir Sadiq is here with our *vakils* from Pune.

TIPU (*aghast*): We talk of the Marathas and our *vakils* from Pune arrive! That doesn't portend well. May God's will be done. Take care of yourself, Ruqayya.

(*Exits.*)

MUIZ: I'm going with Father.

(*Exits.*)

HASINA: Madam, the whole palace is in turmoil—

RUQAYYA: What's it, Hasina?

HASINA: Our *vakils* have been driven out of Pune. The English have succeeded in their manipulation. The Marathas too have declared war on us.

ABDUL: Why, Mother—is it bad for *vakils* to come back?

RUQAYYA: Don't talk, child. I can barely breathe. May it please God it is not the disaster I fear it is.

(*Ruqayya gasps. Hasina anxiously calls out.*)

HASINA: Madam—Madam—

ABDUL: What's happened to Mother?

HASINA: Please wait here, Your Highness. I'll fetch the *hakim*. Please look after her.

(*Runs out. Kirmani and Mackenzie.*)

MACKENZIE: In 1790, Lord Cornwallis invaded Mysore. The Nizam and the Marathas launched parallel attacks. A see-saw war stretched over two years, with no end in sight. Cornwallis reached the foot of the fort of Seringapatam, saw the futility of trying to capture it and retreated disheartened. At one point in the campaign, he wrote to his friend, the Bishop of Lichfield:

CORNWALLIS (*entering*): My spirits are almost worn out and if I cannot soon overcome Tipu, I think the plagues and mortifications of this most difficult war will overcome me. (*Exits.*)

KIRMANI: But on their return journey, the English forces ran into the Marathas with their abundant supplies. The two joined forces and attacked Seringapatam. Tipu Sultan was forced to sue for peace.

Act Two

23 February 1792. The square in front of the big mosque in Seringapatam, packed with senior citizens, generals, and courtiers. A buzz of anxiety and suppressed excitement, which subsides when Poornaiya stands up to speak.

POORNAIYA: Noblemen of the court, the Sarkar-e-Ahmadi has asked me to offer you his most contrite apologies for keeping you waiting. But the senior *hakim* is here with his advisers attending to the Queen. The Sultan will be here with you as soon as the hakims finish their examination.

A NOBLEMAN: Honourable Poornaiya, may we know the state of the Queen's health?

POORNAIYA: The Sultan wishes me to tell you that even the *hakims* do not know what the ailment is. The Queen, as you know, has been ill for a while now and has a fever that refuses to come under control.

NOBLEMAN 2: Could it be that the perils facing our state have affected her?

POORNAIYA: Almost certainly. The Queen loves us all like her children. She is also concerned about the Sultan's health. He is under enormous pressure as you know.

MIR SADIQ (*announces*): His Majesty!

CROWD: God save the King! God grant the Queen a long life!

TIPU: *Inshallah!* (God willing.)

CROWD: *Inshallah!*

(*A long pause.*)

TIPU: I crave your pardon for this delay. You are all noblemen, officers, generals, pillars on whom this kingdom of God rests. You know why I have invited you all here. The enemies hold our city in a python's embrace. The Honourable Ghulam Ali Khan has just returned from France. He knows how to deal with foreigners. I therefore sent him to negotiate with the enemy. It proved to be a most propitious choice. We have three enemies—the English, the Marathas, and the Nizam. But only the English spoke. The other two nodded in respectful silence.

(*Reactions from the crowd.*)

The Honourable Ghulam Ali Khan has returned with the terms of peace. I want your advice on how I should proceed next. We are gathered in front of our chief mosque. I place this Quran Shareef in front of you. With the Holy Book as my witness, I ask you to speak what your heart feels. Honourable Poornaiya, will you please read out the terms dictated by Lord Cornwallis?

POORNAIYA: There are four conditions in the main. One: all English prisoners taken by His Majesty as well as his father of hallowed memory, Haidar Ali, to be released, unconditionally.

TIPU: Let's hear the Honourable Ghulam Ali Khan on that.

GHULAM: Discussions of this condition were accompanied by much vituperation by the English. They said that we had ill-treated our English prisoners of war. We pointed out that we had treated them as we treat our own prisoners—despite much provocation. And then we pointed out that the English who had surrendered to us were at least alive as prisoners of war while our men who surrendered to the enemy—where were they? What happened to them? There was no answer.

(*Angry muttering from the crowd.*)

TIPU: Go on, Honourable Poornaiya.

POORNAIYA: Two: cession of half our domain, adjacent to the territories of the English, the Marathas, and the Nizam.

(*Angry reaction from the crowd.*)

CITIZEN 1: Why should we accept these humiliating terms, Your Majesty? Let's go on with the war—

CITIZEN 2: We'll fight to the last man rather than—

(*Tipu silences them by raising his hand.*)

TIPU: Qilledar Nadeem Khan, you are in charge of our fort. What do you say?

NADEEM (*after a slight hesitation*): If it was a question of facing only the English, we could take the initiative instantly. We could scatter them now as we did a few months ago. But the Marathas are supporting them.

MIR SADIQ: And the Nizam's troops joined them a week ago.

TIPU: We are blocked by our own people. I wrote to the Nizam: 'The benefits of unity and harmony among the followers of Islam are known to you. How can we increase the splendour of our Faith? I shall do as you guide me.'

(*Pause.*)

But we have been snubbed by the lack of even an acknowledgement of our letter. What is the state of the army's morale, Honourable Qamaruddin?

QAMARUDDIN: For two years we have fought and fought well. The soldiers are now tired. For weeks, they've been sleeping on their feet. I do not know how long they can hold out.

TIPU: Do you agree with that, Qilledar Sahib?

NADEEM: Yes, Your Majesty.

TIPU: So we have no alternative but to sue for peace?

(*Pause.*)

God's will be done. Please, do not expend your energies on these matters. Territories come and go. We fight, we gain, we lose. Proceed.

POORNAIYA: An indemnity of six crores.

GHULAM: At this point the English asked us to produce our revenue receipts. Our Chief Peshkar produced them. The English said they doubted the figures...

(*Reaction from the crowd.*)

TIPU: Silence, please! Let the Noble Ghulam Ali Khan complete his report.

GHULAM: We pointed out that if their own allies, the Marathas or the Nizam, had been asked for similar accounts, no such accounts would be forthcoming.

(*Pause.*)

For they have no such system.

(*Laughter from the audience.*)

TIPU: The pity of it is that the representatives of the Nizam and the Marathas were sitting there—swallowing all these jibes without a murmur.

(*Pause.*)

Proceed, Poornaiya.

(*Silence.*)

Poornaiya...

(*Pause.*)

Please!

POORNAIYA (*overcome*): I cannot, Your Majesty. I beg to be excused...

TIPU: All right then. I'll read it out myself. Hand me the paper. (*Reads.*) The last condition: two hostages to be handed over to the English to be kept with them until the terms of the treaty are duly fulfilled.

(*Pause.*)

Two of my sons.

(*Uproar. Angry protests.*)

CITIZEN 1: This is outrageous—

CITIZEN 2: If our soldiers hear of this, they'll rise to a man and fall on the English.

CITIZEN 3: Please, please, Your Majesty, do not accept this humiliation. We would rather die—

CITIZEN 4: This is barbaric.

TIPU: Noblemen, please, silence! I beg of you. Honourable Ghulam Ali Khan, recount to our noblemen what Lord Cornwallis said.

GHULAM: The English Lord in all kindness assured us that having only one son himself, he experienced the affection of a parent in more than an ordinary degree; but even his own child could not be received by him with greater tenderness than ours.

(*Pause.*)

TIPU: Instead of demanding two particular sons, he would accept any two of our sons. Whom can I send? Fath Haidar? Yes, he is the eldest. Old enough to be sent. Though he is dear to me, I would send him. But the English are a very proper nation. They will not accept him, for his mother was not my legal consort.

(*Reaction.*)

So that leaves—Abdul Khaliq, who is eight and Muizuddin, only a few months younger.

(*Reactions of horror, anger, revulsion. Then slow silence.*)

The other children are still at their nurses' breasts. Should I send my two little boys as hostages?

(*Shouts of 'No', 'Please don't accept—'*)

Shall I then accept the destruction of our city?

(*Pause.*)

That's the choice before us.

(*Long silence.*)

This is the new language that has come into our land: English.

This is the culture of that language: English. Boys of seven and eight as hostages of war.

CITIZEN: How can the city wish to remain safe while the lives of our princes are in danger?

TIPU: Danger? Yes. But what danger? Did you not hear what Lord Cornwallis says? The English will not harm our children. They'll not poison them or kill them, for there's no financial profit in it. What will the John Company gain in gold and silver and land by harming my sons? They'll not harm my children.

(*Pause. He is overcome.*)

The danger is: they'll teach my children their language, English. The language in which it is possible to think of children as hostages. All I can try to do is agree to their conditions and conclude the treaty in a hurry—before my children have learnt to think in those terms.

(*Pause.*)

So we accept their demands. Honourable Mir Sadiq, bring the seal. We shall affix our signature. There! Now my dear noblemen, my...

(*His voice cracks. A long pause. To Mir Sadiq*)

Will you please thank the noblemen for coming here and tell them that the meeting is adjourned? Suddenly I seem to have lost my voice.

MIR SADIQ (*in tears*): His Majesty wishes the noblemen to retire—
(*The crowd departs, also in tears. When Mir Sadiq, Poornaiya, Nadeem Khan, Ghulam Ali Khan, and Qamaruddin get up to take leave, Tipu gestures to them to sit down. They sit. There is a very long silence.*)

POORNAIYA: Your Majesty, how will the Queen take the news in her present condition? Will her health be able to bear the shock?

TIPU: God has been angry with us, Poornaiya. But He has not let us down entirely. I was late for this meeting because—I had to bid goodbye to Begum Ruqayya Banu. She left us this morning.

POORNAIYA: God save us!

(*Exclamations of shock and distress from the others.*)

TIPU: I waited till she breathed her last. I am lucky. She died without knowing I had bartered her sons for my kingdom.

MIR SADIQ: But—Your Majesty—

TIPU: And I gave strict orders that there was to be no wailing or weeping till this meeting with the noblemen was over. I didn't want tears to blind the judgement of my advisers.

(*Wailing is heard in the background.*)

The dead are happy. They go. And I've seen too many dead to care about death anymore. It's my sons I have to worry about now. Poornaiya, send for the Chief Astrologer of the Chennapatna temple. Ask him to study the stars and set the most auspicious moment for the departure of my sons. Ghulam Ali Khan, will you accompany your nephews? I don't want my babies to feel their family abandoned them totally—although that's what it amounts to finally.

GHULAM ALI: I shall go with them, Your Majesty. I shall spend every moment with them until they are reunited with you.

TIPU (*getting excited*): Mir Sadiq, tell the British—tell them my sons must be received properly. With full honours. They are princes. There are to be no lapses. Not the smallest—(*Almost angry*) I shall not tolerate it.

MIR SADIQ: Of course, Your Majesty.

TIPU: And we'll send them out as heroes, symbols of the glory of their land. In full splendour. A splendour that'll put the foreigners to shame—and cover up my own sense of shame.

(*The inner chamber of the palace. Ghulam Ali Khan enters.*)

GHULAM ALI: Hasina—Hasina—

HASINA (*enters*): Sir—

GHULAM ALI: Hasina, call the princes Abdul Khaliq and Muizuddin here. Tell them I want to talk to them. Only them, mind you, no one else.

HASINA: Yes, sir.
(*Exits.*)

GHULAM (*murmuring to himself*): I pray to you, God, give me strength to face this moment. Make me strong.
(*Muizuddin, Abdul Khaliq, and Fath Haidar enter with Hasina.*)

CHILDREN (*in a subdued voice*): Our salutations, Uncle.

GHULAM: Oh, Fath Haidar! Er—

HASINA: Sir, what could I do? I said you only wanted to meet—

GHULAM: All right. All right. Leave us now.
(*Hasina withdraws. Pause.*)
Children, there are times when God tests us—to see how strong we are—whether we truly believe in His Will. This is such a time.

ABDUL KHALIQ (*embraces him*): I want to go to Mother—I want Mother—please—

GHULAM: Listen, princes. God has called your mother away. We must not cry about that. We must not question His Will. You have borne that test like princes. There's another test ahead of us now and I want you to face it equally bravely.

FATH: Yes, Uncle.
(*Ghulam Ali pointedly addresses his remarks to the two younger children which is difficult to do without snubbing Fath Haidar.*)

GHULAM: The English have suggested that the two of you visit them and stay with them—as guests. For how long we don't know, but it won't be for too long. Of course, I'll be there with you all the time.

FATH: I am ready, Uncle. And I don't need anyone with me. I'm old enough to go on my own.

(*Pause.*)

GHULAM: I'm sorry, Fath Haidar. The English want only...heirs to the throne.

FATH: Oh, I'm sorry. I'm sorry I offered myself.

GHULAM: No, no, no. Don't take it to heart, son. Your father loves you. We all love you. You, Muizuddin, Abdul Khaliq, you're all the same to us. But this is politics.

FATH: I understand, Uncle. I'm sorry I spoke out of turn.

GHULAM (*helpless*): I'm afraid it has to be Muizuddin and Abdul Khaliq. (*To them*) You see how Fath Haidar volunteered without hesitation? Are you willing to come with me, children?

MUIZ: I'm scared, Uncle. But I will go with you.

GHULAM: That's a good boy. And you, Abdul Khaliq?

(*No answer.*)

I'm sure you are ready too.

ABDUL (*tearful*): I don't want to go, Uncle...I'm frightened...

FATH: He's been listening to all kinds of stupid rumours.

GHULAM: There's nothing to be afraid of. And I'll be there.

ABDUL: I don't want to go.

GHULAM: Look...

ABDUL (*whimpering*): Please, don't make me—Please—

GHULAM: Now, now, Abdul. You are eight years old. A man already! You saw that Fath Haidar volunteered instantly. So did Muizuddin and he's younger than you.

ABDUL: I want Mother—

FATH (*viciously*): Cry-baby. Always a cry-baby!

GHULAM: Please, Fath Haidar, let's be calm...

ABDUL: I want Mother. She wouldn't have let me go—She wouldn't have sent me—

GHULAM: Abdul Khaliq, God has left us no choice. He has taken your mother to his bosom. And you have to go to the English for a few months only. Now, your father will be here any moment. He is already shattered—by everything, but more at the thought of losing you. You have to give him courage. Will you?

HASINA (*enters*): Sir, the Master is here.

GHULAM (*almost panic-stricken*): I told you God is testing us. The test doesn't begin when you face the English. They are our sworn enemies. I'm sure you'll know how to face them. The test is now! Let's see how you pass it.

(*Tipu enters, in a daze.*)

Greetings, Your Majesty.

(*Pause.*)

Your Majesty, I've talked to the princes. They await your orders.

(*Long silence. Tipu stands staring.*)

Your Majesty—

(*Silence. Gently,*)

Prince Muizuddin—

MUIZ: Father, I'm ready to go to the English.

(*Pause.*)

ABDUL: I am too, Father.

TIPU: Oh God!

(*Music. Cheering. Celebrations. A salute of guns. Diwan-i-Aam. Tipu with Kirmani, Poornaiya and Mir Sadiq.*)

TIPU: Then? Then what happened?

KIRMANI: The procession led by camel *harakāras* and standard bearers—followed by a hundred lancers with spears inlaid with silver—entered the English camp. Then came the princes on caparisoned elephants.

TIPU: How beautiful they looked, the two angels! In white muslin robes and pearls and turbans. Ruqayya Banu, you were too much of a queen to stay behind to witness my shame. Still I wish you were here. You would have been proud of them—as the whole city was.

KIRMANI: They were followed by the escort guard of the infantry and cavalry—

TIPU (*impatient*): I know. I know. Janaab Kirmani, I saw all that from the ramparts. Tell me what happened in the English camp.

KIRMANI: The English seemed stunned by our magnificence. The princes were received with a twenty-one-gun salute.

TIPU: Yes, yes, we heard that. That was good. That was proper—

KIRMANI: A battalion of Bengal Sepoys formed a guard of honour as the princes moved down the English lines. Arms were presented, drums were beaten.

TIPU: Excellent! Excellent!

KIRMANI: Lord Cornwallis and his officers received the princes at the entrance of his tent. He took each prince by hand and sat them down on the right and left of his chair—

TIPU: And my children—were they scared? Did they appear nervous?

KIRMANI: No, Your Majesty, not a whit.

TIPU: What about Abdul Khaliq? He was always a little unsure of himself.

KIRMANI: Your Majesty, the dignity of their bearing and their self-possession drew praise from every Englishman. Then the Honourable Ghulam Ali Khan said to Lord Cornwallis: 'These children were this morning the sons of the Sultan, my master. Their situation is now changed and they must look up to Your Lordship as their Father.'

TIPU: Oh God! God! Why didn't I die before I heard these words?

Ruqayya Banu, why didn't you take me with you? How did I come to this?

KIRMANI: Lord Cornwallis assured our Ambassador that the children would not feel the loss of a father's care—

TIPU: He must have known these words would reach me and pull out my entrails—

KIRMANI: —and that his protection was fully extended to them. The princes smiled at that. There was applause. The princes presented Lord Cornwallis with the Persian sword. He inspected it and praised its craftsmanship. And then he gave each prince a gold watch.

TIPU: And what did my children do with the watches?

KIRMANI: They hardly looked at them. They passed them on to the attendants with barely a glance.

TIPU: That's it! That's it! They're well brought up, my sons.

KIRMANI: Then the *attar* of roses and betel leaves were distributed and the princes returned to their tents of fine chintz. And Your Majesty must listen to this. As soon as they were inside the tent—

(*Laughs.*)

TIPU: Yes? Why do you laugh?

KIRMANI: As soon as they were inside the tent, the princes asked for the watches and started busily examining their mechanisms.

(*General laughter.*)

TIPU: They're my sons, after all! My darling princes! Nadeem Khan, fire a salute to the English from the fort tomorrow morning. Let them know we appreciate the way they have received my sons. And Poornaiya, send the English a crore and a half as the first instalment of our payment.

POORNAIYA: Yes, Your Majesty.

TIPU: And Mir Sadiq, send word to the Marathas. I want to visit their camp and see their Commander-in-Chief, Hari Pant Phadke, before they depart.

MIR SADIQ: Is that wise, Your Majesty?

TIPU: Please do as I say. Now goodbye, gentlemen. Thank you. I must retire.

ALL: May God protect the Sultan.

(*They withdraw. Tipu moves to his bed chamber. Sees the mattress spread out on the bed.*)

TIPU: Chamberlain—

CHAMBERLAIN: Your Majesty—

TIPU: Remove the bed from my bed chamber. While my sons are in foreign hands, I shall sleep on the bare stone floor.

(*Tipu undresses, sits on the stone floor. He takes out a string of beads and starts reciting a Sufi Zikr—incantation—to himself. He begins to sway as in a trance. He sways more and more violently as the lights darken. A voice calls out to him softly in the dark.*)

VOICE: Tipu—Tipu—

TIPU: Who's that? Is that you, Father?

HAIDAR: Yes, it's me. Haidar.

(*Lights come on slowly to reveal a spectral landscape. Tipu looks around frantically.*)

TIPU: Where are you, Father?

HAIDAR: Here, under this tree.

TIPU: Under this—? Father, why are you lying there? What's happened to you?

HAIDAR: I'm maimed, Tipu. I have no limbs.

TIPU: But you never lost any limb.

HAIDAR: You have maimed me, Tipu. You have cut off my limbs and handed them over to the enemy.

TIPU (*low*): Yes, Father. I've done that. Have you come to punish me?

HAIDAR: What punishment would be adequate, do you think?

TIPU: I don't know, Father. You remember, once I messed up your campaign and you gave me a lashing, almost skinned me alive. My body still bears those welts—such scars that I'm ashamed to undress in front of anyone. This crime is much worse than that.

HAIDAR: I can't do that now. I have no arms.

TIPU: Shall I lash myself for you?

(*He starts whipping himself.*)

HAIDAR: No melodrama, I pray you. No hysterics. Please. You've gone soft. You spend too much time with your account books.

TIPU: You spent your life on horseback—making conquests. I have to consolidate your gains. That can't be done on horseback. The English are stronger now.

HAIDAR: And whose fault is it?

TIPU: I hate them—and they return the compliment.

HAIDAR: Then why did you let Cornwallis escape? (*No answer.*) When he was retreating from Seringapatam in shame and desperation, your Amirs and Khans begged you to attack. You stood on the ramparts and did nothing.

TIPU: I was paralysed.

HAIDAR: You let Cornwallis go.

TIPU: You would have made mincemeat of him, I know. But I vacillated.

HAIDAR: You're scared of them.

TIPU: No, I'm not. If I were scared, I would have ordered a slaughter. But, Father, often, suddenly, I see myself in them— I see these white skins swarming all over the land and I wonder what makes them so relentless? Desperate? Most of them are no older than Fath Haidar. What drives these young lads to such distant lands through fever, dysentery, alcohol so—often to death—wave after wave? They don't give up. Nor would I. Sometimes I feel more confident of them than my own people. What makes them so unsparing towards themselves? Is it only money?

HAIDAR: You're beginning to think like a trader.

TIPU (*angry*): No, if it was only for money, they would betray each other. But there's never any treachery against their own kind, no back-stabbing. They believe in the destiny of their race. Why can't we?

(*Pause.*)

When our fort was besieged by Cornwallis, I knew several of my officers had already started secret negotiations with him. I even knew who they were. My trusted officers. Yet I couldn't expose them without bringing the whole edifice down. I had to keep saying they were the true pillars of my kingdom, that I depended on their loyalty to me and my family—and hope for the best. Hope that when the moment came, they wouldn't stab me in the back. But the English fight for something called England. What is it? It's not a religion that sustains them, nor a land that feeds them. They wouldn't be here if it did. It's just a dream, for which they are willing to kill and die. Children of England! They have conquered our land, plundered its riches. And now they've started taking away our children. Mine—

(*Haidar laughs.*)

I will not let them. Father, I'll restore your limbs. Father, where are you? Father—Father—Come back—

(*Darkness swallows them up. When lights come on we are in the Maratha camp. Hari Pant Phadke is waiting for Tipu Sultan.*)

HARI PANT: Welcome, Tipu Sultan Khan Saheb. Welcome to the Maratha camp. This is a most pleasant surprise—

TIPU: It's a custom in our land to bid goodbye to guests personally before they leave.

HARI PANT: Even when the guest was unwelcome?

TIPU: I did not make you unwelcome. We met last seven years ago and we parted as friends. We swore there would be everlasting peace between us. I still do not know what changed the situation. But I mustn't be impolite to my guest. I hope your family is well.

HARI PANT: Yes, thank you. And yours?

(*An embarrassed pause as Hari Pant realizes his faux pas.*)

I want to assure you, Khan Sahib, that we Marathas were not party to that deal—about taking your children hostage. We are extremely disturbed by it.

TIPU: You were 'not party'. What does that mean, Hari Pant? You disagreed with it?

HARI PANT: Yes, we did.

TIPU: And you were overruled?

HARI PANT: The Nizam stood by the English. We Marathas were outvoted.

TIPU: Hari Pant, the English were fleeing in despair—I had driven them back—when you came to their aid at Melukote. Without your enormous bazaar of supplies, half their army would have been wiped out, and the other half stumbling towards Madras by now. You are the true victors of this war. Yet you let the English dictate the terms!

HARI PANT: The English are our allies. After all, you have the French working for you. You have sought French friendship.

TIPU: Friendship, yes! Working for me! Not dictating to me. You have seen the new demands made by the English? I've just received them.

HARI PANT (*evasive*): I've had no occasion to doubt the integrity of the English. Cornwallis deals firmly but fairly.

TIPU: I am to cede half my kingdom adjacent to your territories—

HARI PANT: I know that. That was part of the initial agreement between us.

TIPU: And you know what part of my lands they are demanding? The province of Kodagu.

(*Pause.*)

You're silent. To which possession of the English is Kodagu adjacent? Will you tell Cornwallis that this wasn't the geography you had in mind when you discussed the terms of the treaty? You won't. For this is a convenient geography of his own invention, and you go along.

HARI PANT: Cornwallis has been honest with us. That's what counts. We have a third share of our joint conquests—

TIPU (*hoots with laughter*): You have what? Hari Pant, how can you say that without blushing? The share that you've been given is what my father had won from you Marathas forty years ago. What you've got is only a restitution of your earlier possessions. And in return you have given the English new territories: Salem, Dindigul, the Malabar coast with its coconuts and pepper and its magnificent ports. You are back where you were while the English now have the entire coastline of India. And remember, they are a sea-faring power. Mine is a landlocked kingdom, so I thirst for the sea, for today the sea is the key to power, to prosperity. You have the whole of the western coast. And instead of keeping the English out, you've permitted the shark into your waters and are trying to swim along with it.

HARI PANT: We only want what's ours—

TIPU: And how long will it remain yours? Where's the Raja of Tiruvidankoor in whose honour the English mounted this campaign? Thrown on the dung heap.

HARI PANT (*lamely*): He is no concern of ours.

TIPU: I would have torn this treaty and flung it in your faces and died in the breach sooner than consent to the cession of Kodagu. But they have my children! My sons! I asked for time to consider these preposterous terms and you know what their response has been? Instead of returning my children and continuing the battle, they have taken away their Mysore escort— and imprisoned my sons! Made them prisoners of war! How does that strike you, brave leader of the Marathas? Prisoners of war, aged seven and eight! So I'll capitulate—I'll give them what they want. Goodbye, Hari Pant. You are a wise man. And I hope you have given thought to why, when the English could have decimated me, they have left me with my kingdom.

HARI PANT: Khan Saheb, we insisted that your status was not to be touched—

TIPU: Rubbish. Cornwallis has saved me because without me in south India, you Marathas would become too powerful. You are being carefully contained. No, don't reply. And please don't come out of the tent to see me off. I shall find my way. This is still my land. Only one word of caution, Hari Pant. Make sure it's not your children next time.

(*Walks out.*)

(*Mackenzie and Kirmani.*)

MACKENZIE: The defeat of Tipu was a personal triumph for Lord Cornwallis. The stigma of York Town was washed off. The Crown conferred on him the title of 'Marquis'. In a fit of absent-mindedness, the Parliament forgot all about Pitt's India Act.

KIRMANI: It was two years before Tipu's sons were restored to him. When they were reunited, the boys laid their heads on their father's feet and he, leaning forward, touched them on their necks. No words were spoken.

MACKENZIE: Lord Cornwallis was succeeded by Sir John Shore as the Governor General. Seven years of peace ensued. And then came Richard Wellesley, Second Earl of Mornington—an ambitious young man of thirty-eight.

(*1798. Calcutta. Richard Wellesley, Earl of Mornington, the Governor General of India, with his younger brother Arthur Wellesley, a junior colonel in the Indian army and Colonel William Kirkpatrick.*)

MORNINGTON: Before my departure for India, the Board of Control made it clear to me that the East India Company was not to acquire any more territory in India. The Prime Minister, Mr Pitt, was emphatic on that score.

KIRK: Yes, Your Lordship.

MORNINGTON: I've been on the Board myself for the last four years and have had time to reflect on what would be the best course of action for us to take.

KIRK: Yes, Your Lordship.

MORNINGTON: It seems to me self-evident that we have to liquidate Tipu.

(*Kirkpatrick looks up startled, then turns to gauge Arthur Wellesley's reaction. Arthur is impassive.*)

KIRK: But, Your Lordship, Sir John—

MORNINGTON: My saintly predecessor was an evangelical Christian. If you kicked him on his right buttock, he would probably turn his left. He didn't know how to take offence.

WELLESLEY (*laughs*): I gather he preferred Jortin's Sermons to official dispatches.

MORNINGTON: He should have taken offence when Tipu sent a delegation to Napoleon inviting him to invade India. This flirtation with our enemy should not have been tolerated.

KIRK: But now, after the Battle of Nile, that's surely not a cause for concern.

MORNINGTON: In fact, Tipu should have been got rid of after the last Mysore war by Cornwallis. But he didn't. And since then Tipu has grown in power and prestige, which is more than can be said of our dear effete allies. We must hold Cornwallis guilty of grave lapse of judgement and Sir John of deliberate connivance. It's my duty as the new Governor General of India to set things right.

KIRK: Do you think Tipu will want to create trouble, Your Lordship? Madras doesn't think so.

MORNINGTON: Tipu is building a trading empire on the European model and succeeding eminently. We have driven the French and Dutch out of India, contained the Portuguese. Is there any reason why we should tolerate an upstart native? The longer the peace, the stronger will Tipu become.

KIRK: But, Your Lordship, Madras is opposed to any move against Tipu—

MORNINGTON: Kirkpatrick, I will not allow a bunch of incompetent hacks, cowering in fear, to arrogate to themselves the power of governing the empire committed to my care. I'll not let them thwart me. Make that absolutely clear to Madras.

KIRK: Yes, Your Lordship.

MORNINGTON: Good. Now let's start at the beginning and ponder the opening move. Has Tipu had anything to do with the French recently?

(*Pause. Kirkpatrick doesn't know what to say.*)
No dealings with Pondicherry? Chandernagore?

WELLESLEY: What about Mauritius? More romantic, I'd say. Strategically located. The right scale.

MORNINGTON: Anything there?

KIRK: We have information that some forty Frenchmen from Mauritius came to Mysore last year in search of employment—

MORNINGTON: They did? Excellent. So Tipu sends a secret mission to the French Governor of Mauritius. What's his name?

KIRK (*Scottish pronunciation*): Malarctic, sir.

MORNINGTON: Quite! (*French pronunciation.*) Malarctic—asking for a dispatch of ten thousand French and twenty thousand African troops. And Malarctic puts up a proclamation asking for volunteers—

KIRK (*guarded*): Not if the mission were secret, surely?
(*Wellesley smiles.*)

MORNINGTON: No need for subtlety. Let's take the shortest route.

One of our newspapers in Calcutta gets hold of a copy and publishes it—

KIRK: I shall contact a local editor, Your Lordship—

WELLESLEY: Is that necessary? I'm sure the Board of Control will accept Richard's word for it.

(*Kirkpatrick is suitably snubbed.*)

MORNINGTON: Of course, we shan't believe the report initially. We want Tipu's friendship. It gives us time to prepare.

KIRK: But won't Tipu deny such an allegation, Your Lordship?

(*Long silence.*)

I'm sorry, but protocol would seem to demand we give him an opportunity to recant or make amends or at least explain himself.

MORNINGTON: Tipu has had peaceful relations with us for the last seven years, which means he will not expect us to declare war. He is not in a state of preparedness. In fact, he's quite likely to be absorbed in silkworms and sandalwood forests. Shall we then give him adequate warning, William, and face a long-drawn-out, costly war?

WELLESLEY: We know the speed with which he can mobilize.

KIRK (*cowed*): I understand.

MORNINGTON: I shall of course write to Tipu seeking an explanation. But General Harris will despatch the letter only after he and General Stuart have entered the Mysore territory. Tell the Nizam and the Marathas we shall expect their presence, though it scarcely matters either way. As for our Governor in Madras, he gets confused by long messages. So keep our instructions to him brief: Tipu must go.

KIRK: Yes, Your Lordship.

(*Pause.*)

Would that be all?

MORNINGTON: Yes, thank you.

(*Kirkpatrick leaves.*)

WELLESLEY: I'm rearing to leave for Seringapatam.

MORNINGTON: You should indeed.

(*Pause.*)

Baird is keen to lead the assault against Tipu. He has been a prisoner of Tipu's and is eager to avenge himself.

WELLESLEY: I know.

MORNINGTON: I told him it wasn't done to take things so personally. But well, you know Baird. The Scotch temper. And then, perhaps it's just as well. He'll lead the assault. You will command the reserve—

WELLESLEY (*jumping up*): Oh, no, Richard, for goodness' sake. Not the reserve.

MORNINGTON: I know you are keen to prove yourself on the battlefield, but I don't need soldiers at the moment. I have an entire army at my command to throw against Tipu. I want you alive...to take command of Seringapatam after the battle.

WELLESLEY (*horrified*): You can't be serious.

MORNINGTON: You know I'm never not serious. I shall need someone there whom I can trust.

WELLESLEY: But, Richard, the Governor General of India appointing his own brother—

MORNINGTON: And a junior colonel at that! Quite right! Nothing's more reprehensible than nepotism that's half-hearted.

WELLESLEY: Listen, I'd rather—

MORNINGTON: I know what you'd rather. Look, Cornwallis still lumbers across our landscape, a senile rhinoceros, all decked up in finery. This man, who lost us our American colonies, can still 'lumber' because he defeated Tipu!

(*Pause.*)

I shall destroy Tipu. I shall decimate Seringapatam, within six months. If that's not merit, I don't know what public service is. Surely, it would entitle me to the same rank as Cornwallis. Arthur, the eyes of the world will be focussed on Seringapatam and I want my brother there—at the centre. The Commandant of the Fortress! After that, it's up to you.

WELLESLEY (*lamely*): But, Richard, the scandal—

MORNINGTON: Would you rather...crawl up?

(*Diwan-i-Aam. Tipu with Mir Sadiq, Poornaiya, Qamaruddin and Nadeem Khan.*)

TIPU: And now they have asked for four of my sons as hostages. And half my kingdom again—half of the half they left me last time.

(*Pause.*)

By the time the next Governor General takes over, I'll be left with half a street and none of my sons.

(*Pause.*)

Shall I accept?

(*Pause.*)

And don't say, Poornaiya, that you had warned me. I knew the English wouldn't like my extending my hand to the French. So what? Shall I spend the rest of my life looking with anxiety at the English for smiles of approval or frowns of displeasure? Today I am the only one in India who won't bow and scrape before them. So they want to crush me. I'm told England is buzzing with stories of what a monster I am and how I need to be chastised.

(*Pause.*)

Shall I allow myself to be chastised?

(*Pause.*)

The English make impossible conditions. They expect me to reject them. I could throw their whole strategy into confusion by accepting these terms. Shall I be subtle and accept?

MIR SADIQ: No, Your Majesty, we'll fight the English to the bitter end.

POORNAIYA: When your father picked me up, I was a mere clerk in a small god-forsaken town. I am what I am today because of the kindness of your family. No, Your Majesty, we will not yield. We'll fight the English to the last drop of our blood.

TIPU: What do you say, Nadeem Khan?

NADEEM: They have tricked us by declaring war at the last minute. But Seringapatam is impregnable. While I am in charge of the fort, Your Majesty may rest assured the English have no hope of winning.

TIPU: Thank you. Thank you all. That's what I wanted to hear. That's why I haven't called a general meeting like I did last time. I only wanted to know what you all felt. You know I am entirely dependent on your loyalty to me and my family.

MIR SADIQ: Who do we have but you, Sarkar?

TIPU: Your word is enough for me. If you will all stand behind me as one—

QAMARUDDIN AND POORNAIYA: We will, sir, we will.

TIPU (*laughing*): Then the future is ours.

VOICES: *Inshallah!* (God willing.)

POORNAIYA: Your Majesty, the Seer of the Monastery at Sringeri has conveyed his support to you.

TIPU: We are indeed fortunate.

POORNAIYA: Remembering that you gave them shelter when the Marathas sacked the monastery, the Swami has assured you of Goddess Sharada's blessings.

TIPU: We are protected by such blessings.

(*Long silence. No one knows what to say. To a servant*)
Incidentally, why is Bahadur Khan quiet today? Is he all right?

SERVANT: Yes, Sarkar. And resting.

TIPU (*fidgety*): Not even a growl?

(*Gets up.*)

Well then. Let's get ready. The meeting is adjourned.

(*They exit. The stage darkens.*)

KIRMANI: The English surrounded the fort of Seringapatam. On 4th May 1799, dawn broke on its ramparts.

(*Tipu's bedroom. Knocking on the door. Tipu enters tying his sword belt.*)

TIPU: Who is it?

FATH (*from outside*): Good morning, Father, it's me, Fath Haidar. Are you ready?

(*Tipu opens the door and lets his son in.*)

TIPU (*laughs*): Well, you are in a hurry, aren't you?

FATH: Of course I am. Qamaruddin, the Commander-in-Chief has sent word that our forces are assembled and rearing to attack.

TIPU: Good. Good! You know, Fath Haidar, I was a year younger than you when I first rode into battle with my father?

FATH: I was ready a long time ago.

TIPU: I know, I know, it's hard to accept that one's children grow up. You'll see for yourself.

POORNAIYA (*entering*): May God bring victory to Your Majesty.

TIPU: Good morning, Poornaiya. What news?

POORNAIYA: I have just been to see the Chief Astrologer of the Ranganatha Temple—

TIPU: And?

POORNAIYA: He says the stars have never been more propitious. Victory will be ours. The nine planets have been placated and offerings made to the guardians of the eight directions.

TIPU: Thank you, friend. One must pacify the stars. But when you and Mir Sadiq are around, I have little to fear. We must first check on our new French cannons.

POORNAIYA: I just ran into the officer in charge of the battery. He says the cannons are accurate and have an extraordinary range. We'll blow the British attack to smithereens.

MIR SADIQ (*enters, excited*): Your Majesty, Your Majesty, incredible news. I'm so excited I don't know where to start. The heavens are smiling on us.

TIPU: The Lord be praised! What is it, Mir Sadiq?

MIR SADIQ: The Nizam has sent this despatch—I'll read it out—

TIPU: Just tell me in a few words. We have no time to waste.

MIR SADIQ: The Nizam says he has at last seen his folly in backing the English. He's seen through their game. If Your Majesty loses, the next target will be the Nizam.

TIPU: Of course, I've been trying to drum that into that moron for the last sixteen years. Still, it's good he's woken up—

MIR SADIQ: The Marathas too have decided to throw in their lot with us.

TIPU: You're sure I am not dreaming all this!

MIR SADIQ: Here's the Qilledar, Nadeem Khan. What news, Nadeem Khan?

NADEEM: News only of God's smile, Your Majesty. Hari Pant Phadke is here, awaiting your audience. Shall I admit him?

QAMARUDDIN (*entering*): Your Majesty—

TIPU (*angry*): Yes, Commander-in-Chief? But you should not be here. You should—

QAMARUDDIN: Sir, I've just seen with my eyes a sight even my grandchildren will narrate with pride!

TIPU: What is it? Get to the point!

QAMARUDDIN: The English are withdrawing. They're in total disarray. Total confusion rules the ranks of the foreigners. I saw English generals squabbling like women in the market—
(*Cheers from those present.*)

HUBBUB: Congratulations, sir. God be praised! We have done it.

FATH: Let's attack them, Father. Let's not allow the English to get away this time—

TIPU: You speak like your grandfather. He was always one for aggressive tactics.

FATH: So shall we fall on them?

TIPU: Not today. Today we celebrate. We pray and thank God. With the Marathas and the Nizam on our side, we can chase the English into the sea any day.

(*Laughter.*)

Thank you, all. Together we have driven the English back—

POORNAIYA: We did nothing, sir. It's the way Your Majesty led all of us. The vision of the future you gave us.

ABDUL KHALIQ (*entering*): Father, Mother says the rose bush sent to you by the King of Pegu has blossomed. She says you must come and see it.

TIPU: Muizuddin, Fath Haidar, Abdul Khaliq, call the entire zenana out. Invite them to the ramparts to see the white plague depart. Let's all watch a new era dawn. Then we'll go to the garden and see the Pegu roses bloom.

ALL: Long live the Sultan! Allah be praised! Victory to the Sultan!

(*Cheers. They all depart. Music builds up to a crescendo and suddenly stops. A long silence.*)

KIRMANI: That was Tipu's last dream.

That afternoon he was killed in battle.

Mir Sadiq's conduct of the war was so openly treacherous that his own troops lynched him. Nadeem Khan, the Qilledar, had ordered a pay parade for his troops at the very moment of British assault, thus taking them away from the battlefront. Poornaiya slipped with alacrity into the post of Prime Minister under the new regime. Qamaruddin was by his side. The battle of Seringapatam was lost before it had begun.

(*Roar of tigers in the background followed by gunfire and then silence.*)

MACKENZIE: The tigers of the palace were shot dead while the mechanical tiger was shipped off to London.

(*Richard Wellesley enters, followed by Arthur.*)

Richard Wellesley, Earl of Mornington, Governor General of the British possessions in the East Indies said in a letter to the Board of Directors of the Honourable East India company:

MORNINGTON: While the dreadful fate of the fallen ruler could not be contemplated without pain and regret, it should show the Indian princes the danger of inviting foreign invasion— against the British power.

MACKENZIE: Arthur Wellesley, the Commandant of Seringapatam, was launched on a spectacular career which culminated in his becoming the Duke of Wellington, the Conqueror of Napoleon, Prime Minister of England.

(*Richard congratulates Arthur. They exit entirely pleased with themselves.*)

Tipu Sultan's sons were moved out of Seringapatam and ended up in Calcutta, where they could be kept under surveillance.

(*Pause.*)

Within twenty years, the British had annexed the Maratha empire.

KIRMANI: It was not Tipu's dreams but his predictions that came true.

(*Pause.*)

Postscript. When India became independent in 1947, the families of maharajas who had bowed and scraped before the British masters were granted sumptuous privy purses by the Government of India while the descendants of Tipu Sultan were left to rot in the slums of Calcutta.

TWO MONOLOGUES
Flowers/Broken Images

Broken Images was first presented in Kannada as *Odakalu Bimba* by Theatre Ranga Shankara, Bangalore on Tuesday, 22 March 2005, with:

ARUNDHATI NAG   Manjula

Broken Images was first presented in English, as *A Heap of Broken Images* by Ranga Shankara on Friday, 25 March 2005, with:

ARUNDHATI RAJA	Manjula
Directed by	GIRISH KARNAD
Sets by	ARUN SAGAR
Lighting Design by	PRADEEP BELAWADI
Production Control by	JAGDISH MALNAD
Coordination by	GAYATHRI KRISHNA

Flowers was first presented in English at Theatre Ranga Shankara by Company Rage, Bombay on Sunday, 8 October 2006, with:

RAJIT KAPUR	The Priest
Directed by	ROYSTEN ABEL

Flowers

In a few moments from now, Scorpio will start creeping into the
water from the south-eastern corner of the temple tank. There is
a hollow there in the third step under the water, large enough to
hold an unhusked coconut. And I know that on this day of the
year at this precise moment—and I can tell the precise moment
because Scorpio is stretched out in the eastern sky in all his
magnificent glory with the lowest point of his curving tail just
about to take off from the horizon—at this precise moment his
reflection will enter the water at the exact point under which
the hollow lies. As though he were swimming out of that cavity.
And looking up at the constellation from this top step of the tank,
even with my back to the temple, I could tell you what star is
perched on the brass tip of its pinnacle. For I know every nook
and cranny in these grounds. I know where every star will be as
the skies revolve through the year.

This temple, this tank, these rough, grey boulders towering
over them, the flowering shrubs and trees, the birds that come and
go through the seasons—they are my world, a private universe
from which I have never for a moment wanted to step out.

I am the priest here. I have lived here all my life and discouraged
all friendly attentions from the world outside. And in the isolation
of this place, I spend most of my time with the *linga*—talking to
it, singing to it, even discussing recent political developments and

most of all, decorating it with flowers. The *linga* is not ornately carved like some in the neighbourhood. It is essentially a plain phallic stump with a smooth crown and a rough-hewn vulva for the base. Endless ablutions of milk and ghee and oil through the centuries have managed to give it a slippery surface. So making the flowers stay on it is not easy and I have often lost track of the hours devising new ways of covering it with flowers. 'The *linga* is my step-wife,' grumbles my wife.

But she is also proud of the fact that my obsession has brought me recognition. The Chieftain of this region, who lives in the fort up on that hill, is an energetic young man. He is deeply devout and is a great admirer of my floral efforts.

Every day, at sunset, the canon goes off on the ramparts, announcing that the Chieftain has set off from home for the temple. That gives me a full hour to get ready for the pooja. My wife attends to the basic ritual requirements such as jawsticks and camphor and the placement of wicks in different silver plates for the *aarati*. I have a dip in the tank, and in the wet *dhoti*, sit down in the sanctum surrounded by baskets of flowers. Everything else then recedes into hazy, scarcely-felt distance and for an hour there is only the *linga* and me. And a conversation conducted through flowers—*malligai*, *sevanti*, *chendu hoovu*, *sampigai* and *kanakambara*.

By the time the Chieftain arrives with his entourage I am ready. He has a keen eye for beauty, the young Chieftain. If I have managed to lay out the flowers in a particularly innovative pattern, he nods his head in appreciation, turns to his retinue which, needless to add, obediently spouts various standard phrases in agreement. The *pooja* over, he accepts a single flower as God's *prasada*, presses it to his eyes, sticks it behind his right ear and rides home. He is not given to saying much.

They leave. I hear the clatter of hoofs fading up the rocky road. Then I carefully pick the flowers from the *linga*, tie them in a bundle in my thin muslin shoulder-cloth and make my way to

Chandravati's house. Chandravati is a courtesan, the only breach in the invisible defences I have built around my private domain.

She came into my life during the Shivaratri celebrations, which go on for a week. During this period, the Chieftain comes down for the *pooja* in the morning and once he leaves, there are the usual throngs of devotees, milling at the door of the temple to offer coconuts to the *linga*. I crack every one of the coconuts myself and return the halves as *prasada*, with a petal or two and sandal paste in it. I have never used assistants for distributing them, although my wife keeps nagging me to employ one. It is an exhausting task, it prolongs the day and yet I insist on handling every coconut myself. I love doing it for the *linga*, but I am not unaware that people shake their heads in admiration at my passion for the Lord and physical stamina.

The inhabitants of the courtesans' quarters are the last to be admitted, so I knew she was one of them. I was too tired to look at faces and desperate to finish the day. I mechanically took the coconut she offered, broke it, placed the *prasada* inside and turned to hand it back. She was bending, holding the *pallu* of her sari spread out in front of her. The upper half of her bosom was uncovered and as I dropped the shells in her sari, I saw the mole. On her right breast, just near the cleft. I looked up at her. There must have been something unusual in my movement, for she looked up too and caught my eyes. For a moment we stared at each other and then she turned away.

I wanted her. I had never lusted for a woman before and so felt emasculated by this sudden weakness. Yet I could not control the fire raging in my loins. During the rest of that week, I started the day impatient for a glimpse of hers.

Courtesans are noticed and talked about. So I discovered without seeming too curious that her name was Chandravati. She had just moved into a nearby town. She was believed to be wealthy—I knew the house she had rented. It was one of the most spacious there. She is a courtesan, I kept saying to myself, she is a courtesan and so perhaps not beyond reach. But I was a poor priest and had nothing to offer her.

I soon learnt to search her out in the crowds and gulp in quick glimpses of her, feeling my insides cramp every time I caught sight of her. She was of average height. She was always in the company of a much older woman, who I was told lived with her. She was always laughing, her bright teeth set off by her dusky skin.

Every day there was a quick meeting of our eyes. But she never once stayed long enough for me to register her features. So each day, as she received the *prasada*, I noticed the mole and as she looked up, hurriedly made note of a fresh aspect of her face— the brilliant eyes which she quickly averted, the straight nose ending in a slight upward tilt, the lips which like thick petals rimmed her smile with dark sensuousness. Then at night I put them together as in a jig-saw puzzle.

She did not come on the sixth morning, nor on the seventh, and I was in agony. When the festivities on the last day were over and the temple precincts deserted, I went to the *linga* and pleaded, 'I am stupid. I am mad. I don't know why I am doing this. But help me, please. Or at least forgive me.' Then I cracked a coconut, tied the halves in my shoulder cloth and left for her house.

It was dark, but it took no effort to be at her door. I knocked. After a pause, the old woman opened the door. She recognized me, and said in a tone of astonishment, 'Sir! What an honour!'

'You and your mistress haven't been coming to the temple. Is she not well?'

The old woman put a corner of her sari to her mouth and giggled behind it. And I knew I had made a fool of myself.

'Woman, I have brought you the *prasada*,' I said. To include her mistress in that offer would have been to repeat my imbecility.

She took the coconut shells. 'Wait, sir, please,' she said and disappeared into the interior of the house. My idiocy, the inauspiciousness of the encounter and the ridicule I would face if anyone saw me standing on the doorstep of the house were crowding in on me when she reappeared. 'My mistress would like to talk to you,' she said, 'Please, come this way.' And led me through the cavernous house.

She was sitting in a corner of the backyard, on a mat spread out on the floor, her figure shadowed rather than lit by a tiny oil lamp. The light struck a glint off a silver water pot placed next to her, demarcating the boundary beyond which she could not be approached in her menstrual seclusion.

'Thank you for the *prasada*,' her voice declared by its clear timber that it had been trained for singing. 'I am sorry I cannot welcome you personally today. I would never have dared to invite you here. But since you have been kind enough to grace my house, may I ask a favour?'

I did not reply. The only women I had known well were my mother and wife. And I was too frightened of what I might get into if I attempted a reply here.

She paused and then proceeded, 'I had heard of your great skill in flower decoration. I have seen it now for myself and am overwhelmed. I can't step into the inner sanctum and you cannot be seen in my company in public. So would you kindly spare an evening for me, just one evening, come here and show me how you do it?'

I was silent. It surprised me that she should take my silence for acquiescence.

For she went on, 'I will be released from this corner in another day. Would it be brazen of me to expect you the evening after tomorrow?'

I said, 'I'll be here,' because anything else would have been needlessly discourteous and left.

Two feverish days later I was at her door again with the bundle of flowers taken from the *linga*. This time the door opened as though someone was waiting behind it and it was the old woman. Chandravati stood in the hall, half concealed by a pillar. Despite the shadow cast on her by the pillar, I could see that her hair was loose and tumbled in large quantities across her face and shoulders. She clutched her sari close to her body as though she was feeling cold.

'Please, come in, sir,' said she, 'This time at least I can ask you to sit down.' The old woman pointed to the mat on the floor. I sat down, opened the bundle and spread the flowers in front of her. Chandra shoved the fingers of her right hand into her lush hair to push them back from her forehead and with a quick shake of her head settled them on the nape of her neck. She moved nearer to the flowers. And I could see that she had carefully made herself up with kohl in the eyes, and sandal paste and turmeric on her cheeks. The flame of the oil lamp lit a sparkle on her lips which ran like quicksilver as she spoke.

'They are beautiful,' she said. 'I can see your expertise begins with the choice of flowers. Could you please describe the whole process of the *pooja* to me? I want to know every detail.'

'First you bathe the *linga*. Cleaning and preparing the god for the decoration.'

She listened intently to my narration and when I had finished, she said, 'Do you mind displaying for my sake some of your skill?' I looked around to decide how or where I could begin when she said, 'I have just bathed. This evening. A head bath. Do I need to bathe again?'

'No,' I said, unsure of what she meant but trying to make out that I was at least sure of what I meant, 'that is not necessary.'

'We can begin then?' Casually, she put aside the sari she had wrapped herself in and sat down in front of me.

I had never seen a woman completely naked. At home, we all bathed in the open, in the corner formed by the neem and the banyan trees in our backyard, so my wife covered herself with a sari even when she bathed. On the days I wanted her, I would give her a look she had come to recognize and late at night when everyone was fast asleep, she would crawl up to my room for a furtive scuffle in bed which demanded the mimimum of uncovering. There were our two children and my old parents in the house and you never knew who might call out for help. The problem, however, was more basic. My wife would have died of shame than be seen naked, even by herself.

I was trying to come to terms with the bronze vision in front of me. My heart was palpitating so wildly that it threatened to burst my eardrums and my hands so trembled that I couldn't even pick up the garlands. I prayed to God not to let me make a fool of myself. I was supposed to show her how I decorated the *linga*. But I could be playful with the *linga*, while here the natural smell of her body which seeped through the perfumes she had used and the continual touching and smoothing of her naked skin which the job required, demanded that I keep a firm control over myself. Fortunately, Chandravati herself was so calm and immobile that any amorous advances were out of the question. She watched with immense concentration as I selected different lengths of garlands and pondered which limb of hers each should go to. Often, her sculptured sinuousness virtually dictated the design. The strings of *malligai* buds seemed to need no help from me as they ran across her bosom to pass under the armpits and crossed themselves into a loose knot between her shoulder-blades. They then plunged down to the small of her back, flowed along her waist to the front, to the gentle mound below her navel and down her thighs. But I had to use all my ingenuity in devising a filigree that could stay snug against the curvature of her hips. Once or twice when the string dug into her I saw her flinch in pain. But then she smiled, asking me to proceed.

Her breasts were firm and tight. I chose the white *parijata* with their orange stem to loop around her breasts so that they set off her large dark nipples. I merely had to push the ends into the cleft and they held. Then I placed a hibiscus into the opening not so much to secure the loops as to provide a contrast in shape and colour to the *parijata*. But it did not work, so I took it out to replace it with a curling flame of the forest.

'Why did you change it?'

Her only question.

'It obscured the mole on your bosom,' I said.

She laughed.

'The beauty of a design lies in the detail,' I added, flattered by the adulation in her laughter and immediately felt foolish. She noticed that too but a trifle carefully, did not let on.

And even as a whole new world of patterns was opening up to me, thoughts of the *linga* kept passing through my mind. I pitied it, felt exasperated at its unimaginative contours. Why did its shape have to be so bland and unindented that one had to balance garlands precariously on it and improvise superfluous knots to hide some ungainly strings? Why didn't the Lord offer a form which inflamed invention like Chandra did?

Nothing more was said as I went on decking her up. The old woman kept moving in and out of the room which irritated me at first. But Chandra with a wave of her hand suggested I ignore her. It was only when the woman tried to help me with the flowers that I turned on her with such fury that she reared and Chandra laughed out. Thereafter the old woman confined herself to standing by the door, chuckling appreciatively.

When I had finished, Chandravati asked for the large mirror. She looked at herself from different angles, her eyes narrowing as she picked out the details, widening in admiration.

As she silently handed the mirror back to the old woman, I stammered: 'What—do you think?'

Chandra picked a *shevanti* flower and deftly wove it in the sacred thread on my shoulder.

The old woman went out, leaving the door ajar.

This then became the daily routine, never exactly repeatable, and therefore nerve-racking and exhilarating in its unpredictability. 'I have given up putting flowers in my hair,' she laughed. 'You have given me a sense of inferiority.' I had to undress her—she would not help me. Sometimes the knot of her breast-cloth was tied into such a mischievous knot that I threatened to cut it with a knife but she said that was not playing the game, and at other times the cloth fell off without warning at my merest touch, leaving me staring breathlessly at her bare bosom. When I finished decorating her, I would lay her down and kiss the mole. With a sudden movement she came alive.

I would return home quite late, ravenous. Chandravati had given up teasing me about consuming her body but not the food in her house. I would have a dip in the tank and head home. My wife was awake. She never ate before me. As soon as she heard me splashing in the tank, she would start heating up the food. While I ate, she stood rigid by the door, lanky and small-breasted, concerned but still. She never once asked me about Chandravati. I knew she would not.

It had taken only a couple of days for the news to spread through the surrounding villages. I knew the main reaction would be of amazement that a beautiful and obviously wealthy courtesan should take up with such an impecunious lover. Eyebrows would be raised at my good fortune or virility. All this mattered little to me. But I was distressed at the pain I was causing my wife. I loved her. I knew I had made her a target of vicious gossip. I sensed her anger, her humiliation and felt ashamed of myself. Conversation in the house was reduced to fragments and we stopped even looking at each other. But there was nothing I could do.

My wife had caught on to the new element in my daily *pooja*. I looked for a wider variety of flowers now, chose them with greater care and experimented with floral motifs on the *linga* which would be distinct from those I would devise later on Chandra. The garlands were the same, inevitably, but God was not to be a preliminary model for what I would do with her body. Each day I coaxed the flowers to say something special to God and then something entirely different to Chandra.

I tried to explain this to Chandra. I thought she would be

flattered, amused. Instead, she flew into a tantrum. 'Why can't you concentrate on me? I am too gross for you, aren't I? I am not stupid, you know. I can see your mind is somewhere else. Why don't you just stay back, trying things out on that stone *linga*?' And sulked most of the evening. Later she made up, pouting 'I worship you, I can't get angry with you.' But I never brought up the subject again. I felt she had forced me to curtain off an important corner of my soul from her. There was no one with whom I could share the excitement of this new development.

Or so I thought till twelve days ago. That was *tritiya*, the third day after the full moon.

That evening, as every day, my wife and I waited for the cannon to sound so we could start preparing for the *pooja*. But the usual hour passed and there was no cannon. I sent my wife home. 'Better go and feed the children,' I said. 'After all, you can come back as soon as you hear the cannon.' She nodded and left. I sat here, right here, on the top step of the temple tank and waited. After a while the prolonged inactivity and the increasing apprehension began to play upon my nerves. It was unlike the Chieftain to be so late. I had to do something. So I went to the inner sanctum and started to tie the garlands on the *linga*. I felt better. It brought back the warm security of being in the company of an old friend. I was talking to the *linga*, wondering what could be detaining the Chieftain, when my wife arrived. Without a word she attended to the details of the *pooja*. We finished what we had to do. But there was still no movement from the fort. I returned to my watch, worried that by now Chandravati would be anxious, leaning against her front door exactly as my wife was doing in the temple courtyard at the moment.

The three of us, frozen in the act of waiting, waiting for the Chieftain to move, waiting for the cannon to be fired so life could move on. More hours passed. I got tired of sitting. It would have been considerate of him to send a message, but who was to teach etiquette to the royalty?

I went back to the sanctum. My wife was stretched out in front of the main door, fast asleep. I stood there and watched her. She lay there like a wet rag, mouth half open, all excitement for life drained out of her, exhaustion oozing from every limb. I couldn't remember how long it had been since I had seen her sleeping. She looked so much in need of the rest that I didn't have the heart to wake her up, so I came back to continue my vigil on this step.

Another hour. It was nearly midnight. It was unthinkable that the Chieftain would come at this late hour. I went back to the temple. I lightly stepped across the recumbent figure of my wife which woke her up. She sat up clutching her *pallu* to her chest and looked around trying to make sense of the place she found herself in.

'Let's finish the *pooja*.' I said. 'He won't come. I am sure some crisis is keeping him home. And we can't leave our lord waiting for ever.'

She nodded, wearily.

I performed the *pooja*. I was boiling within myself and said to God that I hoped He didn't mind my rather perfunctory rites that evening. After all, the *linga* was Shiva and He was used to austerities.

The formality was over. I put a flower in my wife's outstretched palm. As she straightened to tuck it in the knot of her hair, she looked directly into my eyes. And held the look. My wife and I were there, just the two of us, alone, as we could never be at home. At a time and in a place where nobody could possibly surprise us. And for once, her infinite self-control had slipped and she was baring her desire as brazenly as though she had let her *pallu* drop from her bosom to expose her blouse and let it hang unretrieved. At any other time, just giving quarter to the thought of sex while in the temple would have horrified her, but at this moment she was inviting the shame of it. I could feel my insides reaching out for her and was taken aback that I had forgotten that

I could want her. The *linga* sat there looking at us and I snarled silently at it, 'Isn't it funny? I am going to defile your sanctum and it has to be with my lawful wife, for Chandravati would never be allowed to step in here.'

It would have been the simplest of things, to turn to my wife and take her by the hand. But I felt a constriction inside me, paralysing my movement. Confused, I turned to the *linga* and picked up a garland. Why did I do that? Was it because I had lost the habit of making love without bringing flowers into it?

The gesture proved fatal. The desire faded, the glow went out of her eyes. Bleakness seeped back into her voice as she mumbled: 'Don't go in the dark. Snakes, poisonous insects. Why don't you stay home?'

The whining tone insinuated that she already knew my answer and that infuriated me.

'Go home. I'll be back later. And don't wait up. I am not hungry.'

I turned my back to her and started picking the flowers off the *linga*. She stood, immobile, staring at her toenails. I picked up the bundle and left.

There was no sign of any movement in Chandravati's house, but a faint light spilled out from under the front door. I knocked. I had to knock twice again before there was a rustle of clothes and the old woman's voice asked who was knocking.

'It's me,' I said and the door creaked open. The old woman was there and beside her stood Chandra, her hair rumpled, her sari dishevelled, smiling apologetically.

'I am sorry I woke you up,' I said, irritated. 'I'll go back.' And turned to go. To my eternal regret I didn't. For even at that moment I could have salvaged my fate.

But Chandravati grabbed my arm. 'I'm sorry I fell asleep. But you can see I haven't retired,' she laughed. 'I am still in my best sari.' Then almost plaintively she added, 'I was waiting. You are so late. You can't blame me for falling asleep.'

Suddenly I thought of my poor wife's bleary eyes and melted. I stepped into the house.

'My lord and master failed to turn up,' I growled.

'I'm glad mine didn't do the same thing,' she retorted and laughed one of those laughs against which I had no defence.

We did not make love that night. I wanted Chandravati to go to sleep quietly next to me but she wanted the flowers. 'You have come all the way at this time of the night—through all those snakes and poisonous vermin—I must know what flowers you have brought me today and what you mean to do with them and me,' she insisted. 'So long as you don't mind if I nod off.' And kept struggling to stay awake as I decked her body up. Soon, I sat leaning against the wall, and she was reclining on my shoulder, dozing off, then opening her eyes to smile an apology and then floating away again. As I kissed the marigold I had woven in her tresses and held her breasts cupped in my palms ('You must support them, otherwise they begin to hurt from their weight,' she had said), I watched the mole, poised on the inward plunge of her right breast, peering precariously into the darkness of her cleft. I was longing to kiss it, but didn't dare move for fear of disturbing her. Finally when she had fallen into drugged sleep, I laid her back gently on the carpet, still moaning in defiance and resisting sleep like a child. I bent down and kissed the mole.

The tranquility of the night was shattered by the canon. It was barely more than a distant thud and it didn't even raise a ripple in her sleep. But I had spent years training my ears to catch its faintest reverberation and responded to its peremptory summons instantly. I sprang into action. Frantic, I started pulling out the flowers from her hair and piling them on my shoulder cloth. She sat up, groggy and dazed, yelping in pain as I snatched at the flowers. 'He is coming,' I said without wasting any time on looking at her. 'I must rush.' Every moment was precious. I rapidly calculated in my mind that I would have half an hour to set things right once I reached the temple and hoped my wife had

not slept through the cannon shot. As I turned back to push
the main door shut, I saw Chandravati, naked and on all fours,
staring out stupefied, shivering.

My wife was already standing at the gate of the temple
enclosure.

'Have you got the things ready?' I shouted as I rushed past her.

She didn't know what things I meant.

'Get ready for the *pooja*, woman. Quick. He'll be arriving any
moment.'

'But flowers?'

As I hurriedly opened the bundle and started decorating the
linga, there was a sharp intake of breath. I felt buffeted by the
revulsion I could sense welling up inside her. We had already
performed a *pooja* with these flowers. They were now the leavings,
polluted discards. What further use they had been put to in
Chandravati's house she didn't need to try too hard to imagine.
To place them on the *linga* again was desecration.

She didn't say anything. Just stood staring, and it annoyed me
that she should think I needed that rebuke. I turned on her and
said, 'Get on with it. He'll be here any moment.'

When the Chieftain arrived, the inner sanctum was as fresh and
welcoming as it would have been at sunset. The flowers were a
trifle faded, but that was to be expected at this hour of the night.
The Chieftain was accompanied by only the closest of the courtiers, who all looked exhausted. But he did not. He smiled, apologized for being late and explained that envoys from a neighbouring
kingdom were visiting and had to be looked after. He complimented
me and my wife on how beautiful the *linga* looked.

Relieved, I performed the *pooja*. When it was over, I held out
the plate of flowers so he could pick his choice as *prasada*. Then,
as I turned to the courtier next to him, I heard the Chieftain say,
'I didn't know God had long hair.'

The tired drone of the courtiers sloped off into silence and a
chill invaded the sanctum.

In the flickering light of the hanging lamps inside the sanctum, against the long, dancing shadows it was throwing on the walls, the strand of hair was not visible. There was his right hand dramatically stretched out, the thumb and the forefinger in a pinch, the other fingers stiff and pointing, as in a dance gesture. And then nearly a foot below the fingers, a marigold dangled in the air.

He looked at me and I didn't dare look away.

Yet at that moment I was not frightened by his cold anger as much as anguished that I was subjecting my wife's scraggy knot of hair to public derision. She knew that everyone there knew that the strand by which the illicit flower was swinging in the air was not hers. Could not be hers.

'I did not know God had long hair,' he repeated.

I gave the only reply possible under the circumstances.

'If we believe that God has long hair,' I said, 'He will have long hair.'

There was a pause and then he said, 'Prove it.'

'I will,' I said, 'Would your majesty allow me grace till the next new moon?'

'Done,' he replied, 'I shall be back at the cowdust hour on that day.' He then placed the flower back in the plate and left. I noticed that he hadn't thrown it back contemptuously to exhibit his annoyance at my insolent response. He had put it back, almost respectfully, as though the judge in him was willing to give me half a chance.

That was twelve days ago. What happened thereafter is quickly told. As soon as the Chieftain left, I dispatched my wife home and asked her not to disturb me until I sent for her. I forbade anyone, including her, from stepping into the temple precincts. Then I locked up the door of the sanctum and sat down, cross-legged, in front of it and prayed.

I don't know whether prayer is the right word. I had known the *linga* since my birth. My association with it was the longest and the closest in my life. As a child I had peed on it, and then in remorse wept on it. Even as an adult, I had poured out my woes to it, bragged about how my success with flowers had turned this place into the ruler's favourite shrine. Now I pleaded with it to save my face. Just that. I had disgraced myself and trembled at the thought of facing the world in that state. I didn't know what God could do. I had created a situation which was now beyond even His tinkering. But there was nothing else for me to do except surrender to Him. For twelve days, I cleansed my existence of everything, every name or person, except the *linga*.

This morning, the onlookers started collecting even before it dawned. By the time the Chieftain arrived in the evening, there were such crowds that even he couldn't get in and the guards had to use their sticks to make way for him. I was in a stupor, from hunger, from lack of sleep and from a complete sense of desolation. I dully wondered why they had all come. What did they expect to see? My public humiliation? What did the Chieftain hope to see? Why had he joined the charade? Indeed, what had I hoped to achieve by asking for a grace period?

I led him into the vestibule. Then I shut my eyes in one final prayer and pushed the door of the inner sanctum open. There was a pause and then the Chieftain gasped. I opened my eyes. The lights had not been lit and the sanctum was in darkness, but not such darkness that one could not see the long and thick hair that came cascading from the *linga*, hiding it completely. He stared. I stared. He looked at me for some explanation. I had none. I was as stunned as he was. He ordered the lamps to be lit and asked for torches. But he didn't need them. Now that the sanctum door was open, waves and waves of jet black hair came billowing out, their tips gently eddying and swirling in the evening breeze.

Everything seemed to move in slow motion, blanketed in thick hot mists.

I heard someone say, 'They could be glued.' and the Chieftain respond, falteringly, 'Should we test?' One of his Brahmin courtiers moved in, twisted a tuft of hair round his finger and tugged. He put all his strength into it and suddenly the tuft came out in his hand. He brought the tuft to the Chieftain who inspected it closely and touched its roots. There was blood on his fingers. The Brahmin ran back to the *linga*, felt for the spot from where he had plucked the hair and collapsed, crying hysterically, 'It's bleeding. It's bleeding. I have wounded God.'

I did not faint. But I can barely remember what followed: the Chieftain falling to my feet and begging forgiveness, the crowds surging forward to seek my blessings until my wife suddenly took charge and had me brought home. No one, not even the Chieftain, questioned her authority. I fell into deep sleep and woke up refreshed. It was almost midnight, my usual hour for the evening meal. She served me food and supervised the proceedings, as usual, leaning on the door.

The only thing she said was: 'She is gone. She and her old woman left town the very next day.'

But it was clear Chandravati's disappearance would make no difference to my wife. The courtesan was gone and had been replaced by Lord Shiva. I was among the chosen of the Lord and she could not possibly think of herself as a wife now, only as a slave and guardian, all shades of the marital bond expunged in favour of her devotion to me, her good fortune in having me for her husband.

The food gave me strength and here I am back on the temple tank. On my way, I peeped into the sanctum. The hair is gone but the wound is still fresh where the Brahmin had pulled out the tuft. On top of the hills, I can see the torches of soldiers, stationed to guard the approaches to the temple. I am the state saint now, to be prized, protected and shown off to visiting envoys.

And I have a quarrel to pick with God.

Why has God done this to me? I had only asked Him to give me the courage to live in disgrace, for I knew I had tainted myself.

The Chieftain was right to question me, to humiliate me publicly if he so decided. I am guilty of gross dereliction, of sacrilege. Guilty of cruelty to the two women I loved. Why then should God cast His vote on my behalf? Because I loved Him? Has God the right to mock justice in favour of love for Him? Or does He have a different logic? If He does, it's not fair that He should expect me to abide by it, not demanding to know what that logic is. Such Grace is condescension even it comes from God. Why am I worthy of this burden He has placed on my shoulders? I refuse to bear it. God must understand I simply cannot live on His terms.

Scorpio has crawled out of the recess in the third step under water. His reflection is floating towards me. The hollow is empty. As a boy, I used to shove my head into the hollow to test how long I could hold my breath. I shall do so again now, but not to test my lungs. I shall seek in the narrow confines of that hollow the answers that God has denied me.

Broken Images

...for you know only
A heap of broken images, where the sun beats,
And the dead tree gives no shelter,...

T. S. ELIOT
The Waste Land

The interior of a television studio. A big plasma screen hangs on one side, big enough for a close-up on it to be seen clearly by the audience. On the other side of the stage, a chair and a typically 'telly' table—strong, wide, semi-circular. At the back of the stage are several television sets, with screens of varying sizes.
A small red bulb glows above the table, high enough not to appear on the television screen.
Manjula Nayak walks in. She is in her mid-thirties/forties, and has a confident stride. She is wearing a lapel mike. It is immediately evident that she is at home in broadcasting studios. She looks around.

MANJULA: Nice, very nice. Neat!

(*She goes and sits on the chair. Adjusts the earpiece.*)

But where is the camera?

(*Listens to the reply.*)

Ah! I see. New technology. Isn't it scary? The rate of obsolescence? (*Listens.*) Of course I have. In London. And in Toronto. But when you think of Indian television studios, you always imagine them cluttered. Lots of men and woman scurrying about, shouting orders. Elephantine lights. Headphones. Cameras. You know what I mean. But here...I mean, it's all so spartan...I know. But a bit lonely too. Like a sound studio...All right. All right...No camera. I just look ahead and speak to an invisible audience in front of me...Direct. Fine. Fine...I can hear you. Clearly. Voice test?...'Testing, Testing, One, Two, Three, Four, Five, Hello, Hello!' Shall I tap on the mike?

(*Laughs.*)

My speech will last exactly ten minutes. I have timed it...No, I won't read. 'Look ahead and speak!' Good...But that may take a little longer. A couple of minutes...if I don't fumble too much.

(*Giggles.*)

The yellow light?...Okay, okay, ready, fine!

(*She mouths 'Ten' to 'Zero' silently, emphasizing each count with her forefinger. At the stroke of ten, the light turns yellow. The Announcer appears on the big plasma screen. The other screens remain blank till the last few minutes of the play.*)

ANNOUNCER: Good evening. This is a proud evening for the Shree-TV channel. For tonight we bring to you Ms Manjula Nayak. Many of you will know her as a renowned Kannada short-story writer. Until a year ago, she was a lecturer in English in Bangalore. But she had been writing in Kannada. Not unusual, as you know. It's amazing how many of our Kannada writers are lecturers in English: From the earliest days. B. M. Shree, Gokak, Adiga.

Even modern ones. Lankesh, Shantinath, Anantha Murthy. And of course there is A. K. Ramanujan, who was equally at home in both languages. But last year Mrs Nayak stunned the world—yes, I mean, *the world*—by writing a novel. Her first novel. In English! *The River Has No Memories*. The advance she received from her British publishers made headlines, here and in the West. And then the novel turned out to be a bestseller all over the world. Our heartiest congratulations to Mrs Nayak.

This evening we broadcast a Kannada telefilm based on this remarkable novel. The film will begin in exactly ten minutes. And we have with us in the studio Ms Nayak herself, who has graciously agreed to address our viewers about her work. Ladies and gentlemen, welcome the Literary Phenomenon of the Decade, Mrs Manjula Nayak.

(*Applause on the sound track. The light turns green. The Announcer disappears and Manjula's image appears in his place. She speaks.*)

MANJULA: *Namaskara.* I am Manjula Nayak. I must mention that officially I am Mrs Manjula Murty, but my creative self continues to be Manjula Nayak. There are some areas in which we must not let marriage intrude too much.

(*Laughter.*)

Talking about one's work is a very difficult task. So let me find an easy way out. Let me just take up two questions I constantly come across. They seem to bother everyone—here, abroad. I'll answer them to the best of my ability within the short time at my disposal and shut up. Actually, that's what a writer should do, shouldn't she?—Write and shut up!

(*Laughs.*)

The first question—you have probably guessed it already. After having written in Kannada all your life, why did you choose—suddenly—to write in English? Do you see yourself as a Kannada writer or an English writer? What audience do you write for? And variations on that theme.

Actually, let me confess. If I had foreseen how many people I would upset by writing in English—I really would not have committed that folly.

Intellectuals whom I respected, writers who were gurus to me, friends who I thought would pat me on my back and share my delight—they are all suddenly breathing fire. How dare I write in English and betray Kannada!

(*Laughs.*)

Betray! The answer is simple; if there was betrayal, it was not a matter of conscious choice. I wrote the novel in English because it burst out in English. It surprised even me. I couldn't understand why it was all coming out in English. But it did. That's all. There is no other explanation.

What baffles me—actually, let me confess, hurts me—is why our intellectuals can't grasp this simple fact! I have been accused of writing for foreign readers. Accused! As though I had committed a crime. A writer seeks audiences where she or he can find them! My British publishers said to me: 'We like your book because it's so Indian. We receive any number of manuscripts from India but they are all written with the western reader in view. Your novel has the genuine Indian feel!'

(*Laughs.*)

But who listens here? A pundit for instance has stated that no Indian writer can express herself—or himself—honestly in English. 'For Indian writers, English is a medium of dishonesty.' Of course, one could also ask how many Kannada writers are honest in what they write—in Kannada. But if you did that, you would be immediately condemned as a traitor. You can't win!

Recently the President of the Central Sahitya Akademi—the National Academy of the Letters—(who shall remain nameless) declared that Indians who write in English do so in order to make money. That by writing in English they confess their complicity in the global consumer market economy. He of course spoke in English. Speaking in English, as you know, gives you the authority to make oracular pronouncements on Indian literatures and languages. But my response to the charge that I write in English for money would be: Why not? Isn't that a good enough reason? Would you like to see what royalties I earned when I wrote in Kannada?

(*Pause.*)

Yet the accusation hides—or perhaps reveals—a grim anxiety. As is clear from the dictum of the President of the Akademi, what is at issue is not Creativity but Money. What hits everyone in the eye is the money a writer in English can earn. The advance I received for my novel—the advance only, mind you—helped me resign my job and concentrate on writing. Of course it is a cause for jealousy. Having struggled in Kannada, I can understand that. A Kannada proverb says: 'A response is good. But a meaningful response is better.' Meaningful: *Arthapoorna*. The Kannada word for Meaning is *Artha*—which also means money! And of course, fame, publicity, glamour...power.

(*Laughs.*)

Let me leave it at that.

The second question everyone asks is about the book itself: thank God! How could you—you seem so strong and active—I was a long jump athlete in college, though of course no Anju Bobby George—how could you so vividly recreate the inner life of a person confined to bed all her life? How can a healthy, outdoor woman be so empathetic to the emotional world of a disabled person? Well, it is sad, but I owe that to my younger sister, Malini.

She was physically challenged. Suffered from what is technically called, meningomyelocele—the upper part of her body was perfectly normal; below the waist, the nervous system was damaged. Completely dysfunctional. A series of operations, which started soon after her birth, reduced her existence to misery—she spent her entire life confined to the wheel-chair.

Six years ago my parents died. She came to stay with us in our house in Jayanagar, and I nursed her. During the last few months it was quite clear she didn't have much time left. I am childless and she became my child! Truly, the book is about her. I have dedicated it to her memory. She died last year—just a few months before the book came out. I have tried to

relive what I learnt about her emotional life as I nursed her—
tended to her—watched helplessly as she floated into death.
I miss her. I miss my beautiful, gentle sister.

(*Her eyes moisten.*)

She is the only character in the novel drawn from life. The
other characters and the plot are entirely fictional. Invented.

(*Pause.*)

I must here acknowledge the support I received from one
person while I wrote the novel—my husband, Pramod Murty.
I was working full time as a lecturer then. College chores. And
home was full of her memories. And there was I, suddenly
writing in English. Floundering. Sinking. I was utterly clueless.
There were moments when I broke down, when I felt I couldn't
go on. But he was always there at my side, encouraging me,
prodding me on. Without him, I would never have completed
the novel. Thank you, Pramod.

(*The overhead light turns yellow.*)

Well, that's it. I have committed the cardinal sin of writing
in English.

(*Laughs.*)

There is no *prayashchitta* for it, no absolution. But fortunately
the film you are about to see is in Kannada. That makes me
very happy. After all, the family I have written about is
Kannada. I am a Kannada writer myself, born to the language
and civilization, and proud of it. The Kannada reality I
conceived in English has been translated back into Kannada—
to perfection—by the Director. I couldn't have done it better.
My thanks to the cast and the crew and of course, Shree-TV.
Well, enjoy the telefilm.

Good Night. *Namaskara.*

(*The light turns red. She leans back in her chair. Pause. Then into
the lapel mike.*)

I hope that was okay? I didn't fumble too much, did I?

(*Listens.*)

Thank you, Raza. The pleasure's all mine. See you outside?
(*The red light switches off. She smiles contentedly.*)
Whew! That'll get them. Good. I have taken enough shit from them.
(*Laughs and gets up. Manjula's image on the screen should have given way to the film, but hasn't. Instead, the Image continues as before, watching her calmly. She is of course unaware of it.*
She makes a move to the door.)

IMAGE: Where are you going?

(*Startled, Manjula stops and looks around. Touches her earpiece to check if the sound came from there and moves on.*)

You can't go yet. —Manjula!
(*Manjula looks around baffled and sees that her image continues on the screen. She does a double take.*
From now on, throughout the play, Manjula and her image react to each other exactly as though they were both live characters.)

MANJULA: Oh God! Am I still on?

(*Confused, she rushes back to the chair and stops.*)

IMAGE: You are not. The camera is off.

MANJULA: Is it?... Then...how?

IMAGE: You are standing up. If the camera were on, I would be standing up too. I'm not.

MANJULA: Is this some kind of a trick?
(*Into her lapel mike.*)
Hello! Hello! Can you hear me? How come I'm still on the screen? Raza, hello...
(*Taps her mike. No response.*)
Is there a technical hitch?

IMAGE: No hitch.

MANJULA (*to the Image*): But how... Who are you... How... Has the tape got stuck?
(*Calls out into the mike.*)

Raza, Raza. Help! Help!

IMAGE: What are you screaming for? What are you afraid of? It's only me.

MANJULA: Who are you?

IMAGE: Me? You.

MANJULA (*to herself*): This is absurd.

IMAGE: Quite.

(*A long pause while Manjula refuses to acknowledge the presence of the Image. Then she slowly looks up. The Image smiles.*)

IMAGE: A good speech, I must say. My compliments. An excellent performance. The viewers loved it. All two million of them.

MANJULA: But the film? Hasn't it started?

IMAGE: Aw, screw the film... It's awful anyway.

MANJULA: I told them it won't work. A telefilm needs lots of move-ment. Different locations. Pace. Action. Drama. 'A good novel does not necessarily make a good film,' I argued. But they were persistent. Sponsors were easy to find. (*Pause.*) They paid well.

IMAGE: Your performance now... this introduction... it will be the best thing this evening. You'll be all over the papers. You have managed to upset a lot of people.

MANJULA: Thanks. I meant to.

(*Pause.*)

IMAGE: If one had to comment... in the extreme case that one had to... that bit about your sister Malini... the tears... that could have been played down.

MANJULA: I wasn't pretending. I loved her.

(*Pause.*)

I love her. Still. I don't think I have ever been as close to anyone else.

IMAGE: It was a close bond?

MANJULA: The novel doesn't really do her justice. She was attractive—more attractive than me. Intelligent—more intelligent than me. And vivacious, which I never was. I accepted that. She radiated life from the wheelchair to which she was confined. I have always been reconciled to being the second best.

IMAGE: Her illness was unfortunate. But because of it, she got the best of everything.

MANJULA (*defensive*): She never asked for anything. Soon after her birth, the moment the gravity of her situation was realized, my parents moved to Bangalore. Took a house in the Koramangala Extension. She became the...the (*searches for a phrase and then settles for*)...the apple of their eye. When she was old enough to go to school, a teacher came home to teach her English and Mathematics. Everything else, she read up for herself. History, Philosophy, Anatomy. She was hungry—hungry for life. Gobbled it all up.

IMAGE: And you?

MANJULA: I have often wondered whether I would have been as bright if I'd received all that love and attention.

IMAGE: No, you wouldn't. Let's face it.

MANJULA (*defensively*): I did write a bestseller.

IMAGE: That's true.

MANJULA: But you are right. I wouldn't. They left me with grandparents in Dharwad. An affectionate couple. They fussed over me. But no substitute for parents. When vacations approached I could barely wait to get to Bangalore. And once I finished college, I found a job in Bangalore and came and lived with them. Those were the happiest days of my life! Halcyon! But then I met Pramod. We got married and settled down in Jayanagar. Father helped with the house but he left most of his money in her name—for her care. She was always the focus. Naturally.

IMAGE: But when your parents died, why didn't you move into the Koramangala house? Such a nice, big house. The garden. The sense of space.

MANJULA: The Jayanagar house was my house. I was used to it. My college was in Jayanagar. We had selected a house which was within walking distance. Koramangala would have meant a long haul every morning.

And then such a huge house! Not easy to look after. I would have had to stay home all day like Mother. Give up my job probably.

No, as I said, she was one of the most sensitive people I have known. She realized moving to Koramangala would turn my life upside down. She insisted that we sell the Koramangala house. I was reluctant but she wouldn't listen. She wanted no sacrifices on her account, no compromises. And she adjusted beautifully to the smaller house.

(Pause.)

Actually I couldn't take Koramangala! Non-Kannadigas, most of them. And of course all those empty houses bought as investments by Non-Resident Indians. I fancied myself a Kannada writer in those days. Wanted to breathe the language. Live in the heart of Kannada culture.

IMAGE: Now that you are a success in English, have you bought a big bungalow in Koramangala?

MANJULA: Aw, shut up!

IMAGE: Was Malini at home with Kannada?

MANJULA: Of course, it is our mother-tongue. But she rarely used it. Her Kannada was limited to the cook and the maid.

IMAGE: So Kannada was the one area that became yours?

MANJULA: You could say that. I tried to occupy it and make it mine.

(Laughs.)

Actually, I have never said it publicly, but if you argue that a novel written in English cannot express truth about India because we do not express ourselves in English—

(*Takes a breath. Laughs.*)

God, what a sentence! But if you believe that, then let me say I could not have written about my sister in Kannada. She breathed, laughed, dreamt in English. Her friends spoke only English. Having her in my house for six years helped improve my English.

(*Pause.*)

IMAGE: So when are you going to write your next novel? Will it also be in English?

MANJULA: I think I have already answered that question. Why need I write another novel? Surely one is more than enough?

IMAGE: Critically and financially. But then what are you going to do? You have resigned your job. You are rich—

MANJULA: Well-to-do.

IMAGE: Well-to-do. You have no sister to look after. An empty house. Nothing you can use.

MANJULA: Are you trying to make me feel guilty? Are you implying I 'used' her? It was my life as well you know. I am in the book too, though I would never admit to it publicly. Most readers find the girl's 'first cousin' quite unattractive.

IMAGE: Eek! That odious character! Is that you?

MANJULA: Well! There you are!

IMAGE: A triumph of objective self-analysis, shall we say?

MANJULA: If you must. But I am not that wicked really. It was a narrative necessity to have a negative character. A matter of technique. The sympathetic heroine. A villain as a counter-point. You see?

IMAGE: But Pramod must be pleased by your treatment of his character. He comes across as not very good-looking or striking...

MANJULA: But not bad-looking, either. Good enough for me.

IMAGE: ...but an intelligent, warm and lovable person. Fun-loving. Fond of practical jokes. Noble and simple. Almost simple-minded.

MANJULA: You can say that again! You know, we met soon after I moved to Bangalore. He felt attracted to me. Didn't know how to convey it. So do you know what he did? I had a friend called Lucy. A close friend. He wrote a letter to her about me. And wrote me a letter about Lucy. Then he mailed her letter in an envelope addressed to me and vice versa. So I received this letter addressed to Lucy—moaning and groaning about how I tortured him. And I didn't even know he was interested in me. And of course Lucy received the other letter. He thought he was being absolutely clever—original. We went and confronted him. Lucy tore *her* letter to shreds and flung the pieces on him and stormed off. Melodramatically. I felt sorry for him and said, 'Idiot, every fifteen-year old tries that trick, convinced it's never been done before.' He blushed to the roots of his hair.

IMAGE: But you got married. So the ruse worked.

MANJULA: No ruse. He had made such a fool of himself, he did the only thing he could to save his self-respect. He married me. I didn't mind.

IMAGE: Mind? You would never have got another man of his calibre.

MANJULA: I suppose so.

IMAGE: And what happened to Lucy?

MANJULA: She stopped talking to me.
(*They both laugh.*)
Women found him attractive.

IMAGE: Malini too?

MANJULA: Of course. She was a woman, after all.

IMAGE: They were close to each other?

MANJULA: Very. You must realize Malini wasn't exposed to men. There was Father—not given to expressing much affection. And male teachers who floated in and out. Pramod entered her life like a storm and stayed centre stage. He was in fact the only man in her life.

IMAGE: And you didn't mind?

MANJULA: Mind? Thank God for it. You see, he is in software development. Works from home. She was confined to her chair. Can you imagine what would have happened if they hadn't got on? He is basically a two-woman man. I used to call him Tirupati Thimmappa.

IMAGE: He must be proud of you. That flattering portrayal of him in the novel. The moving acknowledgment in your speech today...

MANJULA: I doubt if he will even hear of my speech. Ever.

IMAGE: Why? Is there a problem?

MANJULA (*explodes*): Who are you, for God's sake? What gives you the right to interrogate me like this—about my private life? Either you are me in which case you know everything. Or you are an electronic image, externally prying. In which case, you can just...just...f...switch off.

(*Manjula strides to the chair and sits down, tight-lipped, ignoring the Image completely.*)

IMAGE: Go on. You were saying...

Go on.

So?

Aren't you going to talk to me? Come on.

Listen, I am sorry I am getting on your nerves. But you could say I am getting on my own nerves—if I had any. But I am not here by choice. I don't know how I got here. All I know is I am here, imprisoned, if you like, in this television frame. Literally boxed. My existential situation. My angst.

And I am here to talk to you. So please...cooperate.

(*Pause.*)

There was a time when critics would have said I was your Conscience. Like in the good old Hindi films. The hero reaches out for the money and suddenly his shadow starts speaking: 'Don't. That money is meant for your father's medicines. Do you want to break your mother's heart?' Or it could be his image in the mirror.

But those simple days are gone. Today I would have to be your Freudian Unconscious. Everything you censored. Repressed material. Forbidden impulses. Taboo recollections. A dream. Bad dream. Actually, I could be an Interpretation of a Bad Dream.

(*Giggles.*)

Sorry about that.

(*Pause.*)

Look. You asked me who I am. Does one ever know who one is? It's the ultimate question, isn't it? Where did I come from? Where am I going? You are the Eng. Lit. person. Hamlet started it all. You should know. No use asking me.

(*Pause.*)

We could go back to Narcissus, of course. He loved his image. Which is more than can be said about you.

—What about the Romantic period? The doppelganger. *Dr Jekyll and Mr Hyde. The Picture of Dorian Gray.* And if you are willing to go beyond Eng. Lit., and consider Russ. Lit., there is Dostoyevsky's *The Double.*

Jacques Lacan would have embraced me if he were here.

I would be quite happy to be a central transcendental signified. You could deconstruct me out of existence.

(*Pause.*)

I don't mind.

(*Long pause. Pleading.*)

Say something. Please.

(*Pause.*)

Sorry. You are now an author of international standing. So perhaps we should analyse me in more...Indian terms? Our myths. Folklore. Oral tales passed on by grandmothers? Indian archetypes.

Sita. Yes. Take Sita. As her 'Other', there was a Maya Sita. The Illusory Sita. According to some versions of the Ramayana, it was actually the Illusory Sita that Ravana carried off. And then in the later sections of the epic, Rama replaces the absent Sita with a golden image.

It seems as though the men in the Ramayana never got to the real Sita.

(*Pause.*)

I am trying to keep myself entertained. One must do something, after all. If you are looking for entertainment, you could do better than be in a television studio.

(*Pause. Suddenly.*)

Think of it. Isn't it fortunate that I am your image and therefore outside you? I could be inside you—part of a multiple personality syndrome. Then we two would be struggling inside your body, trying to push each other down, attempting to be mutually exclusive. We would never get a chance to talk to each other.

Like now.

To quote a scholar:

'Sexuality is a matter of cutting and splitting, falling apart and meeting again. It is a matter of division and recomposition...absence and presence, death and birth. Sexuality is double and divided.'

I like that. Don't you?

(*Pause.*)

So.

Please say something.

I have exhausted all the arguments I know. I am exhausted.

(*Pleading.*)

I am nothing if you don't say anything.

(*The Image sits in a position exactly duplicating Manjula's. A long pause.*)

MANJULA: So what do you want to know?

IMAGE (*relieved*): Whew! What happened to you? You said Pramod may never hear of your excellent speech this evening and I only wanted to know why, and you just exploded.

MANJULA: He is in the States now.

IMAGE: Oh! When did he go?

MANJULA: Last year. He lives in Los Angeles now. He is in demand as a software wizard.

IMAGE: Last year! So has he even read the novel?

MANJULA: The launching of the novel was a major media event in the US. After all, you must remember it had already proved a super hit in Britain. They invited me to New York for the release. There was much fanfare. He sent me an email of congratulations. From Los Angeles. Apologized that he couldn't get leave to attend.

IMAGE: And you didn't go to LA?

MANJULA: He didn't even hint at it.

IMAGE: I'm sorry. But the chronology is beginning to confuse me. When did he decide to go to the States? Was it after Malini's death?

MANJULA: Yes.

IMAGE: Immediately after?

MANJULA: No. But soon after.

IMAGE: How long after?

MANJULA: All right. Let me explain. The offer from the American Software Company had been hanging fire for a while. Even when Malini was alive. In fact, she became quite agitated when he received the offer—although of course she was also happy. I knew he too was dragging his feet because of her. We knew she was dying. Then she died. Then, I wrote the novel and sent it to a literary agent in Britain. Within a couple of weeks we received an email from the agent accepting the novel for publication. Mentioning the advance. That did it. Everything fell apart.

IMAGE: Really? What happened?

MANJULA: I suppose it was to be expected. Until that moment I was essentially dependent on him—emotionally, financially. He was the quiet bread winner. Also the more successful partner—the pillar of the family. Then suddenly, the rave response, the enormous advance. I had achieved a status he did not care for.

IMAGE: So?

MANJULA: His behaviour took an odd turn. I was of course inundated with invitations to public functions, cultural events, literary conferences and so on. He had never attended these events before. He didn't now. That was fine. But one day Lucy called. You know—my friend Lucy—of the mixed-up letters? I knew she was still unmarried—living by herself. She hadn't talked to me since that episode. She rang. Pramod had begun to invite her out in the evenings. To dinner in expensive restaurants.

IMAGE: Were they having an affair?

MANJULA: No, no, no. He would never even make a pass. I knew that. In fact, I wish he had had a full-scale affair with her—with anyone, in fact. That might have eased the tension in the house. But he just isn't the roaming type. Too much a creature of habit.

IMAGE: So they only talked? What about? Did he complain against you?

MANJULA: Lucy said he never so much as mentioned me.

IMAGE: Then?

MANJULA: He told her jokes.

IMAGE: He did what?

MANJULA: He cracked jokes. Of course he talked of other things, but everything was honed to delivering the jokes he had carefully selected, polished, tabulated and fitted into the larger narrative.

IMAGE: Not smutty jokes then?

MANJULA (*exasperated*): No, no, no. That's just not like him. Jokes about his work. About Information Technology. About Bill Gates and Wipro and Infosys. Cyberjokes. And she said he was hilarious. Had her in stitches. She enjoyed the evenings enormously.

It was his inexhaustible gaiety that worried her. Did he tell me jokes too? she wanted to know. I said no, he may have in the early days of marriage, but not any more. So she said: 'If it doesn't worry you, it doesn't worry me. If you don't mind, I would like to continue the evenings. So please don't question him.' That was the last I heard from her.

(*Pause.*)

Then he opened a new office for himself away from home.

(*Pause.*)

I had resigned my job, you see. We were both home all the time. People dropped in to see me now. That disturbed him, or he couldn't stand them. He made remarks about the woodworks they must have crawled out of, which began to annoy me. His complaints multiplied. The maid didn't clean his office properly. Or she was too thorough and he couldn't find anything he needed. The quality of food at home was deteriorating. Then one day he wondered if we could reemploy the nurse.

IMAGE: The nurse?

MANJULA: Yes, the nurse who had attended on Malini. 'Can she just come and go once a day?' he asked. I was taken aback. 'Why?' I asked, 'Malini is dead and neither of us is ill.' He stared at his toes, went out of the room without replying. I don't know if he had the nurse visit him in his new office!

IMAGE: He obviously missed Malini.

MANJULA: Hm...

IMAGE: So the collapse of your marriage may have nothing to do with your literary success. It was her.

MANJULA: There was something insidious in the way she had taken over my home.

IMAGE: You can't blame her. You almost willed it.

MANJULA: How do you mean?

IMGE: You let her take over your home. You were out all day. You didn't have much time for the house or them.

MANJULA: I was a working woman, you know. I wasn't out gallivanting.

IMAGE: You made yourself more and more...or rather less and less a part of the home scene. The cook came and went? (*Manjula nods.*)

The maid came and went? The nurse similarly?

So Malini and Pramod were together—virtually all day. And she was pretty.

MANJULA: Very, with a soft skin, almost translucent. Never exposed to sun or wind.

Most people in her situation would have grown fat— obese. Developed diabetes. I'm told many kill the boredom of confinement by gorging and so put on weight. She didn't. She was never bored. She remained alert and supple and glowed.

IMAGE: A young shapely body? Small but firm breasts. When you bathed or changed her, you must have compared her physique with your own?

MANJULA: Funnily, whenever I sponged her, it was she who looked away.

IMAGE: Perhaps she couldn't bear the look in your eyes?
(*Pause.*)

MANJULA: Was I jealous? Of course not. She was paralysed below
the waist. There was no possibility of any physical intimacy.

IMAGE: Intimacy can mean anything two people agree to.
(*Pause.*)

MANJULA: All right. It bothered me. Shall we say it was that
irritation that produced this novel? What went on between
them? Even if it was only words, what words?
(*Pause.*)

I tried various experiments. If I turned the key in the main
door noisily enough before going in—sure enough I would
find him at his table, studious, a picture of concentration.
She would be deep into her book or her laptop, but never so
absorbed that she couldn't give me that warm, welcoming
smile. If I surprised them by entering silently, animated
conversation would suddenly come to a stop—a guilty pause—
before she picked the exact note effortlessly and continued,
involving me too in their talk. It was always her. He was no
good at subterfuge.

IMAGE: But what were they talking about? After all, six years! They
couldn't have been declaring love all that time.

MANJULA: One day I returned home early. A furious battle was
raging. I eavesdropped. They were squabbling like a married
couple. It was about ethics. He was arguing that any system
of ethics demanded a single universal principle applicable
to everyone. A command that bound every human being without
exception. She was horrified by this. Different human situations called for different principles on which to act. Ethical
demands are ethical because they are conflicting, she said.
She found a universal principal inhuman.

They were screaming their heads off. He said Hinduism
knew no real ethics. She called Immanuel Kant a fascist. But

it all seemed impersonal. Abstruse. Innocuous. So I stepped in. They saw me, a sudden look of guilty horror as though I had caught them making love. Silence. Then she picks up again. She asks my opinion. What did I think?

I couldn't try the experiment too often of course. They knew my timings. There were occasions when I felt, 'This isn't my home. I am an intruder here: someone external to the soul of this house—along with the cook, the maid and the nurse.'

IMAGE: Did Pramod come to your bed willingly?

MANJULA: Almost too willingly. After all, he was not paralysed. (*Suddenly.*)

But the film must be halfway by now. What about the commercial break? I was told advertisers were queuing up. We can't be kept locked in here for ever.

IMAGE (*quietly*): You were talking about your bed.

MANJULA: There were moments when I wondered if he was fantasizing about having Malini instead of me in bed with him.

IMAGE: And she no doubt lay listening, beyond earshot. Imagining the two of you together.

MANJULA: It was painful... There seemed to be no end in sight. No resolution. Critics have commented on the sensually charged atmosphere of the novel. The despair—

(*Pause.*)

IMAGE: You found the perfect 'Objective Correlative' for it.

MANJULA: It sold the book.

IMAGE: But you have to keep protesting that the plot was not taken from life?

(*Manjula shrugs.*)

By the way, did Malini know you were writing a book about her?

MANJULA: How could she? I hadn't even thought of it when she was alive. Have a heart! I was a working woman. English literature. At home, there was Malini. Completely dependant. And a quintessentially Indian husband—caring, but useless. Where was the time? Besides you need distance. 'Emotion recollected', etc.

IMAGE: But once you found Tranquility you must have written at a tremendous pace.

MANJULA: It poured out. It was one way of making up for her absence.

IMAGE: She died. Within a couple of weeks of her death you mailed the typescript to your literary agent. 350 printed pages worth of material within two weeks.

MANJULA: I worked my fingers to the bone.

IMAGE: A gigantic task, worthy of the Guinness Book of World Records. Do you know the publishers of the Guinness Book say they receive the largest number of applications from India? We are a nation that aspires to being the world-record-holder in world-record-holding.

MANJULA (*flares up*): What are you burbling? Are you being willfully obtuse? Or plain stupid? And nasty. All those hints. Jibes. Innuendos.

IMAGE: But one hundred and fifty thousand words in two weeks? Ten thousand words a day! It wasn't inspiration. It was a cataract—of words. A deluge not matched since Noah's Ark!

MANJULA (*explodes*): All right! I didn't write the novel. She did. She wrote it. Every word of it.

IMAGE: Dear me!

MANJULA: Once her health began to collapse, about eighteen months before the end, she began hammering away at the laptop. I knew she was writing something. But I had no time for it. After her death, I found the typescript in her drawer. I read it.

(*Pause.*)

I was decimated.

IMAGE: It was brilliant. A masterpiece. You knew that as a writer you could never dream of such heights. The passion. The clarity. The insights. The total control. A work of genius.

MANJULA: Absolutely. I looked up a Directory of Literary Agents in the British Council and mailed the typescript to them. I didn't know if they would even respond. Then it happened.

IMAGE: What?

MANJULA: I tried to explain to Pramod. But he would have none of it. He was unforgiving.

IMAGE: About stealing the book?

MANJULA: I did *not* steal it. Malini liked to sign herself M. Nayak. My letter accompanying the manuscript was signed Manjula Nayak. The agent obviously thought we were the same person. His reply arrived at Pramod's email address. We shared a computer, you see. Why does a Kannada writer need a computer anyway? He printed off a copy of the reply and left it for me—on the kitchen table.

As I read the email, I could sense him watching me. From his corner. I decided to face him.

'How can you accuse me of plagiarism?' I wanted to demand. 'Are you implying I knowingly stole my sister's novel?'

I knew he would deny any such insinuation. I was rearing to pitch into him—wring the truth out of him.

'Why don't you say what is on your mind?' I wanted to go on. 'You know it was a genuine mistake. The Agent is an Englishman, unfamiliar with Indian names.'

Instead, I heard myself asking, 'Why did you leave the email message on the kitchen table?' He looked nonplussed. And it wasn't what I had meant to ask. But I had to plunge on. 'You know I have a study of my own—a desk at which I work.' 'Oh, I'm sorry,' he said, picked up the message from the kitchen table, took it into my study and plonked it down on my writing desk, 'Here. The message.' That was it. He pretended he didn't know what I was getting at. But he did know. You could see it in his anger. He had never been so angry before—not with me. The subject was never mentioned again.

IMAGE: Then?

MANJULA: We lived entombed in silence. The last real communication between us—the last moment of privacy—was when he'd asked whether we could call the nurse back. I had replied with a flippant why, but as we looked at each other—for a moment only—the room had suddenly filled with the reek of her incontinence, her phlegm and sweat, her perfumes, medicines and disinfectants. This was weeks after she had died! Before long, the press got wind of the deal and invaded our home. The enormous advance. The rave previews. The literary tours. It was all too late...

IMAGE (*gently*): Let's just go back a bit. The plot is a little too neat, don't you agree?

(*Manjula stares dourly.*)

All that spiel about the Literary Agent confusing Malini with Manjula. Such melodrama! Sounds like one of your Kannada short stories.

(*A very long pause.*)

MANJULA: After her death, I looked for her papers. I could not find them in her room. I dashed to Pramod's office. Rifled through his papers. There it was, the typescript. Not even a floppy which you might miss or not recognize. She had printed off the entire novel and arranged the pages, carefully. It lay there, hidden away in his drawer. Or at least he thought so. He is no good at concealment. He did not even know I had filched the typescript until the agent's email arrived... I read the typescript.

IMAGE: You were decimated. It was brilliant, a masterpiece, etc.

MANJULA: It was venomous. I was camouflaged as the first cousin, and not sister. But it was me all right and the portrayal was rancorous. I was a shallow woman, a pretentious mediocrity, a gushy, conniving and devious relative who had taken her in for her inheritance. But there were no adjectives. Just facts. The events were from life. They were accurately described. The conversations were recorded verbatim. I couldn't deny them.

IMAGE: Perhaps that's why Pramod had hidden the script.

MANJULA: Or perhaps they had shared it together? Laughed and exchanged notes? Perhaps he was not simple at all—she had brought out an aspect of him I never suspected? She could not have imagined her work would find the light of day. So it was either meant to be read by me—or to be shared between them.

She despised me. Perhaps they both did. Perhaps she had turned him against me.

At that moment I knew—that I hated the cripple. I had always hated her. I was only waiting for her to die.

IMAGE: And she had recognized the truth all along.

MANJULA: And she was right! Once again! It was maddening. (*Pause.*)

For six years, from her wheelchair, she had watched me, stalked me in every move. Then she had pinned me down in coruscating prose.

(*Pause.*)

From beyond the funeral pyre, my sister was challenging me to burn the script. If I succumbed, I would stand condemned in my own eyes for destroying a masterpiece.

IMAGE: And if you published it, everyone would see who 'the first cousin' was. You would become the laughing stock. Worse still, you would go down in history as a footnote in the life of a brilliant author. Dangling by an insignificant asterix. Malini had nicely crucified you.

MANJULA: I had to do something she could not have possibly

anticipated. I had to solve all problems at one stroke. I had
to survive.

(*Pause.*)

And this time I had one advantage. She was dead and I was
not.

(*Pause.*)

I published the novel in my name. I won!

(*The Image claps. Manjula takes a bow. Smiling.*)

Shall we go then?

(*Makes a move to the door. Suddenly the Image stops clapping.*)

IMAGE: Wait a bit. Perhaps...she did win in the end?

MANJULA: How do you mean?

IMAGE: If she meant to prove *to you* that you were a fraud, she
certainly succeeded.

MANJULA: You—you—I'll show you.

(*She rushes to the screen and looks for the cable connecting it.*)

IMAGE: What are you doing?

MANJULA: I've had enough of you. I want to unplug you. I want
to wipe you out.

(*She goes behind the screen looking for the connections, so that the
Image seems to become the upper part of her body. Suddenly,
Manjula's body, gesticulating in sync with the words of the Image,
almost becomes an extension of the Image. The Image intones the
following speech.*)

IMAGE: I am Malini Nayak, the English novelist. Manjula Nayak,
the Kannada short-story writer, was decimated the moment
she read my novel. She thus obliterated all differences of ink
and blood and language between us and at one full stroke
morphed into me.

(*If there is a revolving stage available, it begins to revolve taking
Manjula-cum-the-Image with it, as the television sets at the back
come alive one after another. Every screen shows a different Image
of Manjula, silent but gesticulating.*)

Of course, I shall continue with the name of Manjula Nayak. As Manjula Nayak, I have been invited as Visiting Professor to seven prestigious American Universities. I use that nomenclature for my passport, my bank accounts, property and financial investments. However I am in truth Malini, my genius of a sister who loved my husband and knew Kannada and wrote in English.

(*Suddenly all the screens start speaking loudly, some in Kannada, the others in English. The cacophony is deafening. The revolving stage moves Manjula out into the dark. Then one by one, the sets switch off, leaving the studio, dark and empty.*)

APPENDIX 1
Note on *The Fire and the Rain**

The myth of Yavakri (or Yavakrita) occurs in Chapters 135–8 of the Vana Parva (Forest Canto) of the Mahabharata. It is narrated by the ascetic Lomasha to the Pandavas as they wander across the land during their exile. I have met Sanskrit scholars who were unaware of the existence of the myth: it is easy to lose track of a short narrative like this in the tangled undergrowth that covers the floor of that epic.

I first came across the story of Yavakri and Paravasu, while still in college, in C. Rajagopalachari's abridgment of the Mahabharata.[1] That Rajaji, confronted with the stupendous task of abridging the world's longest epic to about four hundred pages, should not have discarded this seemingly peripheral tale is a tribute to his sensitivity and judgement.

It was fortunate for me that Rajaji did not do so, for the moment I read the tale, I knew it had to be turned into a play. For the next thirty-seven years, I struggled with it, trying to fit all the ramifications of the myth within some sort of a manageable shape.

What literally forced my hand was a commission, in 1993, from the Guthrie Theater, Minneapolis, USA, to write a play for them. In October 1994, a workshop was organized in Minneapolis in which I worked with professional American actors at making the script stageworthy. My

---

* Taken from Preface, *The Fire and the Rain*, Girish Karnad, Oxford University Press, Delhi, 1998.

[1] C. Rajagopalachari: *Mahabharata*, Bharatiya Vidya Bhavan, Bombay, 1951.

grateful thanks are therefore due to Garland Wright, Artistic Director of the Theater (who also directed my play, *Naga-Mandala²*), Madeline Puzo, who supervised the entire enterprise and Sumitra Mukherjee, who started it all by introducing my work to them. Barbara Field, with her sensitivity to nuances of another culture, commitment to theatre and pragmatic good sense proved an excellent dramaturge at the workshop and has continued to be a close and valued friend. The actors could not have been more understanding and co-operative in helping me reshape the text, but I should like to mention Amy Kane who brought such sympathy and understanding to the character of Nittilai.

While writing the play, I tried the patience of innumerable pundits, friends and scholars. I should particularly like to acknowledge my debt to Vidyalankara Professor S. K. Ramachandra Rao who analysed the story for me word by word; my guru, Mahamahopadhyaya Professor K. T. Pandurangi, to whom I turned again and again for guidance; Professor Ramachandra Gandhi who read the manuscript and criticized it and finally Shri Arunacharya Katti of Dharwad, a practising *purohit*, who explained to me what a *yajña* feels like from the 'inside' to a practitioner. My thanks are also due to Professor Sheldon Pollock of the University of Chicago, Professor Heidrun Brückner of Tübingen University and Shri Suresh Awasthi, former secretary of the Sangeet Natak Akademi, for drawing my attention to some important publications on *yajña* and '*natya*'.

About the Play

The following notes are appended at the suggestion of the Publisher.

The Translation

The Fire and the Rain is a translation of my Kannada play, *Agni Mattu Malé*. English is the language of my adulthood: inevitably the translation is only an approximation to the original. But there is also another kind of loss.

Agni is the Sanskrit word for fire. And being a Sanskrit word, it carries, even when used in Kannada, connotations of holiness, of ritual status, of ceremony, which the Kannada word for fire (*benki*) does not

---

² Oxford University Press, 1970.

possess. *Agni* is what burns in sacrificial altars, acts as a witness at weddings and is lit at cremations. It is also the name of the god of fire. Conversely, when a match is struck, a gas-burner is lit or when a house goes up in flames, you see *benki*.

Malé is a Kannada word. It means rain, pure and simple. It has none of the aura of romance, mystery and grandeur that surrounds Sanskrit words for rain when used in Kannada.

Mattu means 'and'. It is usually left out in spoken Kannada.

Thus the phrase, *Agni Mattu Malé*, in addition to counterpointing two physical elements normally seen as antagonistic, also sets up several other oppositions: between an Indo-Aryan (Sanskrit) and a Dravidian (Kannada) language, between the pan-Indic and the regional points of view, between the classical *marga* and the less exalted *desi* traditions, between the elevated and the mundane, and even perhaps between (here one needs to tread cautiously) the sacred and the secular.

Nothing of this can come through in English—a despair not confined to the title.

So bearing in mind Robert Frost's maxim that poetry is what gets left out in a translation, we proceed.

The Myth of Yavakri

There were two sages, Bharadwaja and Raibhya, who were good friends. Raibhya was a learned man who lived with his two sons while Bharadwaja concentrated on his ascetic practices. Yavakri, Bharadwaja's son, nursed a grievance against the world for he felt his father did not receive the respect and recognition which was his due.

He therefore went off to the forest and did *tapasya* (penance) so that he could obtain the knowledge of the Vedas from the gods directly. The rigours of his ascetic practice were such that Indra, the lord of gods, appeared to him, but only to persuade him that there were no such short cuts to knowledge. Knowledge has to be obtained by studying at the feet of a guru. But Yavakri was so adamant that Indra ultimately relented and let him have his wish.

Bharadwaja, being a wise man, was anxious lest the triumph turn his son's head and cautioned Yavakri against delusions of omnipotence. But his fears unfortunately proved well-founded. For one of the first things

Yavakri did was to corner Raibhya's daughter-in-law in a lonely spot and molest her.

Yavakri's misdemeanour incensed Raibhya. He invoked the *kritya* spirit. He tore a hair from his head and made an oblation of it to the fire. From it sprang a woman who looked exactly like his daughter-in-law. From another hair he similarly brought forth a *rakshasa* (demon). Then he sent the two to kill Yavakri.

The spirit in the form of the daughter-in-law approached Yavakri seductively and stole the urn which contained the water that made him invulnerable to danger. The *rakshasa* then chased him with a trident.

Yavakri ran toward a lake in search of water, but the lake dried up. Every spot with a bit of water in it went dry at his approach. Finally Yavakri tried to enter his father's hermitage. But a blind man of the Sudra caste, who was guarding the gate, barred Yavakri's entry. At that moment the *rakshasa* killed Yavakri.

When Bharadwaja learnt from the Sudra how his son had died, he was naturally distressed. Although he knew his son was to blame for all that had happened, he cursed Raibhya that he would die at the hand of his elder son. And then shocked at his own folly in cursing a friend, he entered fire and immolated himself.

Raibhya's two sons, Paravasu and Aravasu (spelt Arvasu in the play) were conducting a fire sacrifice for the king. One night when Paravasu was visiting his home, he mistook the black deerskin which his father was wearing for a wild animal and unintentionally killed him.

When he realized what he had done, he cremated his father and returned to the sacrificial enclosure. There he said to his brother Aravasu: 'Since you are not capable of performing the sacrifice alone, go and perform the penitential rites prescribed for Brahminicide. I'll carry on with the sacrifice.'

Aravasu did his brother's bidding. But when he returned to the sacrifice, Paravasu turned to the king and said: 'This man is a Brahmin-killer. He should not be allowed to enter the sacrificial enclosures.'

The king promptly ordered his servants to throw Aravasu out, although the latter kept protesting loudly that he was innocent.

Aravasu retired to the jungle and prayed to the Sun God. When the gods appeared, he asked them to restore Yavakri, Bharadwaja and

Raibhya back to life and make Paravasu forget his evil act. The gods granted him the boon. When Yavakri came back to life, the gods reprimanded him on his folly and asked him to pursue knowledge in the right manner.

The *Yajña*: Fire Sacrifice

In Vedic thought, as in the Iranian tradition, there was a conception of the world as due not to a chance encounter of elements but as governed by an objective order, inherent in the nature of things, of which the gods are only the guardians... The sacrifice (*yajña*) is performed on behalf of an individual householder, technically called the sacrificer, accompanied by his wife, but all the ritual acts are performed by priests, varying in number from one to sixteen and ultimately seventeen officiants in the full... sacrifice... A special area is consecrated for each performance of a ritual and the sacrificer undergoes a consecration setting him apart from the profane world. In essence, the sacrifice can be regarded as a periodic ritual by which the universe is recreated, with the sacrificer like his prototype Prajapati incorporating the universe.

Indeed, the construction of the altar is conceived as a creation of the world from the basic elements of earth and water. In this cyclical process the gifts to the priests in attendance... came to be seen as the fee paid for the performance of the ritual... Originally, as indeed in the myth of the cosmic sacrifice of *purusha* (RV 10.90), the sacrifice was a sacrifice of the sacrificer himself and then successively of increasingly remote substitutes [like the horse, the ox, the sheep and then the goat and finally the rice-cake.][3]

The expenses of a fire sacrifice are met by a king or a wealthy man (known only as the *dikshita* or *yajamana*) who arranges for one in order to obtain certain benefits: sons, cattle, wealth or even to postpone old age, avoid death, or 'shine in glory like the Adityas'.

There are four Chief Priests, each associated with a Veda and specializing in a particular branch of the ritual, helped by the other

[3] J. L. Brockington: *The Sacred Thread: A Short History of Hinduism*, Oxford University Press, 1992, pp. 34–5.

priests. The conduct of the participants is regulated by stringent rules. They cannot go outside the sacrificial precincts. They cannot indulge in sexual dalliance. They cannot speak to 'lower-caste' people, etc.

There is one aspect of the idea of divinity in this period to which we should call particular attention, viz. its intimate association with what is described as *rita*. *Rita* which etymologically stands for 'course', originally meant 'cosmic order', the maintenance of which...is the purpose of all the gods; and later it also came to mean 'right', so the gods were conceived as preserving the world not merely from physical disorder but also from moral chaos...

This [initially] simple form of worship became more and more complicated and gave rise, in course of time, to elaborate sacrifices as also to a special class of professional priests who alone, it was believed, could officiate at them.

More noteworthy...was the change that came over the spirit with which offerings were made to the gods... What prompted the performance of sacrifices was no longer the thought of prevailing upon the gods to bestow some favour or to ward off some danger; it was rather to compel or coerce them to do what the sacrificer wanted to be done. This change of spirit is explained by many among modern scholars as importing of the magical element into Vedic religion and...as a sign of the transfer of power from the gods to the priests. [But it would seem more correct to see the power as] transferred from the gods not to the priests but directly to the Veda itself!

It is this sacrificial correctness that constitutes the third meaning of *rita*... Ritualistic punctilio thus comes to be placed on the same level as natural law and moral rectitude.[4]

Yajña and Entertainment

The duration of a fire sacrifice varied and some stretched over years. The Mahabharata opens with a sacrifice that was to go on for twelve years.

[4] M. Hiriyanna: *The Essentials of Indian Philosophy*, George Allen & Unwin, 1949, pp. 12, 16, 17.

The daily activity of a sacrifice is cyclical. And there are intervals between the ritual actions when the priests are free and can devote their time to other activities, not directly connected with the sacrifice.

Story-telling was an activity that often occupied the intervals between the actions of the rite. The whole of the Mahabharata, for instance, was narrated during such intervals between rites. The space could also be devoted to the performance of plays. In the last chapter of the *Natyashastra*, King Nahusha expresses his intention to arrange for dramatic performances at *yajñas*.

A Kannada reviewer of *The Fire and the Rain* based his entire analysis on the assumption that in the play, the *yajña* represented the sacred while the dramatic performance represented its secular counterpoint. This is not just simplistic. It is wrong. The *Natyashastra* lists ten forms of theatre and some may have been secular. But no truly secular performance would be permitted as entertainment at a fire sacrifice.

Indra

Indra is the king of gods, the lord of rains and the wielder of the thunderbolt.

> Indra was clearly the most popular deity among the poets of the Rigveda..., for almost a quarter of all the hymns are addressed to him. He is the dominant deity of the middle region, the region between the Earth and Heaven... A few [of the hymns] make him the son of Tvastri, the Great Father and Creator of all creatures... His chief characteristic, accorded unstinted praise, is his powers, both on the human plane as the god of battle... and mythologically as the thunder god who conquers the demons of drought and darkness, thus liberating the waters or winning the light.
>
> The most basic myth connected with Indra concerns his battle with the serpent Vritra, who is obstructing the waters and the sky...[5]

Indra and Vritra

The slaying of the demon Vritra by Indra is one of the archetypal myths of India. We find it in the Rigveda: it appears again, needless to say with

[5] Brockington, 1992, pp. 10–11.

variations, in the Mahabharata nearly a thousand years later. In the Rigveda, Vritra, 'the shoulderless one' (a serpent) swallows rivers and hides the waters inside him. Indra, by killing him, releases the waters and 'like lowing cows, the rivers flow out'. The importance of this deed to Vedic culture is borne out by the epithet, 'Vritrahan' or the slayer of Vritra, by which Indra is repeatedly hailed. Yet a passing reference in the myth to how Indra, frightened, fled 'like a falcon across ninety-nine rivers' suggests that even the Rigvedic version probably had elements not entirely complimentary to Indra.[6]

> The exact nature of [the] liberation of the waters has given rise to much speculation. In the nineteenth century it was interpreted as bringing down rain... But the Vritra myth is now generally accepted as a creation myth with Vritra symbolizing chaos...[7]

By the time we come to the version recorded in the Mahabharata, Indra has lost his central position in the Hindu pantheon. The sectarian gods, Vishnu and Shiva, now hold sway. In the later version of the myth, Indra is anxious that Vishwarupa (also called Trishiras, the three-headed one), son of Tvastri, may dislodge him from his throne. He therefore destroys Vishwarupa treacherously. Tvastri then gives birth to another son, Vritra, by a female demon, and tells him: 'Kill Indra'. Indra, unable to overcome the new enemy, again has to resort to ignominious trickery to survive. Having killed Vritra, he suffers from the guilt of Brahminicide.

The myth can be seen as expressing a deep anxiety which informs the whole of Indian mythology, the fear of brother destroying brother. This fear branches out fully and nakedly in the Mahabharata, where the bonding of brothers within the Pandava and the Kuru clans is as close as the enmity between the cousins is ruthless and unrelenting. In the Ramayana, the fraternal bonding in the Raghu family—Rama and his brothers—expresses another facet of the same anxiety, with the betrayals of Sugriva and Vibhishana (interestingly in the cause of the ethically correct side) marking the counterpoint.

The tale of Aravasu and Paravasu fascinated me as an unusual variant of this Indian obsession with fratricide and it seemed logical too that

---

[6] Wendy O'Flaherty, *Hindu Myths*, Penguin, 1975, pp. 74–86.

[7] Brockington, 1992, p. 11.

Yavakri should be their cousin, though the Mahabharata does not explicitly say so. I cannot remember when I decided to incorporate the Indra–Vritra legend in my plot, but years later, while re-reading the original version, I was astonished to find that right at the beginning of the tale of Yavakri, Lomasha mentions that the whole story took place on the banks of a river in which Indra had bathed to cleanse himself of the sin of killing Vritra! One of the fascinating aspects of dealing with myths is their self-reflexivity. A myth seems complete in itself and yet when examined in detail, contains subconscious signals which lead you on to another myth which in turn will act as a conduit to a third one while illuminating the one you started with.

Yajña and Theatre

The fire sacrifice was a rite of such central importance in the Vedic society and so completely dominated the mode of thinking that it became the central metaphor, used to underline the importance of any activity. Thus the *yajña* metaphor has been employed while talking of academic study, love-making, the epics, marriage, indeed of life itself. One need hardly mention then that it is also a favourite metaphor for theatre. Kalidasa talks of theatre as the 'desirable fire sacrifice of the eyes' (*Kantam kratum chakshusham*).

The parallel is striking in so far as both activities involve human performances, precise gestures, speech, and a carefully worked out action leading to a predetermined dénouement. But an additional characteristic common to both is the perennial possibility of disruption. The disruption may come from outside, either from a human agency (unruly audiences, mischief-mongers, intruders, those unable to understand what is happening, demons) or from a more general calamity (rain, storm, political upheavals). Or the source of disruption could be within: the performers may forget their lines, mispronounce words, or quite simply may not have prepared themselves properly for their roles.

To guard against the first two hazards, the *yajña* is performed inside a sacrificial enclosure, the play inside a theatre building. The third possibility is guarded against by the vigilance of the Chief Priest, the director, the *guru*.

The parallels are so close that many scholars[8] have argued that the steps by which the narrative of the Birth of Drama proceeds in the first chapter of the *Natyashastra* actually mirror the progression in similar myths about the *yajña*:

> Performance → disruption by demons → building of a protective enclosure → discussion → second performance inside the enclosure.

One of the principle differences between the two activities lay in the fact that drama was open to and became the prerogative of castes and communities excluded from the *yajña*. Abhinavagupta, a tenth-century critic, author of the only extant pre-modern commentary on the *Natyashastra*, brings home to us both this identity and difference when he explains that in the Prologue of a Sanskrit play the Sutradhara (Stage Manager) is addressed as 'Aryaputra' (a scion of an Arya family), although the actor is a Sudra by birth, because he is the host of the great sacrifice of the Natya Veda (*natyavedamahasattradikshita*).

The Birth of Drama

The first chapter of Bharata's *Natyashastra* gives us the myth of the origin of drama. The chapter itself has been attributed to 500 BC though the other chapters of the book may be of later date.

It was a time when the moral fibre of the society had weakened, irrational passions held sway and people had surrendered themselves to their baser instincts. Knowledge of the Vedas (which presumably could have saved the situation) being restricted to the upper strata of the society, a medium was required that entertained and could restore the health of the society by reaching out to all the people, regardless of their position in the social hierarchy. On being implored by Indra and the other gods to provide such an instrument, Brahma, the Father of the Universe, took the text from the Rigveda, the art of performance from the *Yajurveda*, the song from the *Samaveda* and *rasa* (aesthetic experience) from the *Atharvaveda* and created a fifth Veda called the *Natyaveda*).

But Indra realized that the gods were unable (or unfit) to deal with this new form and passed it on to a human preceptor, Bharata. And

[8] M. Christopher Byrsky, *Concept of Ancient Indian Theatre*, Munshiram Manoharlal, 1974, pp. 41–51; 76–90.

Bharata, with the help of his hundred sons and some nymphs specially created by Brahma for the purpose, staged the first play.

The play was performed on the occasion of the Banner Festival, held to celebrate Indra's victory in a battle over the demons. The theme of the play was the victory of the gods over the demons, the event which the festival was meant to celebrate. This did not please the demons who were present. They took umbrage and using supernatural powers, 'paralysed the speech, movement as well as the memory of the actors'. (Notice that the demons do not attack the actors physically but rather render the training they had received for performance ineffective.)

Indra, engaged by the mischief of the demons, laid into the demons with his thunderbolt, killing many. (Notice again that thus Indra, the god, re-enacts what Indra, in Bharata's play, was enacting in imitation of what Indra, the god, initially had done in battle.) But the demons persisted in their obstructive tactics.

At this point Bharata again approached Brahma, whose immediate reaction was to suggest that a theatre building should be built within which the performance could proceed uninterrupted. He placed the various gods at the vulnerable points of the building to ensure security. And then he addressed the demons on the nature of drama: 'In it (*natya*) there is no exclusive representation of you or the gods', he said, 'for the drama is a re-enactment of the state of the Three Worlds.'[9] Drama serves varied functions—providing for instruction, entertainment, enlightenment, happiness, peace and moral upliftment. It teaches one one's duty and relieves one's sorrow. There is no maxim, no learning, no art or craft that is not found in drama. For it is the joys and sorrows of human nature expressed through gestures and other techniques.

Then Brahma instructed Bharata to consecrate the stage for the next performance.

Drama and the *Purusharthas*

The *Purusharthas* are the four ethical goals of human existence: *dharma*, *artha*, *kama* and *moksha*. Very roughly, *dharma* relates to the spiritual

[9] M. M. Ghosh (tr.), *The Natyashastra*, The Royal Asiatic Society of Bengal, 1950 and 1961, p. 14. The word used by Dr Ghosh is 'representation'. But I prefer 're-enactment' as a translation of *anukeertanam*.

sphere, *artha* to the realm of political and economic power, and *kama* to that of sexual or aesthetic gratification. In these cases, what a person understands as his or her *Purushartha* could vary according to his or her background, stage of and station in life, sex etc., as well as the nature of the crisis he or she is facing. The fourth goal, *moksha*, is release from the cycle of births and deaths and hence final liberation from human bondage. This is the supreme goal, the achievement of which relates the human being to the Absolute. The concept therefore belongs to a realm beyond where the first three are relevant. Thus the harmony of the first three may be seen as a means to realizing the fourth.

The Nature of Drama

The opening chapter of the *Natyashastra*, as we saw, ends with Brahma telling Bharata to get ready for the next performance. It does not tell us whether this performance was any more successful, or at least less troublesome, than the first one. But that is the curious aspect of the myth. Here is the most ancient, most revered text on drama telling us about what was in fact the very first dramatic performance in history. The performance was the result of a collaboration between men and gods, working on a combination of the most appropriate elements drawn from the Vedas. The result should have been a resounding success, unmatched in the history of Time.

Instead, we are told the show was a disaster.

The last chapter of the *Natyashastra*—admittedly a later addition— tells us of another performance, again staged by the sons of Bharata. This time it is the Brahmins who are offended and they curse the actors to be outcastes. The Brahmanic tradition which handed down the *Natyashastra* does not concede that these irate Brahmins may have been as wrong in their understanding of drama as the demons were in chapter one. But it is significant that the *Natyashastra* is sandwiched between two performances, neither of which could be described as a success.

There is an implicit statement here about the nature of drama itself, which modern scholars have refused to look at: possibly, it embarrasses them. The point being made is that drama is a precarious, potentially disruptive, event. The possibility of being misunderstood is built into it because of its social character. Before it can be made to yield *rasa* or pleasure, all the parties need to undergo rigorous and disciplined training. One has to train oneself to 'recognize' the form for what it is and appreciate its finer points.

Let me now quote a tale by one of the great storytellers of our time as summarized by another storyteller, Umberto Eco, concerning drama.

According to Jorge Luis Borges, Abulgualid Mohammed Ibn Ahmed Ibn Mohammahd Ibn Rushd, better known as Averroes, was thinking—something like one thousand years ago, more or less—about a difficult question concerning Aristotle's *Poetics*. As you probably know, Averroes was a specialist on Aristotle, mainly on the *Poetics*. As a matter of fact, Western civilization had lost this book and had rediscovered it only through the mediation of Arab philosophers. Averroes did not know about theatre. Because of the Muslim taboo on representation, he had never seen a theatrical performance. At least, Borges, in his short story, *The Quest of Averroes*, imagines our philosopher wondering about two incomprehensible words he had found in Aristotle, namely 'tragedy' and 'comedy'. A nice problem, since Aristotle's *Poetics* is nothing else but a complex definition of those two words, or at least of the first of them.

[One day] Averroes is disturbed by some noise coming from downstairs. On the patio a group of boys are playing. One of them says, 'I am the Muezzin', and climbs on the shoulders of another one, who is pretending to be a minaret. Others are representing the crowd of believers. Averroes only glances at this scene and comes back to his book, trying to understand what the hell 'comedy' means.

In [another] episode, Averroes and the Koranist Farach are talking with the merchant Albucasim, who has just come back from remote countries. Albucasim is telling a strange story about something he has seen in Sin Kalan (Canton): a wooden house with a great salon full of balconies and chairs, crowded with people looking towards a platform where fifteen or twenty persons, wearing painted masks, are riding on horseback, but without horses, are fencing, but without swords, are dying, but are not dead. They were not crazy, explains Albucasim they were 'representing' or 'performing' a story. Averroes does not understand, and Albucasim tries to explain it: 'Imagine', he says, 'that someone *shows* a story instead of telling it.' 'Did they speak?'

asks Farach. 'Yes, they did', answers Albucasim. And Farach remarks, 'In such a case they did not need so many persons. Only one teller can tell everything, even if it is very complex.' Averroes approves. At the end of the story, Averroes decides to interpret the words 'tragedy' and 'comedy' as belonging to encomiastic discourse.

Averroes touched twice upon the experience of theatre, skimming over it without understanding it. Too bad, since he did have a good theoretical framework ready to define it.[10]

Conclusion

Thirty-seven years is a long time to live with a myth for company. It inevitably grows and changes with one. Somewhere along the line I became aware that the shape of the myth I was dealing with had uncanny parallels with that of Aeschylus's *Oresteia*.

The plot naturally fell into three parts, like a trilogy, each part with its own central action and lead character. The first two parts opened with the protagonist returning home after a prolonged absence while the third part culminated, not in some dramatic event, but in a debate on human frailty and divine grace. Then there was the presence in both of a supernatural agency bent on avenging a crime.

These are of course only external similarities but the shape of a myth cannot be isolated from its meaning, and once I saw the parallel, I was irresistibly drawn to delve deeper into the *Oresteia* and then the rest of Aeschylus. A deeper appreciation of that joyous genius has been one of the major benefits I have personally derived from writing *The Fire and the Rain*.

---

[10] Umberto Eco: 'Semiotics of Theatrical Performance'. (Source unknown to author).

APPENDIX 2

Note on *The Dreams of Tipu Sultan**

In 1996, the BBC commissioned me to write a radio play to celebrate the Fiftieth Anniversary of Indian Independence. The plot obviously had to deal with some aspect of Indo-British relations and I immediately thought of Tipu Sultan, one of the most politically perceptive and tragic figures in modern Indian history. It was the late A. K. Ramanujan who drew my attention to the secret record of his dreams maintained by this warrior.

Tipu has always fascinated playwrights. *Tipu Saib or British Valour in India* was put on at Covent Garden, London, as early as 1791 and was followed by a series of spectaculars. In Karnataka, Tipu has continued to inspire folk ballads and I have, in my lifetime, seen three Kannada stage versions of his life, two of them by itinerant troupes of rural actors.

The radio play was broadcast by the BBC on 15 August 1997 and was directed by Jatinder Verma of Tara Arts with Saeed Jaffrey playing Tipu Sultan. Karnataka Nataka Rangayana, the state repertory, staged the Kannada version in the precincts of Daria Daulat, Tipu's summer palace in Srirangapatna, to commemorate his 200th death anniversary in May 1997. It was directed by C. Basavalingaiah, with Hulugappa Kattimani in the lead role.

The present text has been entirely rewritten for the stage.

---

* Taken from Preface, *The Dreams of Tipu Sultan, Bali: The Sacrifice: Two Plays by Girish Karnad*, Oxford University Press, 2004.

APPENDIX 3

Note on *Flowers*

Flowers is based on a folk-tale from the Chitradurga region in Karnataka. My grateful thanks to the Late Ta. Ra. Subbanna, Kannada novelist, who drew my attention to it thirty-five years ago.

Plays by Girish Karnad
in English

Translation

Dates refer to the year of publication. All the plays have been published by Oxford University Press, except *Talé-Danda*, which was initially published by Ravi Dayal, Publisher.